THE HIDDEN INNS OF
EAST ANGLIA

By Peter Long

© Travel Publishing Ltd.

Regional Hidden Places

Cambs & Lincolnshire
Chilterns
Cornwall
Derbyshire
Devon
Dorset, Hants & Isle of Wight
East Anglia
Gloucs, Wiltshire & Somerset
Heart of England
Hereford, Worcs & Shropshire
Kent
Lake District & Cumbria
Lancashire & Cheshire
Lincolnshire & Nottinghamshire
Northumberland & Durham
Sussex
Thames Valley
Yorkshire

National Hidden Places

England
Ireland
Scotland
Wales

Hidden Inns

East Anglia
Heart of England
Lancashire & Cheshire
North of England
South
South East
South and Central Scotland
Wales
Welsh Borders
West Country
Yorkshire
Wales

Country Living
Rural Guides

East Anglia
Heart of England
Ireland
North East of England
North West of England
Scotland
South
South East
Wales
West Country

Published by: Travel Publishing Ltd, 7a Apollo House, Calleva Park, Aldermaston, Berks, RG7 8TN

ISBN 1·904·43421·5

© Travel Publishing Ltd

First published 2002, second edition 2005

Printing by: Scotprint, Haddington

Maps by: © Maps in Minutes ™ (2005)
© Crown Copyright, Ordnance Survey 2005

Editor: Peter Long

Cover Design: Lines & Words, Aldermaston

Cover Photograph: The Cock Inn, Polstead, Suffolk

Text Photographs: © www.britainonview.com

FOREWORD

The *Hidden Inns* series originates from the enthusiastic suggestions of readers of the popular *Hidden Places* guides. They want to be directed to traditional inns "off the beaten track" with atmosphere and character which are so much a part of our British heritage. But they also want information on the many places of interest and activities to be found in the vicinity of the inn.

The inns or pubs reviewed in the *Hidden Inns* may have been coaching inns but have invariably been a part of the history of the village or town in which they are located. All the inns included in this guide serve food and drink and some offer the visitor overnight accommodation. A full page is devoted to each inn which contains a coloured photograph, full name, address and telephone number, directions on how to get there, a full description of the inn and its facilities and a wide range of useful information such as opening hours, food served, accommodation provided, credit cards taken and details of entertainment. *Hidden Inns* guides however are not simply pub guides. They provide the reader with helpful information on the many places of interest to visit and activities to pursue in the area in which the inn is based. This ensures that your visit to the area will not only allow you to enjoy the atmosphere of the inn but also to take in the beautiful countryside which surrounds it.

The *Hidden Inns* guides have been expertly designed for ease of use and are printed in full colour. *The Hidden Inns of East Anglia* is divided into four chapters each of which is laid out in the same way. To identify your preferred geographical region refer to the contents page overleaf. To find a pub or inn and details of facilities they offer simply use the index to the rear of the guide or locator map at the beginning of each chapter which refers you, via a page number reference, to a full page dedicated to the specific establishment. To find a place of interest, again use the index to the rear of the book or list found at the beginning of each chapter which will guide you to a descriptive summary of the area that includes details of each place of interest.

We do hope that you will get plenty of enjoyment from visiting the inns, pubs and places of interest contained in this guide. We are always interested in what our readers think of the inns or places covered (or not covered) in our guides so please do not hesitate to write to us. This is a vital way of helping us ensure that we maintain a high standard of entry and that we are providing the right sort of information for our readers. Finally if you are planning to visit any other corner of the British Isles we would like to refer you to the list of Travel Publishing guides to be found at the rear of the book.

Travel Publishing

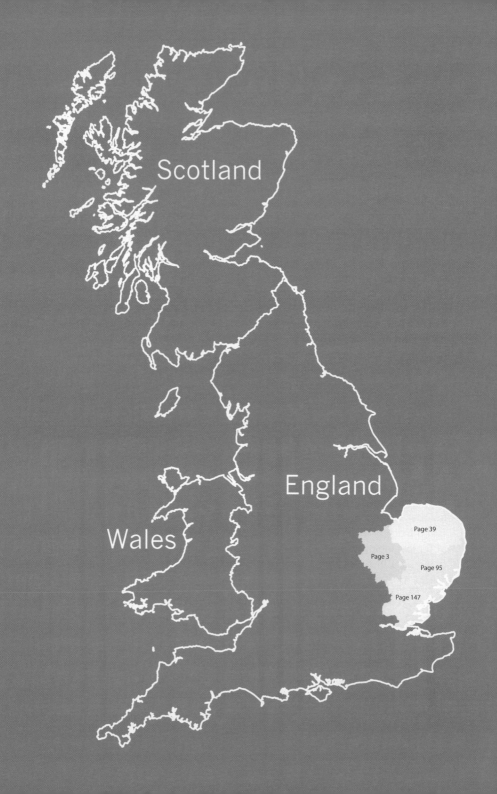

Scotland

England

Wales

Page 39

Page 3

Page 95

Page 147

CONTENTS

iii   Foreword

iv   Regional Map

1   Contents

GEOGRAPHICAL AREAS:

3   Cambridgeshire

39   Norfolk

95   Suffolk

147   Essex

INDEXES AND LISTS:

200   Alphabetical List of Pubs and Inns

204   Special Interest Lists

     204   Accommodation

     205   Open All Day

     207   Childrens Facilities

     208   Accepts Credit Cards

     211   Garden, Patio or Terrace

     214   Occasional or Regular Live Entertainment

     216   Separate Restaurant or Dining Area

218   Places of Interest

ADDITIONAL INFORMATION:

222   Order Forms

223   Reader Comment Forms

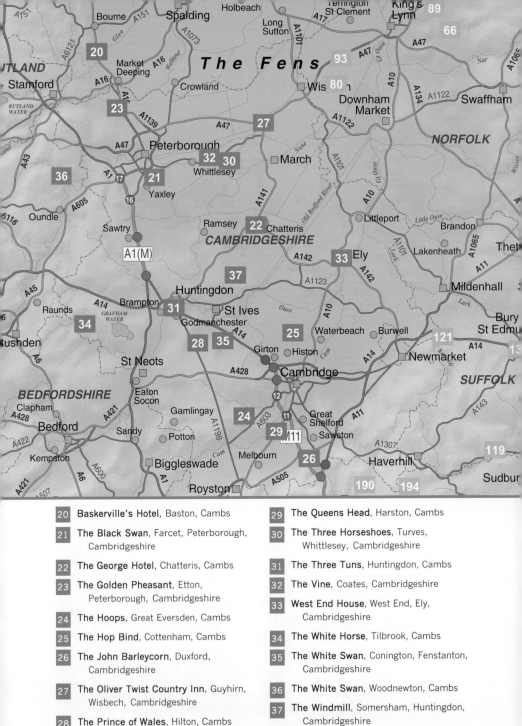

20	Baskerville's Hotel, Baston, Cambs	29	The Queens Head, Harston, Cambs
21	The Black Swan, Farcet, Peterborough, Cambridgeshire	30	The Three Horseshoes, Turves, Whittlesey, Cambridgeshire
22	The George Hotel, Chatteris, Cambs	31	The Three Tuns, Huntingdon, Cambs
23	The Golden Pheasant, Etton, Peterborough, Cambridgeshire	32	The Vine, Coates, Cambridgeshire
24	The Hoops, Great Eversden, Cambs	33	West End House, West End, Ely, Cambridgeshire
25	The Hop Bind, Cottenham, Cambs	34	The White Horse, Tilbrook, Cambs
26	The John Barleycorn, Duxford, Cambridgeshire	35	The White Swan, Conington, Fenstanton, Cambridgeshire
27	The Oliver Twist Country Inn, Guyhirn, Wisbech, Cambridgeshire	36	The White Swan, Woodnewton, Cambs
28	The Prince of Wales, Hilton, Cambs	37	The Windmill, Somersham, Huntingdon, Cambridgeshire

Please note all cross references refer to page numbers

CAMBRIDGESHIRE

Cambridgeshire is a county with a rich rural heritage, with attractive villages strung along the banks of the Great Ouse and the flat land of the Fens stretching north towards the Wash. Far removed from the hustle and bustle of modern life, the Fens are like a breath of fresh air. Extending over much of Cambridgeshire from the Wash, these flat, fenland fields contain some of the richest soil in England.

Before the Fens were drained, this was a land of mist, marshes and bogs, of small islands inhabited by independent folk, their livelihood the fish and waterfowl of this eerie, watery place. The region is full of legends of web-footed people, ghosts and witchcraft. Today's landscape is the result of human ingenuity, with its constant desire to tame the wilderness and create farmland. This fascinating story spans the centuries from the earliest Roman and Anglo-Saxon times, when the first embankments and drains were constructed to lessen the frequency of flooding. Throughout the Middle Ages large areas were reclaimed, with much of the work being undertaken by the monasteries, and, later, the significant influence of the Dutch lives on in some of the architecture and place names of the Fens. The Fens today offer unlimited opportunities for exploring on foot, by car, bicycle or by boat. Anglers are well catered for, and visitors with an interest in wildlife will be in their element. The jewel in the crown of the Fens is Ely, with its magnificent Cathedral. A few miles south of Ely, Wicken Fen is the oldest nature reserve in the country - 600 acres of undrained fenland that is famous for its varied plant, inscet and bird life.

PLACES OF INTEREST

Arrington	5	Madingley	13
Burghley	5	March	13
Cambridge	5	Peterborough	13
Crowland	8	Prickwillow	15
Duxford	8	Ramsey	15
Ely	8	St Ives	16
Fenstanton	10	St Neots	16
Godmanchester	10	Thorney	17
Grafham	10	Waterbeach	18
Grantchester	11	Welney	18
Huntingdon	11	Whittlesey	18
Kimbolton	12	Wicken	18
Linton	12	Wisbech	19
Lode	12		

Southeastern Cambridgeshire covers the area around the city of Cambridge and is rich in history, with a host of archaeological sites and monuments to visit, as well as many important museums. At the heart of it all is Cambridge itself, one of the leading academic centres in the world

Bridge of Sighs, Cambridge

and a city which deserves plenty of time to explore - on foot, by bicycle or by the gentler, more romantic option of a punt.

The old county of Huntingdonshire is the heartland of the rural heritage of Cambridgeshire. Here, the home of Oliver Cromwell beckons with a wealth of history and pleasing landscapes. Many motorists follow the Cromwell Trail, which guides tourists around the legacy of buildings and places in the area associated with the man. The natural start of the Trail is Huntingdon itself, where he was born the son of a country gentleman. Other main stopping places are covered in this chapter.

The 26-mile Ouse Valley Way follows the course of the Great Ouse through pretty villages and a variety of natural attractions. A gentle cruise along this area can fill a lazy day to perfection, but for those who prefer something more energetic on the water there are excellent, versatile facilities at Grafham Water. The Nene-Ouse Navigation Link, part of the Fenland

Ely Cathedral at Sunset

Waterway, provides the opportunity for a relaxed look at a lovely part of the region. It travels from Stanground Lock near Peterborough to a lock at the small village of Salters Lode in the east, and the 28-mile journey passes through several Fenland towns and a rich variety of wildlife habitats.

ARRINGTON

Arrington's 18th century **Wimpole Hall**, owned by the National Trust, is probably the most spectacular country mansion in the whole county, and certainly the largest 18th century country house in Cambridgeshire. The lovely interiors are the work of several celebrated architects, and there's a fine collection of furniture and pictures. The magnificent formally laid-out grounds include a Victorian parterre, a rose garden and a walled garden.

Landscaped **Wimpole Park**, with hills, woodland, lakes and a Chinese bridge, provides miles of wonderful walking and is perfect for anything from a gentle stroll to a strenuous hike.

A brilliant attraction for all the family is **Wimpole Home Farm**, a working farm that is the largest rare breeds centre in East Anglia.

BURGHLEY

"The largest and grandest house of the Elizabethan Age", **Burghley House** presents a dazzling spectacle with its domed towers, walls of cream coloured stone, and acres of windows. Clear glass was still ruinously expensive in the 1560s so Elizabethan grandees like William Cecil, Lord Burghley, flaunted their wealth by having windows that stretched almost from floor to ceiling. Burghley House also displays the Elizabethan obsession with symmetry - every tower, dome, pilaster and pinnacle has a corresponding partner.

The eighteen State Rooms at Burghley house a vast treasury of great works of art. The walls are crowded with 17th century Italian paintings, Japanese ceramics and rare examples of European porcelain grace every table, alcove and mantelpiece, and the wood carvings of Grinling Gibbons and his followers add dignity to almost every room. Also on display are four magnificent State Beds along with important tapestries and textiles.

Throughout the summer season, Burghley hosts a series of events of which the best known, the Burghley Horse Trials, takes place at the end of August.

CAMBRIDGE

There are nearly 30 Cambridges spread around the globe, but this, the original, is the one that the whole world knows as one of the leading university cities. Cambridge was an important town many centuries before the scholars arrived,

Burghley House

King's College Gatehouse, Cambridge

standing at the point where forest met fen, at the lowest fording point of the river. The Romans took over a site previously settled by an Iron Age Belgic tribe, to be followed in turn by the Saxons and the Normans.

Soon after the Norman Conquest, William I built a wooden motte-and-bailey castle; Edward I built a stone replacement: a mound still marks the spot. The town flourished as a market and river trading centre, and in 1209 a group of students fleeing the Oxford riots arrived.

The Colleges are all well worth a visit, but places that simply must not be missed include **King's College Chapel** with its breathtaking fan vaulting, glorious stained glass and Peter Paul Rubens' *Adoration of the Magi*; **Pepys Library**, including his diaries, in Magdalene College; and Trinity's wonderful **Great Court**. A trip by punt along the 'Backs' of the Cam brings a unique view of many of the Colleges and passes under six bridges, including the **Bridge of Sighs** (St John's) and the extraordinary wooden **Mathematical Bridge** at Queens.

Cambridge has nurtured more Nobel Prize winners than most countries - 32 from Trinity alone - and the list of celebrated alumni covers every sphere of human endeavour and achievement: Byron, Tennyson, Milton and Wordsworth; Marlowe and Bacon; Samuel Pepys; Sir Isaac Newton and Charles Darwin; Charles Babbage, Bertrand Russell and Ludwig Wittgenstein; actors Sir Ian McKellen, Sir Derek Jacobi and Stephen Fry; Lord Burghley; Harold Abrahams, who ran for England in the Olympics; and Burgess,

May Week Celebrations, Cambridge

University Botanic Garden, Cambridge

Technology, housed in a Victorian sewage pumping station, features an impressive collection of steam, gas and electric pumping engines and examples great and small of local industrial technology. Anyone with an interest in fossils should make tracks for the **Sedgwick Museum of Earth Sciences**, while in the same street (Downing) the **Museum of Zoology** offers a comprehensive and spectacular survey of the animal kingdom. The **Whipple Museum of the History of Science** tells about science through instruments; the **Scott Polar Research Institute** has fascinating, often poignant exhibits relating to Arctic and Antarctic exploration; and the **University Botanic Garden** boasts a plant collection that rivals those of Kew Gardens and Edinburgh.

The work and life of the people of Cambridge and the surrounding area are the subject of the **Cambridge and County Folk Museum**, housed in a 16th century building that for 300 years was the White Horse Inn. One of the city's greatest treasures is the **University Library**, one of the world's great research libraries with 6 million books, a million maps and 350,000 manuscripts.

Cambridge also has many fine churches, some of them used by the Colleges before they built their own chapels.

Maclean, Philby and Blunt, who spied for Russia.

The Colleges apart, Cambridge is packed with interest for the visitor, with a wealth of grand buildings both religious and secular, and some of the country's leading museums, many of them run by the University. The **Fitzwilliam Museum** is renowned for its art collection, which includes works by Titian, Rembrandt, Gainsborough, Hogarth, Turner, Renoir, Picasso and Cezanne, and for its antiquities from Egypt, Greece and Rome. **Kettle's Yard** has a permanent display of 20th century art in a house maintained just as it was when the Ede family donated it, with the collection, to the University in 1967. The **Museum of Classical Archaeology** has 500 plaster casts of Greek and Roman statues, and the **University Museum of Archaeology and Anthropology** covers worldwide prehistoric archaeology with special displays relating to Oceania and to the Cambridge area. The **Museum of**

CROWLAND

It is hard to imagine that this whole area was once entirely wetland and marshland, dotted with inhospitable islands. Crowland was one such island, then known as Croyland, and on it was established a small church and hermitage back in the 7th century, which was later to become one of the nation's most important monasteries. The town's impressive parish church was just part of the great edifice which once stood on the site. A wonderful exhibition can be found in the **Abbey** at Crowland, open all year round. The remains cover a third of the Abbey's original extent.

Crowland's second gem is the unique Trinity Bridge - set in the centre of town on dry land! Built in the 14th century, it has three arches built over one overarching structure. Before the draining of the Fens, this bridge crossed the point where the River Welland divided into two streams.

DUXFORD

Part of the Imperial War Museum, **Duxford Aviation Museum** is probably the leader in its field in Europe, with an outstanding collection of over 150 historic aircraft from biplanes through Spitfires to supersonic jets.

The American Air Museum, where aircraft are suspended as if in flight, is part of this terrific place, which was built

on a former RAF and US fighter base. Major air shows take place several times a year, and among the permanent features are a reconstructed wartime operations room, a hands-on exhibition for children and a dramatic land warfare hall with tanks, military vehicles and artillery. Everyone should take time to see this marvellous show - and it should be much more than a flying visit!

ELY

Ely is the jewel in the crown of the Fens, in whose history the majestic **Cathedral** and the Fens themselves have played major roles. Ely owes its existence to St Etheldreda, Queen of Northumbria, who in AD673 founded a monastery on the 'Isle of Ely', where she remained as abbess until her death in AD679. It was not until 1081 that work started on the present Cathedral, and in 1189 this remarkable example of Romanesque architecture was completed. The most outstanding feature in terms of both scale and beauty is the Octagon, built to

Duxford Aviation Museum

Boats Moored by the Riverside, Ely

attractions that should not be missed are the Brass Rubbing Centre, where visitors can make their own rubbings from replica brasses, and the **Museum of Stained Glass**. The latter, housed in the south Triforium of the Cathedral, is the only museum of stained glass in the country and contains over 100 original panels from every period, tracing the complete history of stained glass.

replace the original Norman tower, which collapsed in 1322.

Alan of Walsingham was the inspired architect of this massive work, which took 30 years to complete and whose framework weighs an estimated 400 tons. Many other notable components include the 14th century Lady Chapel, the largest in England, the Prior's Door, the painted nave ceiling and St Ovin's cross, the only piece of Saxon stonework in the building.

The Cathedral is set within the walls of the monastery, and many of the ancient buildings still stand as a tribute to the incredible skill and craftsmanship of their designers and builders. Particularly worth visiting among these are the monastic buildings in the College, the Great Hall and Queens Hall.

Just beside the Cathedral is the **Almonry**, in whose 12th-century vaulted undercroft visitors can take coffee, lunch or tea - outside in the garden if the weather permits. Two other

Ely's **Tourist Information Centre** is itself a tourist attraction, since it is housed in a pretty black-and-white timbered building that was once the home of Oliver Cromwell. It is the only remaining house, apart from Hampton Court, where Oliver Cromwell and his family are known to have lived; parts of it trace back to the 13th century, and its varied history includes periods when it was used as a public house and, more recently, a vicarage. There are eight period rooms, exhibitions and videos to enjoy.

Tourist Information Centre, Ely

The Old Gaol, in Market Street, houses **Ely Museum**, with nine galleries telling the Ely story from the Ice Age to modern times. The tableaux of the condemned and debtors' cells are particularly fascinating and poignant.

Ely is not just the past, and its fine architecture and sense of history blend well with the bustle of the streets and shops and the riverside. That bustle is at its most fervent on Thursdays, when the largest general market in the area is held.

FENSTANTON

Lancelot 'Capability' Brown (1716 – 1783) was Lord of the Manor from 1768, and he, his wife and his son are buried in the medieval church. Born in Northumberland, Brown started his working life as a gardener's boy before moving on to Stowe, where he worked under William Kent. When Kent died, Brown set up as a garden designer and soon became the leading landscape artist in England, known for the natural, unplanned appearance of his designs. His nickname arose from his habit of remarking, when surveying new projects, that the place had 'capabilities'.

GODMANCHESTER

Godmanchester is linked to Huntingdon by a 14th century bridge across the River Ouse. It was a Roman settlement and one that continued in importance down the years, as the number of handsome buildings testifies. One such is **Island Hall**, a mid-18th century mansion built for John Jackson, the Receiver General for Huntingdon; it contains many interesting pieces. This family home has lovely Georgian rooms, with fine period detail and fascinating possessions relating to the owners' ancestors since their first occupation of the house in 1800. The tranquil riverside setting and formal gardens add to the peace and splendour - the house takes its name from the ornamental island that forms part of the grounds.

Wood Green Animal Shelter at Kings Bush Farm, Godmanchester, is a purpose-built, 50-acre centre open to the public all year round. Cats, dogs, horses, donkeys, farm animals, guinea pigs, rabbits, llamas, wildfowl and pot-bellied pigs are among the many creatures for visitors to see, and there is a specially adapted nature trail and restaurant.

GRAFHAM

Created in the mid-1960s as a reservoir, **Grafham Water** offers a wide range of outdoor activities for visitors of all ages, with 1,500 acres of beautiful countryside, including the lake itself. The ten-mile perimeter track is great for jogging or cycling, and there's excellent sailing, windsurfing and fly-fishing.

The area is a Site of Special Scientific Interest, and an ample nature reserve at the western edge is run jointly by Anglian Water and the Wildlife Trust. There are nature trails, information boards, a wildlife garden and a dragonfly pond. Many species of waterfowl stay here at various times of the year, and bird-watchers have the use of six hides, three of them accessible to wheelchairs. An exhibition centre has displays and video presentations of the reservoir's history, a gift shop and a café.

GRANTCHESTER

A pleasant walk by the Cam, or a punt on it, brings visitors from the bustle of Cambridge to the famous village of Grantchester, where Rupert Brooke lived and Byron swam. The walk passes through Paradise Nature Reserve.

'Stands the church clock at ten to three

And is there honey still for tea?'

The Orchard, with its Brooke connections, is known the world over. Brooke spent two happy years in Grantchester, and immortalised afternoon tea in The Orchard in a poem he wrote while homesick in Berlin. Time should also be allowed for a look at the Church of St Andrew and St Mary, in which the remains of a Norman church have been incorporated into the 1870s main structure.

HUNTINGDON

Oliver Cromwell was born in Huntingdon in 1599 and attended Huntingdon Grammar School. The schoolhouse was originally part of the Hospital of St John the Baptist, founded during the reign of Henry II by David, Earl of Huntingdon. Samuel Pepys was also a pupil here.

Cromwell was MP for Huntingdon in the Parliament of 1629, was made a JP in 1630 and moved to St Ives in the following year. Rising to power as an extremely able military commander in the Civil War, he raised troops from the region and made his headquarters in the Falcon Inn.

Appointed Lord Protector in 1653, Cromwell was ruler of the country until his death in 1658. The school he attended is now the **Cromwell Museum**, located on Huntingdon High Street, housing the only public collection relating specifically to him, with exhibits that reflect many aspects of his political, social and religious life. **All Saints Church**, opposite the Cromwell Museum, displays many architectural styles, from medieval to Victorian. One of the two surviving parish churches of Huntingdon, All Saints was considered to be the church of the Hinchingbrooke part of the Cromwell family, though no memorials survive to attest to this. The Cromwell family burial vault is contained within the church, however, and it is here that Oliver's father Robert and his grandfather Sir Henry are buried. The church has a fine chancel roof, a very lovely organ chamber, a truly impressive stained-glass window and the font in which Cromwell was baptised, as it's the old font from the destroyed St John's church, discovered in a local garden in 1927!

About half a mile southwest of town stands **Hinchingbrooke House**, where visitors can see examples of every period of English architecture from the 12th to early 20th centuries. King James I was a regular visitor, and Oliver Cromwell spent part of his childhood here. The 1st Earl of Sandwich was a central figure in the Civil War and subsequent Restoration, while the 4th Earl (inventor of the lunchtime favourite that bears his name) was one of the most flamboyant politicians of the 18th century. The House is open for guided tours, including lovely cream teas served in the Tudor kitchens.

Hinchingbrooke Country Park covers 180 acres of grassy meadows, mature woodland, ponds and lakes.

KIMBOLTON

History aplenty here, and a lengthy pause is in order to look at all the interesting buildings. St Andrew's Church would head the list were it not for **Kimbolton Castle**, which, along with its gatehouse, dominates the village. Parts of the original Tudor building are still to be seen, but the appearance of the castle today owes much to the major remodelling carried out by Vanbrugh and Nicholas Hawksmoor in the first decade of the 18th century. The gatehouse was added by Robert Adam in 1764. Henry VIII's first wife Catherine of Aragon spent the last 18 months of her life imprisoned here, where she died in 1536.

The castle is now a school, but can be visited on certain days in the summer (don't miss the Pellegrini murals).

LINTON

The village is best known for its zoo, but visitors will also find many handsome old buildings and the church of St Mary the Virgin, built mainly in Early English style.

A world of wildlife set in 16 acres of spectacular gardens, **Linton Zoo** is a major wildlife breeding centre and part of the inter-zoo breeding programme for endangered species. Collections include wild cats, birds, snakes and insects.

LODE

Anglesey Abbey dates from 1600 and was built on the site of an Augustinian priory, but the house and the 100-acre garden came together as a unit thanks to the vision of the 1st Lord Fairhaven. The garden, created in its present form from the 1930s, is a wonderful place for a stroll, with 98 acres of landscaped gardens including wide grassy walks,

Lode Watermill at Anglesey Abbey

open lawns, a riverside walk, a working water mill and one of the finest collections of garden statuary in the country. There's also a plant centre, shop and restaurant. In the house itself is Lord Fairhaven's magnificent collection of paintings, sumptuous furnishings, tapestries and clocks.

MADINGLEY

The American Cemetery is one of the loveliest, most peaceful and most moving places in the region, a place of pilgrimage for the families of the American servicemen who operated from the many wartime bases in the county. The cemetery commemorates 3,800 dead and over 5,000 missing in action in the Second World War.

MARCH

March once occupied the second-largest 'island' in the great level of Fens. As the land was drained the town grew as a trading and religious centre, and in more recent times as a market town and major railway hub. **March and District Museum**, in the High Street, tells the story of the people and the history of March and the surrounding area, and includes a working forge and a reconstruction of a turn-of-the-century home.

St Wendreda's uniquely dedicated church, at Town End, is notable for its magnificent timber roof, a double hammerbeam with 120 carved angels, a fine font and some impressive gargoyles.

St Wendreda's, March

John Betjeman declared the church to be 'worth cycling 40 miles into a headwind to see'.

The **Nene-Ouse Navigation Link** runs through the town, affording many attractive riverside walks and, just outside the town off the B1099, Dunhams Wood comprises four acres of woodland set among the fens. The site contains an enormous variety of trees, along with sculptures and a miniature railway.

PETERBOROUGH

The second city of Cambridgeshire has a long and interesting history that can be traced back to the Bronze Age, as can be seen in the archaeological site at Flag

Bridge Street, Peterborough

Fen. Although a cathedral city, it is also a New Town (designated in 1967), so modern development and expansion have vastly increased its facilities while retaining the quality of its historic heart.

Peterborough's crowning glory is, of course, the Norman **Cathedral**, built in the 12th and 13th centuries on a site that had seen Christian worship since AD655. Henry VIII made the church a cathedral, and his first queen, Catherine of Aragon, is buried here, as for a while was Mary Queen of Scots after her execution at Fotheringay. Features to note are the huge (85-foot) arches of the West Front, the unique painted wooden nave ceiling, some exquisite late15th century fan vaulting, and the tomb of Catherine.

The **Peterborough Museum and Art Gallery** covers all aspects of the history of Peterborough from the Jurassic period to Victorian times.

There are twin attractions for railway enthusiasts in the shape of **Railworld**, a hands-on exhibition dealing with modern rail travel, and the wonderful **Nene Valley Railway**, which operates 15-mile steam-hauled trips between Peterborough and its HQ and museum at Wansford. A feature on the main railway line at Peterborough is the historic Iron Bridge, part of the old Great Northern Railway and still virtually as built by Lewis Cubitt in 1852.

Just outside the city, by the river Nene, is **Thorpe Meadows Sculpture Park,** one of several open spaces in and around the city with absorbing collections of modern sculpture. **Flag Fen Bronze Age Centre**, on the outskirts of Peterborough, comprises massive 3,000-year-old timbers that were part of a major settlement and have been preserved in peaty mud. The site

River Nene, Peterborough

includes a Roman road with its original surface, the oldest wheel in England, recreations of a Bronze Age settlement, a museum of artefacts, rare breed animals, and a visitor centre with a shop and restaurant. Ongoing excavations, open to the public, make this one of the most important and exciting sites of its kind.

PRICKWILLOW

On the village's main street is the **Prickwillow Drainage Engine Museum**, which houses a unique collection of large engines associated with the drainage of the Fens. The site had been in continuous use as a pumping station since 1831, and apart from the engines there are displays charting the history of Fens drainage, the effects on land levels and the workings of the modern drainage system.

RAMSEY

A pleasant market town with a broad main street down which a river once ran, Ramsey is home to the medieval **Ramsey Abbey**, founded in AD969 by Earl Ailwyn as a Benedictine monastery. The Abbey became one of the most important in England in the 12th and 13th centuries, and as it prospered, so did Ramsey, so that by the 13th century it had become a town with a weekly market and an annual three-day festival at the time of the feast of St Benedict. After the Dissolution of the Monasteries in 1539, the Abbey and its lands were sold to Sir Richard Williams, great-

grandfather of Oliver Cromwell. Most of the buildings were then demolished, the stones being used to build Caius, King's and Trinity Colleges at Cambridge, the towers of Ramsey, Godmanchester and Holywell churches, the gate at Hinchingbrooke House and several local properties. In 1938 the house was converted for use as a school, which it remains to this day.

The **Church of St Thomas à Becket of Canterbury** forms an impressive vista at the end of the High Street. Dating back to about 1180, it is thought to have been built as a hospital or guesthouse for the Abbey. It was converted to a church to accommodate the many pilgrims who flocked to Ramsey in the 13th century. The church has what is reputed to be the finest nave in Huntingdonshire, dating back to the 12th century and consisting of seven bays. The church's other treasure is a 15th century carved oak lectern, thought to have come from the Abbey.

Most of **Ramsey Rural Museum** is housed in an 18th century farm building and several barns set in open countryside. Among the many fascinating things to see are a Victorian home and school, a village store, and restored farm equipment, machinery, carts and wagons. The wealth of traditional implements used by local craftsmen such as the farrier, wheelwright, thatcher, dairyman, animal husbandman and cobbler offer an insight into bygone days.

ST IVES

An ancient town on the banks of the Great Ouse which once held a huge annual fair and is named after St Ivo, said to be a Persian bishop who came here in the Dark Ages to spread a little light. In the Middle Ages, kings bought cloth for their households at the village's great wool fairs and markets, and a market is still held every Monday. The Bank Holiday Monday markets are particularly lively affairs, and the Michaelmas fair fills the town centre for three days.

Seagoing barges once navigated up to the famous six-arched bridge that was built in the 15th century and has a most unusual two-storey chapel in its middle. Oliver Cromwell lived in St Ives in the 1630s; the statue of him on Market Hill, with its splendid hat, is one of the village's most familiar landmarks. It was made in bronze, with a Portland stone base, and was erected in 1901. It was originally designed for Huntingdon, but

they wouldn't accept it!

The beautiful parish church in its churchyard beside the river is well worth a visit. The quayside provides a tranquil mooring for holidaymakers and there are wonderful walks by the riverside.

The **Norris Museum**, in a delightful setting by the river, tells the story of Huntingdonshire for the past 175 million years or so, with everything from fossils, mammoth tusks and models of the great historic reptiles through flint tools, Roman artefacts and Civil War armour to lace-making and ice-skating displays, and contemporary works of art.

Just outside St Ives are **Wilthorn Meadow**, a Site of Natural History Interest where Canada geese are often to be seen, and **Holt Island Nature Reserve**, where high-quality willow is being grown to reintroduce the traditional craft of basket-making. Take some time for spotting the butterflies, dragonflies and kingfishers.

ST NEOTS

St Neots dates back to the founding of a **Saxon Priory**, built on the outskirts of Eynesbury in AD974. Partially destroyed by the Danes in 1010, it was re-established as a Benedictine Priory in about 1081 by St Anselm, Abbot of Bec and later Archbishop of Canterbury. For the next two centuries the Priory

Hemingford Grey Near St Ives

Riverside Walk, St Neots

Victorian stained-glass and a Holdich organ, built in 1855.

St Neots Museum - opened in 1995 - tells the story of the town and the surrounding area. Housed in the former magistrates' court and police station, it still has the original cells. Eye-catching displays trace local history from prehistoric times to the present day. Open Tuesday to Saturday.

flourished. Charters were granted by Henry I to hold fairs and markets. The first bridge over the Great Ouse, comprising 73 timber arches, was built in 1180. The name of the town comes from the Cornish saint whose remains were interred in the Priory some time before the Norman Conquest. With the Dissolution of the Monasteries, the Priory was demolished. In the early 17th century the old bridge was replaced by a stone one. This was then the site of a battle between the Royalists and Roundheads in 1648 - an event sometimes re-enacted by Sealed Knot societies.

St Neots has many interesting sites and old buildings tucked away. The magnificent parish **Church of St Mary the Virgin** is a very fine edifice, known locally as the Cathedral of Huntingdonshire. It is an outstanding example of Late Medieval architecture. The gracious interior complements the 130-foot Somerset-style tower, with a finely carved oak altar, excellent

THORNEY

Thorney Abbey, the church of St Mary and St Botolph, is the dominating presence even though what now stands is but a small part of what was once one of the greatest of the Benedictine abbeys. Gravestones in the churchyard are evidence of a Huguenot colony that settled here after fleeing France in the wake of the St Bartholomew's Day massacre of 1572 and to settle the drained fenland at the request of Oliver Cromwell.

The **Thorney Heritage Museum** is a small, independently-run museum of great fascination, describing the development of the village from a Saxon monastery, via Benedictine Abbey to a model village built in the 19th century by the Dukes of Bedford. The main innovation was a 10,000-gallon water tank that supplied the whole village; other villages had to use unfiltered river water.

WATERBEACH

Denny Abbey, easily accessible on the A10, is an English Heritage Grade I listed Abbey with ancient earthworks. On the same site, and run as a joint attraction, is the **Farmland Museum**. The history of Denny Abbey runs from the 12th century, when it was a Benedictine monastery. It was later home to the Knights Templar, Franciscan nuns and the Countess of Pembroke, and from the 16th century was a farmhouse. The old farm buildings have been splendidly renovated and converted to tell the story of village life and Cambridgeshire farming up to modern times. The museum is ideal for family outings, with plenty of hands-on activities for children and a play area, gift shop and weekend tearoom.

WELNEY

The **Wildfowl & Wetlands Trust** in Welney is a nature reserve that attracts large numbers of swans and ducks in winter. Special floodlit 'swan evenings' are held, and there is also a wide range of wild plants and butterflies to be enjoyed.

WHITTLESEY

The market town of Whittlesey lies close to the western edge of the Fens and is part of one of the last tracts to be drained. Brick-making was a local speciality, and 180-foot brick chimneys stand as a reminder of that once-flourishing industry. The **Church of St Andrew** is mainly 14th century, with a 16th century tower; the chancel, chancel chapels and naves still have their original roofs.

A walk around this charming town reveals an interesting variety of buildings: brick, of course, and also some stone, thatch on timber frames, and rare thatched mud boundary walls.

The **Whittlesey Museum**, housed in the grand 19th century Town Hall in Market Street, features an archive of displays on local archaeology, agriculture, geology, brick-making and more. Reconstructions include a 1950s corner shop and post office, blacksmith's forge and wheelwright's bench.

WICKEN

Owned by the National Trust, **Wicken Fen** is the oldest nature reserve in the country, 600 acres of undrained fenland famous for its rich plant, insect and bird life and a delight for both naturalists and ramblers. Features include boardwalk and nature trails, hides and watchtowers, a cottage with 1930s furnishings, a working wind pump (the oldest in the country), a visitor centre and a shop. Open daily, dawn to dusk.

St Lawrence's Church is well worth a visit, small and secluded among trees. In the churchyard are buried Oliver Cromwell and several members of his family. One of Cromwell's many nicknames was 'Lord of the Fens': he defended the rights of the Fenmen against those who wanted to drain the land without providing adequate compensation.

Wicken Windmill is a fine and impressive smock windmill restored back to working order, one of only four smock windmills making flour by wind in the UK.

WISBECH

One of the largest of the Fenland towns, a port in medieval times and still enjoying shipping trade with Europe, Wisbech is at the centre of a thriving agricultural region. The 18th century in particular saw the building of rows of handsome houses, notably in North Brink and South Brink, which face each other across the river. The finest of all the properties is undoubtedly **Peckover House**, built in 1722 and bought at the end of the 18th century by Jonathan Peckover, a member of the Quaker banking family. The family gave the building to the National Trust in 1948. Behind its elegant façade are splendid panelled rooms, Georgian fireplaces with richly carved overmantels, and ornate plaster decorations. At the back of the house is a beautiful walled garden with summerhouses and an orangery.

No 1 South Brink Place is the birthplace of Octavia Hill (1838-1912), co-founder of the National Trust and a tireless worker for the cause of the poor, particularly in the sphere of housing. The house is now the **Octavia Hill Museum** with displays and exhibits commemorating her work.

More Georgian splendour is evident in the area where the Norman castle once stood. The castle was replaced by a bishop's palace in 1478, and in the 17th century by a mansion built for Cromwell's Secretary of State, John Thurloe. Local builder Joseph Medworth built the present Regency villa in 1816; of the Thurloe mansion, only the gate piers remain.

The **Wisbech and Fenland Museum** is one of the oldest purpose-built museums in the country, and in charming Victorian surroundings visitors can view displays of porcelain, coins, rare geological specimens, Egyptian tomb treasures and several items of national importance, including the manuscript of Charles Dickens' *Great Expectations*, Napoleon's Sèvres breakfast set captured at Waterloo, and an ivory chess set that belonged to Louis XIV.

Croquet at Peckover House

BASKERVILLE'S HOTEL

BASTON, SOUTH LINCOLNSHIRE PE6 9PB
TEL: 01778 560010 FAX: 01778 561147

Cambridgeshire

Directions: Baston lies on the A15 about 6 miles north of Peterborough.

Built in 1842, and a prominent landmark in the quiet village of Baston, **Baskerville's Hotel** is a very handsome redbrick building set back from the main road. Its facade sports an attractive covering of creeper, and at the back is a lovely garden complete with a fish pond. Inside, the well-stocked public and lounge bars are very roomy and comfortable, and there's also plenty of space to relax over a meal in the elegant restaurant. Vic Slater, here since 1998, runs a very well-established pub, equally popular as a village 'local', a comfortable hotel and a fine destination restaurant that brings those in the know from all over the region. The menu makes excellent use of the best fresh produce, much of it locally sourced, in dishes that look as good as they taste. The fine food, which is served from noon to 9.30 seven

days a week, is complemented by a good selection of ales and wines. Wednesday is quiz night, and Fridays in winter are livened by live music nights.

The overnight accommodation comprises eight well-appointed bedrooms, all with modern en suite facilities, television and hospitality tray. With the A15 on the doorstep and the A16 nearby, access is easy in all directions, making Baskerville's Hotel a very convenient stopover for business travellers and as a base for a relaxed tour of the region. Market Deeping and Peterborough are to the south along the A15, while the typical Fenland town of Bourne is a few miles to the north. The waters around Bourne and the Deepings have long been said to have curative powers; that may or may not be true, but there's no doubt at all that an excellent way of quenching a thirst is to visit to Baskerville's Hotel.

- 🕐 11.30-11
- 🍴 All day menu of home-cooked dishes
- £ Major cards accepted
- 🛏 8 en suite rooms
- Ⓟ Car park, beer garden
- 🎵 Quiz Wednesday, music Friday in winter
- ❓ Bourne Heritage Centre and Bourne Wood 4 miles, Peterborough 6 miles, Grimsthorpe Castle 6 miles

THE BLACK SWAN

77 MAIN STREET, FARCET, NR PETERBOROUGH,
CAMBRIDGESHIRE PE7 3DF
TEL: 01733 240387

> **Directions:** Farcet is on the B1091 2 miles south of Peterborough. The Black
> Swan is on the main street.

A short drive from Peterborough brings visitors to **The Black Swan**, which stands on the main street at the lower end of the Fenland village where Colman's grows its mustard seeds. The tenants of this substantial roadside inn, which dates from the 18th century, are the husband and wife team of Steve and Jan Thurston, who since their arrival have made many new friends with their warm welcome and excellent hospitality. Steve is in charge of the drinks side of the business, and he keeps connoisseurs of cask ales happy with a selection that changes each week and is chalked up behind the bar; typical options on tap might be John Smiths Cask (3.8%), Highlander (4.6%) and Bass (4.4%). Jan does the cooking, offering a choice of well-priced, generously served dishes between 12 and 2 from Tuesday to

Thursday, Friday 12-3 and Saturday and Sunday 12-4. Theme nights are held on the first Wednesday of each month e.g. Curry, Italian or Mexican and Friday night is fish & chip night – another very popular time of the week. Pool and darts are played in the bar.

The inn is very much at the heart of life in Farcet and Farcet's 850-year-old church is well worth a visit. The inn is close to many other places of interest; these include the cathedral town of Peterborough with attractions both old and new, the marvellous Church of St Peter in the neighbouring village of Yaxley, and the Bronze Age Centre at Flag Fen, one of Europe's most important Bronze Age sites.

The Black Swan has no guest accommodation but it is registered with the Touring Caravan Club and has a few spaces for caravans on an adjoining site.

- 🕐 Tuesday to Thursday 12-2, Monday to Thursday 5-11, Fri, Sat & Sun open all day
- 🍴 Home cooking (no food Mon)
- 💷 Major cards accepted
- 🅿 Car park, patio
- ❓ Peterborough 2 miles, Yaxley 2 miles, Stilton 5 miles, Whittlesey 5 miles, Flag Fen Bronze Age site 5 miles

Cambridgeshire

THE GEORGE HOTEL

2 HIGH STREET, CHATTERIS, CAMBRIDGESHIRE PE16 6BE
TEL: 01354 692208

Directions: The George lies on the main street of Chatteris, 8 miles south of
March off the A141.

The George Hotel is a fine-looking and substantial redbrick building standing prominently in the centre of the friendly little Fenland town of Chatteris. Proprietor Robbie Lyons, a cheerful Irishman from County Laios, has devoted much time and effort to refurbishing the spacious interior, giving it a stylishly updated look that has widened its appeal from the traditional pub regulars to a younger generation.

It remains a popular 'local', with a wide range of cask ales, beers and lagers always available, and is also establishing a growing reputation for its excellent cooking; the varied menus are served every session except Sunday evening.

Robbie's jovial disposition, flair and enthusiasm, along with the friendly presence of manageress Sarah Thompson, have helped to create a very relaxed ambience, with plenty of lively conversation, and in fine weather the patio is a popular spot for a little party or get together. The George is also an excellent base for business or leisure visitors, and the eight guest bedrooms (five with en suite facilities) are all equipped with television and tea/coffee trays. There's plenty to see in Chatteris, and the Chatteris Museum and Council Chamber features a series of interesting displays on Fenland life and the development of the town. The Church of St Peter and St Paul is also well worth a visit, with a number of original 14th century features surviving extensive modernisation.

- 🕐 11-11 (Sun 12-10.30)
- 🍴 Home cooking
- 💷 Major cards accepted
- 🛏 8 letting rooms (5 en suite)
- 🅿 Car park, patio
- @ e-mail: robbielyons2@hotmail.com
- ❓ Chatteris Museum and Church of St Peter & St Paul; March 8 miles

THE GOLDEN PHEASANT

1 MAIN ROAD, ETTON, NR PETERBOROUGH,
CAMBRIDGESHIRE PE6 7DA
TEL/FAX: 01733 252387

Cambridgeshire

> **Directions:** From Peterborough take the A15 north, left on to the B1443
> Stamford road, then first right on to minor road signposted Etton.

Those in the know come from near and far to the **Golden Pheasant**, where they can be certain that a warm welcome awaits from Henry, Joann and family. Henry, a local farmer, now devotes his time to running this fine old inn. The inn is a sturdy 18th century stone building set back from the road at the end of a drive, with an extensive outside area, lawns, picnic benches and a children's play area. The spacious interior is very comfortable and full of character, a great place to take a break and relax with a glass of ale and something to eat. Food is take very seriously here, and the blackboard offers an extensive daily-changing choice of home-cooked dishes. There is a special menu of discounted dishes for senior citizens, and a kids' menu. Sunday lunch with traditional roasts is particularly popular, and booking is strongly recommended.

Equally in demand are the summer barbecues centred round a special barbecue hut in the garden. Fresh fish, prime beef and lots of other local produce are to the fore, and the chef can always be relied on to provide the best variety to offer something for everyone, whatever their taste and appetite. Food is served every session except Sunday evening and Monday. All in all, this splendid inn is one of the best for miles around, a place that it's always a pleasure to visit for its really terrific atmosphere – and even the resident ghost Caspar never causes any problems. The Golden Pheasant is located about 4 miles from Peterborough off the B1443 Stamford road and almost adjacent to the A15.

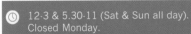

- 🕐 12-3 & 5.30-11 (Sat & Sun all day). Closed Monday.
- 🍴 Home cooking
- £ Major cards accepted
- Ⓟ Car park, garden, children's play area, barbecue
- ❓ Peterborough 4 miles, Stamford 7 miles

THE HOOPS

HIGH STREET, GREAT EVERSDEN, CAMBRIDGESHIRE CB3 7HN
TEL: 01223 264008 FAX: 01223 262710

> **Directions:** The inn is located in the main street of Great Eversden, 5 miles south of Cambridge just off the A603 (turn right).

On the main street of the village of Great Eversden, on the corner with Chapel Road, **The Hoops** has the outward appearance of a quintessential 19th century village inn. But step inside and there are a few surprises! Tim Richards spent much of his career as an engineer in the Far East, and when he returned to England it was with his lovely wife Anna. She has transformed the traditional decor inside the inn with a fascinating collection (still growing) of Oriental artefacts that adorn the public areas, from fabulous prints of her native home to elaborate gilded mirrors, ebony elephants and many other eyecatching pieces.

The East-meets-West theme continues through to the kitchen, turning this fine old village 'local' into an increasingly popular destination restaurant. Anna and her family are all excellent cooks, and as word spreads, The Hoops is attracting a clientele not just from the villages and its neighbours but from further afield. The menu continues to offer classic English pub dishes while tempting the taste buds with some Thai and other Oriental specialities. The best Thai food is fresh, full of flavour and very easy to enjoy, and the best is what visitors to The Hoops can definitely expect! Food is served from 6 o'clock onwards on Monday and all day on other days. Great Eversden is situated a few miles southwest of Cambridge, off the A603 - turn right at Little Eversden.

- 🕐 12-11 (Sun 12-10.30, Mon 6-11)
- 🍴 Home-cooked English and Thai food
- 💷 Major cards accepted
- 🅿 Car park, beer garden
- ❓ Harlton (Church of St Mary) 2 miles, Wimpole Hall and Home Farm NT 5 miles, Cambridge 5 miles

THE HOP BIND

HIGH STREET, COTTENHAM, CAMBRIDGESHIRE CB4 8RZ
TEL: 01954 200701

> **Directions:** The inn is situated on the main street of Cottenham (the B1049) 5 miles north of Cambridge.

The inviting cream-painted facade of **The Hop Bind** marks it out from its neighbours on the main street of Cottenham. Inside, the long carpeted bar features beams, handsome fireplaces and a panelled serving counter, while at the back of the pub is a charming courtyard with smart wooden garden furniture. The Hop Bind has been providing hospitality and refreshments to the elegant village of Cottenham since 1851, and today it remains a very comfortable and convivial place to meet. It's the first venture into the licensed trade for William Wallace, and the combination of the pleasant ambience, friendly staff, good ale and well-priced food attracts a large band of regulars.

The pub is open all day, every day for drinks, and home-cooked food is served every lunchtime and evening. Favourite dishes include a slap-up breakfast, ham, egg and chips, bangers & mash, steak & ale cobbler and steak or chicken in a Portuguese flour roll. Tuesday is steak night, Wednesday fish & chips. The Hop Bind is very much at the heart of village life, with cribbage and darts teams playing in the local leagues, summer barbecues and musical Sunday evenings featuring blues, rockabilly, rock 'n' roll and other styles. There are plenty of places of interest nearby, including the important archaeological site of Giant's Hill and Denny Abbey and its Farm Museum. In Cottenham itself, All Saints Church, with its distinctive yellow and pink Jacobean brick tower, is well worth a look.

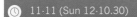

- 🕐 11·11 (Sun 12·10.30)
- 🍴 Home cooking
- £ Major cards accepted
- 🅿 Patio
- 🎵 Occasional live music evenings
- @ website: www.hopbind.co.uk
- ❓ Giant's Hill Archaeological Site 1 mile, Waterbeach (Denny Abbey & Farm Museum) 3 miles

THE JOHN BARLEYCORN

MOORFIELD ROAD, DUXFORD, CAMBRIDGESHIRE CB2 4PP
TEL: 01223 832699 FAX: 01223 830330

Directions: Duxford is located 8 miles south of Cambridge, very close to Junction 10 of the M11. The inn is at the eastern end of the village 1 mile from the A1301.

Named after the legendary figure who travelled round the country sowing seeds, the **John Barleycorn** is a wonderful thatched pub with a history that goes back to 1660 - the date is inscribed above a first-floor window. Hanging baskets and flower tubs make a pretty sight even prettier, and inside all is old-world charm, with low beamed ceilings, pew benches and heavy wooden refectory-style tables with brass nameplates such as 'Poachers Corner' and 'Smugglers Retreat'. Old proverbs are painted on the beams, and on one wall is a list of all the landlords from 1720 to the present day. The current incumbents are Doug and Paula Bollen, ably assisted by experienced, willing and friendly staff. Doug has been in the licensed trade for most of his working life, and both he and the John Barleycorn are recipients of prestigious awards: Doug has been voted Licensee of the Year for the Anglia region, and the

inn was National Pub of the Year 2002, an award earned for its splendid atmosphere and hospitality, for its well-kept real ale and for its outstanding food.

This is deservedly one of the popular pubs in the region, and a team of chefs are kept busy providing seriously good food from 11am to 10pm, from light snacks to daily fish specials, sizzling chicken, classic Irish stew with dumplings and the house special roast leg of lamb. The pub has an attractive garden with picnic benches and a safe children's play area. Four pleasant timber-framed guest bedrooms in chalet style offer very comfortable accommodation and an excellent base for both business people and tourists. With the M11 (J10) a short drive away, access north and south is easy, and among the nearby attractions is the marvellous Duxford Aviation Museum, an offshoot of the Imperial War Museum.

- 🕐 8am-midnight daily
- 🍴 Light snacks to full à la carte menu
- 💷 Major cards accepted
- 🛏 4 en-suite rooms
- 🅿 Garden, children's play area
- ❓ Duxford Aviation Museum 2 miles, Cambridge 8 miles

THE OLIVER TWIST COUNTRY INN

HIGH ROAD, GUYHIRN, NR WISBECH, CAMBRIDGESHIRE PE13 4EA
TEL: 01945 450523 FAX: 01945 450009

Directions: Guyhirn is located 6 miles south of Wisbech on the A47; 4 miles north of March. The pub is signposted from the A47/A141 Guyhirn roundabout.

The Oliver Twist is a smart redbrick, tile-roofed pub nestling below the bank on the Peterborough side of the River Nene. Mick and Jacqui Thornton took over the reins in 1996, and in the years since they have turned the Oliver Twist into a thriving country inn of wide appeal. The interior is tastefully decorated in half wood panelled cottage style. Fully air conditioned public rooms with real fires keep things snug in winter. Mick is a connoisseur of good beer and a champion cellarman, so it comes as no surprise that the cask ales and other beers are kept in tip-top condition. Food is also an important part of the business, and the generous servings mean that no-one need ask for more.

The choice runs from filled rolls, baguettes and ploughman's platters to plain and sauced chicken and steak dishes, salmon en croûte and medallions of lamb. There's plenty for the visitor to see and do in the region, and the Oliver Twist has recently added another string to its bow with the opening of a sympathetically designed accommodation block that came on stream in March 2004. The six bedrooms are well-equipped and very comfortable, providing an ideal base for a business trip or for exploring the area. Walking and cycling are popular activities in the area round the pub, and fishing is available on the Morton's Leam. The A47 and A141 put the towns of Wisbech, March and Peterborough within an easy drive, and other local places of interest include Thorney Abbey and Heritage Museum, and the lovely old Fenland village of Parson Drove.

- ⏱ 11.30-2.30 & 6-11 (Sun 12-3 & 6-10)
- 🍴 Snacks and full à la carte menu
- £ Mastercard, Visa
- 🛏 6 en suite rooms
- 🅿 Car park
- @ website: www.theolivertwist.com
- ❓ Thorney Abbey 6 miles, Wisbech 6 miles

THE PRINCE OF WALES

POTTON ROAD, HILTON, HUNTINGDONSHIRE PE28 9NG
TEL: 01480 830257

Directions: Hilton is located on the B1040, 1 mile off the A14 and about 6 miles southeast of Huntingdon.

The Prince of Wales is an attractive, well-kept roadside inn dating from 1870, with a prominent princely crest of feathers on the sign and few picnic tables set out at the front. Inside, the bar has a homely, traditional appeal, making it a very pleasant and inviting spot to enjoy a chat and a drink. The Prince of Wales, which is owned by prominent local businessman Simon Perry, has also earned a well-deserved reputation as an excellent place for a snack or a meal, and such is its popularity that booking is advisable at the weekend. The choice runs from sandwiches and jacket potatoes with a choice of fillings to steaks and hearty braised lamb shanks. The facilities of the Prince of Wales do not end at food and drink, as it also has four very comfortable en suite letting rooms.

It is a convenient place to stay for anyone who has come a long way to visit a friend or relative at Papworth Hospital in nearby Papworth Everard. It is also a pleasant, civilised base for a leisurely tour of the region. Papworth Everard and Papworth St Agnes both have notable churches, and Huntingdon and St Ives, both with strong Oliver Cromwell connections, are within a short drive. The chief attraction in Hilton itself is its famous maze. Cut out of turf to a popular medieval design, this compact circular maze was the work of a certain William Sparrow, and at the centre is an obelisk with English and Latin inscriptions about Sparrow and his maze. Those finding their way out of the maze could head for nearby Fenstanton and look at the grave of the garden designer Lancelot 'Capability' Brown in the graveyard of the medieval church.

- 🕐 12-3 Fri, Sat & Sun; 7-11 every day
- 🍺 Bar meals
- 💷 Major cards accepted
- 🛏 4 en suite bedrooms
- 🅿 Car park, beer garden
- ❓ Turf Maze in Hilton; Papworth St Agnes 2 miles, Fenstanton 2 miles, Papworth Everard (Papworth Hospital) 4 miles, Huntingdon 6 miles

THE QUEENS HEAD

ROYSTON ROAD, HARSTON, CAMBRIDGESHIRE CB2 5NH
TEL/FAX: 01223 870693

Directions: Harston lies 4 miles south of Cambridge on the A10, close to Junction 11 of the M11.

Flanked by handsome trees, **The Queens Head** is an attractive white-painted building with a distinctive slate roof. It dates from the last years of the 19th century, and the promise of the exterior is more than fulfilled inside, where the very smart public bar and the lounge/dining area are in traditional style. Neil Clements and Michele Hoyland are the young, go-ahead tenants who took over here in the summer of 2004, bringing with them a good deal of experience and bags of enthusiasm. The inn's reputation was well established, and Neil and Michele clearly intend to stay here and enhance its appeal still further. The food is definitely the star of the show, and Neil, who masterminds that side of the

enterprise, has recruited a second chef. Between them they provide a fine variety of wholesome, freshly prepared dishes that cater for all tastes and appetites (no food Sunday evening).

The Queens Head, which hosts musical evenings at the weekend and occasionally during the week, has a huge car park and adjoining beer garden. The village of Harston is very easy to reach, being situated on the A10, with Junction 11 of the M11 just a few minutes away. Cambridge is only five miles up the road, and other places of interest in the vicinity include the nature reserves at Shepreth and Fowlmere, the renowned Aviation Museum at Duxford, and Wimpole Hall, a spectacular country mansion set in equally spectacular grounds.

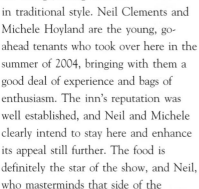

- 🕐 12-2 & 6-11 (Sun 12-3 & 7-10.30)
- 🍴 Home cooking (no food Sunday evening)
- £ Major cards accepted
- Ⓟ Car park, beer garden
- @ e-mail: neil051@hotmail.com
- ❓ Fowlmere Nature Reserve 3 miles, Duxford 4 miles, Cambridge 4 miles

THE THREE HORSESHOES

344 MARCH ROAD, TURVES, NR WHITTLESEY,
CAMBRIDGESHIRE PE7 2DN
TEL: 01733 840414

Directions: The inn is located in the village of Turves, signposted off the A605 between Whittlesey and March.

Melanie and Tim Fletcher, both from a farming background, left the land in 2002 to put all their energies into running **The Three Horseshoes**. Their quintessential country pub stands in the village of Turves about a mile south of the busy A605, which runs from Peterborough to meet the A141 and March to the south and Wisbech to the north. Behind the long, distinctive white-painted frontage, the extensive bar space offers the comfort of a good hotel while retaining the style and atmosphere of a rural pub. The 50-cover dining area is particularly intimate and inviting, with carpets, curtains, candlelit tables and sparkling glass and cutlery. Melanie is in charge of the restaurant, from where the chef produces great-value lunches

and a splendidly varied evening menu with a major showing of local ingredients. Lunch is served Thursday to Sunday, dinner every evening except Monday.

A brisk walk in the Fens will soon generate a thirst and an appetite which Melanie and Tim are only too willing and able to take care of. For motorists, Whittlesey, with its 14th century Church of St Andrew, its museum of local archaeology and history, and its famous Straw Bear procession in the January Festival, is a short drive away, and a little further on are the many attractions of the cathedral town of Peterborough. Perhaps the most interesting place of all to visit is Flag Fen Bronze Age Centre, one of Europe's most important Bronze Age sites.

- Mon-Wed 6-11, Thurs & Fri 12-2 & 6-11, Sat 12-11, Sun 12-10.30
- Home cooking served Tues & Wed evening, Thurs-Sat lunch and evening, Sun 12 to 4
- Major cards accepted
- Car park, beer garden, barbecue
- Occasional live music evenings
- Whittlesey 4 miles, March 5 miles

THE THREE TUNS

HIGH STREET, HUNTINGDON, CAMBRIDGESHIRE PE29 3NF
TEL: 01480 356309 OR 437644

Cambridgeshire

> **Directions:** The inn stands on the main street of Huntingdon, which is located close to the A1 and A14.

In the main street of Huntingdon, a short stroll from the shops and the town's many places of interest, **The Three Tuns** is open throughout the day, every day, for the dispensing of hospitality and liquid refreshment. Crawford Boyd, who hails from Edinburgh, has been here for seven years, his regular patrons appreciate the warm welcome, the relaxed atmosphere and the general air of bonhomie that prevails. The handsome redbrick building dates from the middle of the 17th century and has a traditional, unpretentious feel that appeals to everyone - even the several resident ghosts are very much at home and invariably well behaved. It's a down-to-earth place with good beer, plenty of

lively conversation and live music at the weekend.

There's always plenty going on in Huntingdon, and business people and tourists will find The Three Tuns a very convenient base of operations. The inn has four guest bedrooms, one of them with en suite facilities. The former county town of Huntingdonshire, first settled by the Romans, has many fine Georgian buildings including a splendid three-storey town hall. Oliver Cromwell was born in the town and went to school in the town, as did Samuel Pepys. The two churches are both well worth a visit, and so is the Cromwell Museum, and visitors looking to build up a thirst can take a walk in nearby Hinchingbrooke Country Park before repairing to The Three Tuns.

- 🕐 11-11
- 💷 Major cards accepted
- 🛏 4 rooms (1 en suite)
- 🅿 Car park, patio
- 🎵 Live music at the weekend
- ❓ All the attractions of Huntingdon are close by.

THE VINE

SOUTH GREEN, COATES, CAMBRIDGESHIRE PE7 2BJ
TEL/FAX: 01733 840343

Cambridgeshire

Directions: The inn lies on the A605 about 9 miles east of Peterborough.

A short drive east of Whittlesey along the A605 brings visitors to the village of Coates and **The Vine** public house. Overlooking the village green, this early 19th century coaching inn has quickly found a new lease of life since Bruce and Denise Roan arrived as tenants in the spring of 2004. Their neat

redbrick pub, which sits discreetly back from the main road behind trim hedges and bushes, has a very traditional appeal in the cosy little public bar and the attractive lounge/dining area. It's a popular place for locals to gather to chat over a drink, and it also does a good line in food, including an excellent Sunday lunch that's a treat not to be missed for many of the regulars.

Over the last few years Coates has put

itself on the map as a major centre for petanque, a game similar to the French boules that is said to have originated in the Netherlands. 2004 saw the tenth anniversary of the Coates petanque tournament, and residents of the village set up petanque pitches in their gardens and driveways as no fewer than 126 teams competed. The tournament was centred round The Vine, with a barbecue and refreshments provided, and the community spirit engendered by the event was a source of great pride and satisfaction to everyone in the village. Apart from this annual sporting occasion, the region is very popular with walkers and cyclists, and those interested in the history of the region and in particular the Fens will find all the answers in the museums in Whittlesey and Peterborough.

- Mon,Tues, Wed 4.30 to 11, Thurs, Fri 12 to 2.30 and 4.30 to11.
- Bar Meals
- Car park, garden, children's play area, petanque
- Occasional live entertainment
- Whittlesey 2 miles, Peterborough 9 miles

WEST END HOUSE

16 WEST END, ELY, CAMBRIDGESHIRE CB6 3AY
TEL: 01353 662907   FAX: 01353 659101

Directions: The inn lies a quarter of a mile to the west of Ely Cathedral.

A pub has stood on this corner site in the centre of Ely for several centuries, and behind its smart cream and red facade the present **West End House** has many fine period features. Kim and Stephen Baxter took over the licence in the spring of 2003 and run the pub with the help of their daughter Philippa and the active participation of the dogs Murphy and Paddy. Stephen is in charge of the drinks side of the business, and in the comfortable bar, with its feature brick walls, beams, wooden floor and smart country furniture, he dispenses a good variety of cask ales, including brews from Morland's (Old Speckled Hen), Greene King, Adnams, Websters and the Fenland Brewery. Kim looks after the food preparation, which comprises a straightforward selection of sandwiches,

filled baguettes and some light snacks (food is not available on Sunday).

An important asset of West End House is its proximity to Ely's greatest attractions. The house where Oliver Cromwell lived, which is now the Tourist Information Centre, is literally just a few steps away, and a little further on stands the glorious Ely Cathedral. This remarkable example of Romanesque architecture stands within the walls of a monastery, and many of the ancient buildings stand as a tribute to the amazing skills of their designers and builders - definitely not to be missed. Ely, the jewel in the crown of the Fens, is easily reached from any direction, standing at the junction of the A10 up from Cambridge and down from King's Lynn, and the A142, which runs west to Chatteris and southeast to Newmarket.

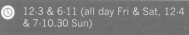

🕐 12-3 & 6-11 (all day Fri & Sat, 12-4 & 7-10.30 Sun)

🍴 Bar snacks (no food Sunday)

🅿 Beer garden

@ e-mail: kimbaxter9@aol.com

❓ In Ely: Oliver Cromwell's House, Ely Cathedral, Brass Rubbing Centre, Museum of Stained Glass

THE WHITE HORSE

HIGH STREET, TILBROOK, CAMBRIDGESHIRE PE28 0JP
TEL: 01480 860764

Directions: Tilbrook lies on the B645 about 8 miles northwest of St Neots. From the A14 about 7 miles west of Huntingdon take the B660 signposted Catworth and Kimbolton; take the second right to Tilbrook.

The White Horse is an attractive traditional village pub dating from 1738, with a large car park and a lawned area set with picnic benches under parasols. Since 2002 it has been run by Michael and Julia Higgs, who love every aspect of pub life; their staff are equally dedicated, and their joint efforts are rewarded by a growing band of regular patrons. The bar and dining area are neat, pretty and immaculate, and the feature conservatory blends harmoniously with the old-fashioned style of the inn. Michael and Julia both cook, and everything is prepared to order, from hot and cold snacks and light meals to a mixed grill that will satisfy the heartiest outdoor appetite.

The main menu is supplemented by some more elaborate specials on Thursday to Saturday evenings, and senior citizens can enjoy a bargain menu on weekday lunchtimes; food is not served on Sunday evening or Monday. Walking and cycling are popular activities in the region, and a walk round nearby Grafham Water is a good way to build up a thirst and an appetite. This reservoir was created in the mid-1960s and offers beautiful country walks, numerous outdoor activities, nature trails, bird habitats and exhibitions. Even closer than Grafham Water is Kimbolton, a village filled with history and well worth a lengthy pause. The splendid Church of St Andrew would head the list of attractions were it not for Kimbolton Castle, a much-modified Tudor mansion where Catherine of Aragon spent the last years of her life and where she died in 1536.

- 🕐 11-3 & 5.30-11 (Sat 12-3 & 6-11, Sun 12-3 & 7.10.30)
- 🍴 Home cooking
- £ Major cards accepted
- Ⓟ Car park, beer garden, children's play area
- ❓ Kimbolton Castle 2 miles, Grafham Water 4 miles, St Neots 8 miles

THE WHITE SWAN

ELSWORTH ROAD, CONINGTON, NR FENSTANTON,
CAMBRIDGESHIRE CB3 8LN
TEL/FAX: 01954 267251

> **Directions:** Conington is situated off the A14 between Cambridge and
> Huntingdon, signposted at Fenstanton.

Hospitality is in liberal supply at **The White Swan**, a handsome 18th century redbrick building at a quiet crossroads on the edge of the village of Conington. The short detour off the busy A14 (at Fenstanton or the next turning south) will be rewarded with a friendly welcome from Kevin and Teresa Parfett and a comfortable, civilised ambience for enjoying a chat, a drink and something good to eat. The hosts are a very hardworking couple who have widened the appeal of The White Swan from a charming village 'local' into a popular pub for all the family. Greene King IPA heads the list of cask ales, and there's a good selection of wines to enjoy by the glass on their own or to accompany Teresa's excellent home cooking. The bar-lounge is roomy and comfortable, and in the non-smoking restaurant generously served, well-priced dishes, using local produce as far as possible. A varied menu is available from bar snacks to three course meals. The Sunday roasts are deservedly very popular, and Teresa's fruit crumbles round off a meal in style.

The inn has a huge car park and a lawned area with picnic benches and space for children to play. Here, too, is a unique feature for children - the Cygnet Bar, where kids can buy soft drinks and snacks. This bar is open at the weekend during the summer months. The city of Cambridge, with all its many attractions, is an easy drive along the A14, and even closer is the village of Fenstanton, where the landscape gardener Lancelot 'Capability' Brown is buried in the churchyard of St Peter & St Paul. This is also a good area for walking, and Kevin and Teresa are always ready with advice on local walks and tours.

- ⏰ 12-3 & 6-11
- 🍴 Home cooking
- £ Not Amex
- 🅿 Car park, garden, children's play area and Cygnet Bar
- @ e-mail: enquiries@WhiteSwanConington.co.uk website: www.WhiteSwanConington.co.uk
- ❓ Fenstanton 2 miles, Cambridge 6 miles, Huntingdon 7 miles

THE WHITE SWAN

MAIN STREET, WOODNEWTON, NORTHAMPTONSHIRE PE8 5EB
TEL: 01780 470381   FAX: 01780 470177

Cambridgeshire

> **Directions:** Woodnewton can be reached from the A605 Peterborough-Oundle road (leave at Warmington roundabout), from the A43 Corby-Stamford road or from the A1/A47 junction on to minor road through Yarwell and Nassington.

The White Swan endured a precarious few months when in 1988 it was closed and bought by a developer. The villagers thought that they had lost their pub, but after a sustained campaign it was saved, renovated and re-opened in 1990. It is now in the safe hands of Jenni Chalkley and Adrian Downing, who have lived in Woodnewton for many years. In this, their first venture into the licensed trade, they are assisted by Jenni's daughter Vicki, and between them the trio have established a wide and growing reputation for excellent hospitality. A large white swan on a red background announces the immaculately kept 18th century inn, which features beautiful original stonework that reaches right back to the beer garden. Picnic benches are set out under parasols to take advantage of sunny weather, and the inn has ample off-road parking and a petanque pitch. Inside, the darkwood bar-lounge has a pleasantly traditional look and feel that is continued in the dining area, where Jenni has quickly made her mark on the cooking as well as the decor.

Jenni and her chef are of a like mind, producing a selection of dishes prepared from the best raw materials that local suppliers and local markets can provide (food is served every day except Monday). The village and the inn can be approached from almost any direction, and the surrounding area is particularly rich in places of historic interest. Notable among these are Fotheringhay Castle, where Mary Queen of Scots was imprisoned and executed, Prebendal Manor House, the oldest dwelling in Northamptonshire, and Elton Hall, a Gothic revival house with a fine art collection.

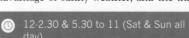

- 🕐 12-2.30 & 5.30 to 11 (Sat & Sun all day)
- 🍽 Home cooking (no food Monday)
- 💷 Major cards accepted
- Ⓟ Car park, garden, petanque
- 🎵 Quiz first Sunday of month
- ❓ Prebendal Manor House 2 miles, Fotheringhay 2 miles, Rockingham Forest 3 miles, Oundle 5 miles, Elton Hall 6 miles

THE WINDMILL

ST IVES ROAD, SOMERSHAM, NR HUNTINGDON,
CAMBRIDGESHIRE PE28 3ET
TEL/FAX: 01487 840328

Cambridgeshire

Directions: The Windmill is situated on the western edge of Somersham, 5 miles east of Huntingdon.

The Windmill is a fine-looking cream-painted country inn on the edge of the village of Somersham, five miles east of Huntingdon and surrounded by many scenic and historic locations and visitor attractions. Stuart Clements and Natalie Leaden arrived in the spring of 2003 to take charge of this splendid traditional pub, which dates from the 1840s. The Windmill is very much food-driven, and the compact interior has a real restaurant feel, with neatly laid tables clad in dark blue tablecloths over pristine white linen. The good-value home cooking brings in an impressive lunchtime trade, and the menu is supplemented by regularly changing dishes of the day. The daily fish specials and the super home-

made savoury pies are particularly popular, but everything is fresh and appetising, and the food is complemented by an excellent wine list. The Windmill is also a great place for a relaxing evening meal (food is served every session) and with space at a premium booking is essential at the weekend and other peak times. The inn hosts live jazz nights most weekends, and the murder mystery and other themed nights also bring in the crowds.

The Fenland village of Somersham, home to artists, potters and classic car owners, has an attractive square where brass bands sometimes play. It once had a palace for the Bishops of Ely, and the splendid Church of St John is well worth a visit. Close by is the Raptor Foundation, sanctuary for owls and other birds of prey. At nearby Earith are the Ouse Washes, a special protection area of wetland and the natural habitat of many species of birds.

- 11.30-3 & 6-11 (open all day Sat & Sun)
- Home cooking lunchtime and evening
- Major cards accepted
- Car park, beer garden
- Weekend jazz evenings, regular theme evenings
- e-mail: thewindmill@ukonline.co.uk
- In Somersham: Raptor Foundation, Church of St John; Ouse Washes wetland 2 miles, Huntingdon 5 miles, St Ives 4 miles

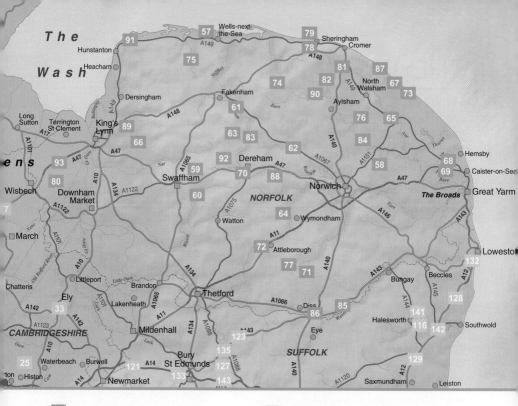

57	**The Ark Royal**, Wells-next-the-Sea
58	**The Bell Inn**, Salhouse, Norwich
59	**The Black Swan**, Little Dunham
60	**The Blue Lion**, North Pickenham
61	**The Boar Inn**, Great Ryburgh
62	**The Bridge Inn**, Lenwade, Norwich
63	**The Brisley Bell Inn**, Brisley, Norfolk
64	**The Cherry Tree**, Wicklewood
65	**The Cross Keys**, Dilham, North Walsham
66	**The Crown**, Gayton, Kings Lynn
67	**The Duke of Edinburgh**, Bacton
68	**The Eels Foot Inn**, Ormesby St Michael
69	**The Fox & Hounds**, Filby
70	**The Gemini Pub & Restaurant**, Dereham
71	**The Greyhound**, Tibenham, Norwich
72	**The Griffin Hotel**, Attleborough
73	**The Hill House**, Happisburgh
74	**The John H Stracey**, Briston
75	**The Jolly Farmers**, North Creake
76	**The Jolly Farmers**, Swanton Abbott
77	**The Kings Head**, New Buckenham
78	**The Lobster**, Sheringham, Norfolk
79	**The Stables Restaurant**, Sheringham
80	**The Marshlands Arms**, Marshland St James, Wisbech,
81	**The New Inn**, Roughton
82	**The Old Red Lion**, Aldborough
83	**The Railway Freehouse**, North Elmham
84	**The Red Lion**, Coltishall
85	**The Red Lion**, Needham, Harleston
86	**The Scole Inn**, Scole, Diss
87	**The Ship Inn**, Mundesley, Cromer
88	**The Swan**, Mattishall, Dereham
89	**The Three Horseshoes**, Roydon
90	**The Walpole Arms**, Itteringham, Norwich
91	**The White Horse**, Holme by the Sea
92	**The White Horse at Longham**, Dereham
93	**The Woolpack**, Terrington St John

Please note all cross references refer to page numbers

NORFOLK

The area that lies between the county capital of Norwich and the border with Suffolk is mainly flat farmland, with quiet villages, handsome old farmhouses and the charming spires and towers of churches. The valleys of the Rivers Nar and Wensum display some of the most enchanting scenery in the county, and the area boasts one of the finest Gothic parish churches in England, at Cawston. The major centres of population include Diss, an old market town with a mix of Tudor, Georgian and Victorian houses, and Wymondham, with its timber-framed houses, picturesque market place and an Abbey church that stands up well to comparison even with the majestic Norwich Cathedral. Norwich, once an important centre of the worsted trade, retains many medieval buildings, a number of which now serve as museums relating the fascinating history of the region.

The area to the east of this fine city contains the unique Norfolk Broads, beautiful stretches of shallow water, most of them linked by navigable rivers and canals. This is Britain's finest wetland area, a National Park in all but name. Broadland covers some 220 square miles in a rough oval to the northwest of Great Yarmouth. Three main rivers – the Ant, the Thurne and the Bure – thread their way through the marshes, providing some 120 miles of navigable waterways. The Broads, long popular for restful, relaxing holidays, remain none the less a refuge for many species of endangered birds and plants, and during the spring and autumn they are a favourite stopping-off place for migrating birds.

On the coast due east of Norwich is the old port and modern holiday resort

PLACES OF INTEREST

Attleborough	41	Norwich	47
Aylsham	41	Potter Heigham	51
Blakeney	41	Sandringham	51
Bressingham	42	Sheringham	52
Burnham Market	42	Snettisham	52
Burnham Thorpe	42	South Walsham	52
Caister-on-Sea	43	Swaffham	53
Coltishall	43	Terrington St	
Cromer	44	Clement	53
Diss	44	Thetford	53
Fakenham	45	Wells Next-the-Sea	
Great Yarmouth	45	55	
Holkham	46	West Runton	55
Hunstanton	46	Wymondham	55
King's Lynn	47		

Norfolk Broads

of Great Yarmouth, where the visitor will find miles of sandy beaches, a breezy promenade, two grand old traditional piers and all the fun of the fair, as well as a rich maritime heritage that lives on to this day.

Miles of sandy beaches, spectacular sea views and fresh sea air are the rewards awaiting visitors to the Norfolk coast, which stretches from Great Yarmouth in the east up to Cromer on the edge of the county and west to Sheringham, Hunstanton and beyond. The northeast coast includes what are sometimes known as 'the Highlands of Norfolk' - the Cromer Ridge, which rise to the not-so-dizzy heights of 330 feet above sea level.

The most important town on the northwest coast is the busy seaside resort of Hunstanton, which has cliffs comprising red, white and brown geological layers. Another curious thing about Hunstanton: it is the only east coast resort that actually faces west! King's Lynn, on the Great Ouse three miles inland from The Wash, was one of England's most important ports in medieval times, sitting at the southern end of an underwater maze of sandbanks. To the northeast of King's Lynn is the prosperous market town of Fakenham, around which lie a remarkable variety of places of interest. To the north, in the valley of the River Stiffkey, the Shrine of Our Lady of Walsingham was in medieval times second only to that of Thomas à Becket at Canterbury as a pilgrim destination.

Breckland, which extends for more than 360 square miles in southwest Norfolk and northwest Suffolk, is underlain by chalk with only a light covering of soil. The name 'Breckland' comes from the dialect word *breck*, meaning an area of land which has been cultivated for a while and then allowed to revert to heath after the soil has become exhausted. This quiet corner of the county is bounded by the Rivers Little Ouse and Waveney, which separate Norfolk from Suffolk.

ATTLEBOROUGH

The greatest glory of this pleasant market town is to be found in its church of **St Mary**. Here, a remarkable 15th century chancel screen stretches the width of the church and is beautifully embellished with the arms of the 24 bishoprics into which England was divided at that time. The screen is generally reckoned to be one of the most outstanding in the country, a remarkable survivor of the Reformation purging of such beautiful creations from churches across the land.

A couple of miles west of Attleborough, the **Tropical Butterfly Gardens and Bird Park** is set in 2,400 square feet of landscaped tropical gardens and provides a congenial home for hundreds of exotic tropical butterflies. There's also a Falconry Centre, waterside walk, garden centre, gift shop, coffee shop and tea gardens.

AYLSHAM

The attractive little town of Aylsham is

set beside the River Bure, the northern terminus of the **Bure Valley Railway**. It has an unspoilt **Market Place**, surrounded by late 17th and early 18th century houses, reflecting the prosperity the town enjoyed in those years from the cloth trade, and a 14th/15th century church, St Michael's, said to have been built by John O'Gaunt. In the churchyard is the tomb of one of the greatest of the 18th century landscape gardeners, Humphry Repton, the creator of some 200 parks and gardens around the country.

One of Repton's many commissions was to landscape the grounds of **Blickling Hall**, a 'dream of architectural beauty' which stands a mile or so outside Aylsham. Inside this outstanding Jacobean mansion, the most spectacular feature is the Long Gallery, which extends for 135 feet and originally provided space for indoor exercise in bad weather.

BLAKENEY

One of the most enchanting of the North Norfolk coastal villages, Blakeney was a commercial port until the beginning of the 20th century, when silting up of the estuary prevented all but pleasure craft from gaining access. The silting has left a fascinating landscape of serpentine creeks and channels twisting their way through mud banks and sand hills. In a side street off the quay is the

Blickling Hall, Aylsham

Seals at Blakeney

14th century **Guildhall** (English Heritage), which was probably a private house and contains an interesting undercroft, or cellar, which is notable as an early example of a brick-built vaulted ceiling.

The beautifully restored Church of St Nicholas, set on a hill overlooking village and marshland, offers the visitor a lovely Early English chancel, built in 1220, and the magnificent west tower, 100 feet high, a landmark for miles around. In a small turret on the northeast corner of the chancel a light would once burn as a beacon to guide ships safely into Blakeney Harbour.

BRESSINGHAM

Bressingham Gardens and Steam Museum boasts one of the world's finest collections of British and Continental locomotives, some of them on loan from the National Railway Museum at York. All are housed under cover in the museum's extensive locomotive sheds,

which also contain many steam-driven industrial engines, traction engines, and **The Fire Museum**, whose collection of fire engines and fire-fighting equipment could form a complete museum in its own right. Visitors can view the interior of the Royal Coach and ride along five miles of track through the woods and gardens.

The six acres of landscaped grounds are notable in themselves, since they are planted with more than 5,000 alpine and other types of plants.

BURNHAM MARKET

There are seven Burnhams in all, strung along the valley of the little River Burn. Burnham Market is the largest of them, its past importance reflected in the wealth of Georgian buildings surrounding the green and the two churches that lie at each end of its broad main street, just 600 yards apart. In the opinion of many, Burnham Market has the best collection of small Georgian houses in Norfolk, and it's a delight to wander through the yards and alleys that link the town's three east-west streets.

BURNHAM THORPE

From the tower of All Saints' Church, the White Ensign flaps in the breeze; the only pub in the village is the *Lord Nelson*; and the shop next door is called the Trafalgar Stores. No prizes for deducing that Burnham Thorpe was the birthplace of Horatio Nelson. His father, the Revd Edmund Nelson, was the Rector here for 46 years; Horatio was the sixth of his eleven children.

Parsonage House, where Horatio was born seven weeks' premature in 1758, was demolished during his lifetime, but the pub (one of more than 200 hostelries across the country bearing the hero's name) has become a kind of shrine to Nelson's memory, its walls covered with portraits, battle scenes and other marine paintings.

There's more Nelson memorabilia in the church, among it a crucifix and lectern made with wood from *HMS Victory*, a great chest from the pulpit used by the Revd Nelson, and two flags from *HMS Nelson*.

A little over a mile to the south of Burnham Thorpe stand the picturesque ruins of **Creake Abbey**, an Augustinian monastery founded in 1206. The Abbey's working life came to an abrupt end in 1504 when, within a single week, every one of the monks died of the plague.

CAISTER-ON-SEA

In Boudicca's time, this modern holiday resort with its stretch of fine sands was an important fishing port for her people, the Iceni. After the Romans had vanquished her unruly tribe, they settled here sometime in the 2nd century and built a *castra*, or castle, or Caister, of which only a few foundations and remains have yet been found. **Caister Castle**, which stands in a picturesque setting about a mile to the west of the town, is a much later construction, built in 1435 and the first in England to be built of brick. The 90-foot tower remains, together with much of the moated wall and gatehouse, now lapped by still waters and with ivy relentlessly encroaching. The castle is open daily from May to September and, as an additional attraction, there is a Car Collection in the grounds which features an impressive collection of veteran, Edwardian and vintage cars, an antique fire engine, and the original car used in the film of Ian Fleming's *Chitty Chitty Bang Bang*.

COLTISHALL

This charming village beside the River Bure captivates visitors with its riverside setting, leafy lanes, elegant Dutch-gabled houses, village green and thatched church. Coltishall has a good claim to its title of 'Gateway to Broadland', since for most cruisers this is the beginning of the navigable portion of the Bure. Anyone interested in Norfolk's industrial heritage will want to seek out the **Ancient Lime Kiln**, next door to the Railway Tavern in Station Road.

A couple of miles south of Coltishall, on the B1150, is the **Redwings Horse Sanctuary**, founded in 1984 to provide a caring and permanent home for horses, ponies, donkeys and mules rescued from neglect and slaughter.

CROMER

As you enter a seaside town, what more reassuring sight could there be than to see the pier still standing? **Cromer Pier** is the genuine article, complete with Lifeboat Station and the Pavilion Theatre, which still stages traditional end-of-the-pier shows. The Pier's survival is all the more impressive since it was badly damaged in 1953 and 1989, and in 1993 sliced in two by a drilling rig which had broken adrift in a storm.

Cromer has been a significant resort since the late 1700s and in its early days even received an unsolicited testimonial from Jane Austen. In her novel *Emma* (1816), a character declares that 'Perry was a week at Cromer once, and he holds it to be the best of all the sea-bathing places.' A succession of celebrities, ranging from Lord Tennyson and Oscar Wilde to Winston Churchill and the German Kaiser, all came to see for themselves.

The inviting sandy beach remains much as they saw it (horse-drawn bathing machines aside), as does the Church of **St Peter & St Paul**, which boasts the tallest tower in Norfolk. Cromer Crabs are reckoned to be the most succulent in England. During the season, between April and September, crab-boats are launched from the shore (there's no harbour here), sail out to the crab banks about 3 miles offshore, and there the two-man teams on each boat deal with some 200 pots.

The **Lifeboat Museum** tells the dramatic story of the courageous men who manned the town's rescue service.

Also well worth visiting is the **Cromer Museum**, housed in a row of restored fishermen's cottages near the church

DISS

The late Poet Laureate, John Betjeman, voted Diss his favourite Norfolk town, and it's easy to understand his enthusiasm. The River Waveney running alongside forms the boundary between Norfolk and Suffolk, but this attractive old market town – winner of Best Kept Market Town in Norfolk, whose town centre is now a designated conservation area - keeps itself firmly on the northern bank of the river. The town is a pleasing mixture of Tudor, Georgian

Beach at Cromer

and Victorian houses grouped around **The Mere**, which gives the town its name, derived from the Anglo-Saxon word for 'standing water'.

FAKENHAM

Fakenham is a busy and prosperous-looking market town, famous for its National Hunt Racecourse, antique & bric-a-brac markets and auctions, and as a major agricultural centre for the region. Straddling the River Wensum, this attractive country town has a number of fine late 18th and early 19th century brick buildings in and around the Market Place. And it must surely be one of the few towns in England where the former gasworks (still intact) have been turned into a **Museum of Gas & Local History**, housing an impressive historical display of domestic gas appliances of every kind.

Southeast of Fakenham, off the A1067, **Pensthorpe Waterfowl Park** is home to Europe's best collection of endangered and exotic waterbirds.

GREAT YARMOUTH

The seaward side of Great Yarmouth is a 5-mile stretch of sandy beaches, tourist attractions and countless amusements, with a breezy promenade from which one can watch the constant traffic of ships in Yarmouth Roads. There are two fine old traditional piers, the Britannia (810 feet long) and the Wellington (600 feet long), as well as The Jetty, first built in the 16th century for landing goods and passengers. A host of activities are on offer for families: **The Sealife Centre** with many kinds of marine life including octopus and seahorses, and an underwater viewing channel passing through shark-infested 'oceans'; **Amazonia**, an indoor tropical paradise featuring the largest collection of reptiles in Britain; **Merrivale Model Village** which offers an acre of attractive landscaped gardens with over 200 realistic models of town and country in miniature, which are illuminated at dusk, and the **Pleasure Beach**, featuring over 70 rides and attractions combining all the thrills of modern high-tech amusement park rides with the fun of traditional fairground

Harbour at Great Yarmouth

attractions.

For heritage enthusiasts, Great Yarmouth has a rich and proud maritime history. The **Norfolk Nelson Museum** on South Quay features displays, paintings and contemporary memorabilia relating to the life and times of Horatio Lord Nelson.

At South Denes the 144-foot high **Nelson's Monument** crowned by a statue, not of Norfolk's most famous son, but of Britannia.

HOLKHAM

If the concept of the Grand Tour ever needed any justification, **Holkham Hall** amply provides it. For six years, from 1712 to 1718, young Thomas Coke (pronounced Cook) travelled extensively in Italy, France and Germany, studying and absorbing at first hand the glories of European civilisation. And, wherever possible, buying them. When he returned to England, Coke realised that his family's modest Elizabethan manor

could not possibly house the collection of treasures he had amassed. The manor would have to be demolished and a more worthy building erected in its place. Building began in 1734 but was not completed until 1762, three years after Coke's death. The completed building, its classical balance and restraint emphasised by the pale honey local brick used throughout, has been described as 'the ultimate achievement of the English Palladian movement'.

Each room reveals new treasures: Rubens and Van Dyck in the Saloon , the Landscape Room with its incomparable collection of paintings by Lorrain, Poussin and other masters, the Brussels tapestries in the State Sitting Room and, on a more domestic note, the vast, high-ceilinged kitchen which remained in use until 1939 and still displays the original pots and pans.

HUNSTANTON

The busy seaside resort of Hunstanton can boast two unique features: one, it has the only cliffs in England made up of colourful levels of red, white and brown strata, and two, it is the only east coast resort that faces west, looking across The Wash to the Lincolnshire coast and the unmistakable

Holkham Hall

Cliffs at Hunstanton

tower of the 272-foot high Boston Stump (more properly described as the Church of St Botolph).

The huge stretches of sandy beach, framed by those multi-coloured cliffs, are just heaven for children who will also be fascinated by the **Sea Life Sanctuary**, on Southern Promenade, where an underwater glass tunnel provides a wonderful opportunity to watch the varied and often weird forms of marine life that inhabit Britain's waters. A popular excursion from Hunstanton is the boat trip to Seal Island, a sandbank in The Wash where seals can indeed often be seen sunbathing at low tide.

KING'S LYNN

The best place to start an exploration of the town is at the beautiful church of **St Margaret**, founded in 1101 and with a remarkable leaning arch of that original building still intact. The architecture is impressive, but the church is especially famous for two outstanding 14th century brasses.

Alongside the north wall of St Margaret's is the **Saturday Market Place**, one of the town's two market places, where visitors can explore The Old Gaol House, an experience complete with the sights and sounds of the ancient cells. A few steps further is one of the most striking sights in the town, the **Guildhall of the Holy Trinity** with its distinctive chequerboard design of black flint and white stone. The Town Hall houses the **Museum of Lynn Life** where the greatest treasure is King John's Cup, a dazzling piece of medieval workmanship with coloured enamel scenes set in gold. The Cup is said to be part of King John's treasure which had been lost in 1215 when his overburdened baggage train was crossing the Nene Estuary and sank into the treacherous quicksands.

NORWICH

'Norwich has the most Dickensian atmosphere of any city I know,' declared J B Priestley in his *English Journey* of 1933. 'What a grand, higgledy-piggledy, sensible old place Norwich is!' More than half a century later, in a European Commission study of 'most habitable' cities, Norwich topped the list of British

Norwich Castle and Market Square

gallery with its mummy Ankh Hor, and interactive displays in the Castle keep and keep basement.

The Art Gallery has an incomparable collection of paintings by the celebrated Norwich artist, John Sell Cotman (1782-1842), and others in the group known as the Norwich School. Their subjects were mostly landscape scenes, such as John Crome's *The Poringland Oak*. Quite apart from the artistic quality of their works, they have left a fascinating pictorial record of early 19th century Norfolk.

The **Bulwer and Miller** collection of more than 2,600 English china teapots makes its home in a brand new gallery called the Twinings Gallery, while the museum's Langton collection of around 100 cats fashioned in porcelain, ivory, bronze, glass and wood, originating from anywhere between Derbyshire and China, and Margaret Elizabeth Fountaine's mind-boggling accumulation of 22,000 butterflies which she had personally netted during her travels around the world, are available to view by appointment at the Shirehall Study Centre, next door to the Royal Norfolk Regimental Museum on Market Avenue.

contenders, well ahead of more favoured candidates such as Bath and York.

The first **Norwich Castle**, a wooden structure, was replaced in the late 1100s by a mighty fortress in stone which, unlike most blank-walled castles of the period, is decorated with a rich façade of blind arcades and ornamental pilasters. This great fort never saw any military action, and as early as the 13th century was being used as the county gaol, a role it continued to fill until 1889. From its walls, in December 1549, the leader of the rebellion against land enclosures, Robert Kett, was hung in chains and left to starve to death.

The Castle is now home to the **Castle Museum and Art Gallery**, home to some of the most outstanding regional collections of fine art, archaeological exhibits and natural history displays. Among the many fascinating exhibits are those devoted to Queen Boudicca, which features the life of the Iceni tribe with an interactive chariot ride, the Egyptian

Dominating the western side of the Market Square is **City Hall**, modelled on

Stockholm City Hall and opened by King George VI in 1938. Opinions differ about its architectural merits, but there are no such doubts about the nearby **Guildhall**, a fine example of 15th century flintwork that now houses a tea room.

Around the corner from London Street, in Bridewell Alley, is the **Bridewell Museum**, a late 14th century merchant's house now dedicated to Norfolk's crafts and industries. Another museum/shop, this one located in the **Royal Arcade**, a tiled riot of Art Nouveau fantasy, celebrates the county's great contribution to world cuisine: mustard. Back in the early 1800s, Jeremiah Colman perfected his blend of mustard flours and spice to produce a condiment that was smooth in texture

and tart in flavour. Together with his nephew James he founded J & J Colman in 1823; 150 years later **The Mustard Shop** was established to commemorate the company's history. The shop has an appropriately late-Victorian atmosphere and a fascinating display of vintage containers and advertisements, some of them from 'Mustard Club' featuring such characters as Lord Bacon of Cookham and Miss Di Gester, created by no less distinguished a writer than Dorothy L Sayers. All in all, a most appetising exhibition.

Millennium Plain just off Theatre Street is where visitors will find **The Forum**, an architecturally stunning new building designed by Sir Michael Hopkins. At the **Origins** Visitor Centre, an attractive multi-media display on three floors affords the opportunity to experience the life and times of Norwich and the wider Norfolk region. Here can also be found the Tourist Information Centre. The new **Norfolk & Norwich Millennium Library** houses 120,000 books and offers the best in information and communication technology.

The Assembly House in Theatre Street is one of the city's finest historical houses and also a leading venue for the arts. With two concert halls, three galleries featuring changing exhibitions and a restaurant and tea rooms, this magnificent Georgian home must be included in any visit to the city.

Royal Arcade, Norwich

Norwich Cathedral

While the Castle has been used for many purposes over the years, the **Cathedral** remains what it has always been: the focus of ecclesiastical life in the county. It's even older than the castle, its service of consecration taking place over 900 years ago, in 1101. This peerless building, its flint walls clad in creamy-white stone from Caen is, after Durham, the most completely Norman cathedral in England, its appeal enhanced by later Gothic features such as the flying buttresses. The Norman cloisters are the largest in the country and notable for the 400 coloured and gilded bosses depicting scenes from medieval life. Another 1,200 of these wondrous carvings decorate the glorious vaulted roof of the nave.

It's impossible to list all the Cathedral's treasures here, but do seek out the **Saxon Bishop's Throne** in the Presbytery, the lovely 14th century altar painting in St Luke's Chapel, and the richly carved canopies in the Choir.

Outside, beneath the slender 315-foot spire soaring heavenwards, the **Cathedral Close** is timeless in its sense of peace.

Norwich is home to some 32 medieval churches in all, every one of them worth attention, although many are now used for purposes other than worship. Outstanding among them are **St Peter Mancroft**, a masterpiece of Gothic architecture built between 1430-55 (and the largest church in Norwich), and **St Peter Hungate**, a handsome 15th century church standing at the top of **Elm Hill**, a narrow, unbelievably picturesque lane where in medieval times the city's wool merchants built their homes, close to their warehouses beside the River Wensum.

The **Inspire Discovery Centre**, housed in the medieval church of St Michael in Coslany Street, just across the Wensum northeast of the city centre, is full of exciting hands-on displays and activities that make scientific enquiry come to life.

There are also a large number of beautiful and well-maintained parks in the city, some of which offer chess, lawn tennis and hard tennis courts, bowls, pitch and putt, rowing and more, together with a programme of entertainment ranging from theatre to concerts.

On the western edge of the city stands the **University of East Anglia**, where the **Sainsbury Centre for Visual Arts** contains the eclectic collection of a 'passionate acquirer' of art, Sir Robert Sainsbury.

To the south of Norwich in the village of Caistor St Edmund are the remains of **Venta Icenorum**, the Roman town established here after Boudicca's rebellion in AD61. Most of the finds discovered during excavations in the 1920s and 1930s are now in **Norwich Castle Museum**, but the riverside site still merits a visit.

Just to the north of the city, on the Cromer road, lies the **City of Norwich Aviation Museum**.

POTTER HEIGHAM

Generally regarded as one of the liveliest of the Broadland boating centres, Potter Heigham is also home to the **Museum of the Broads**, located in boat sheds in the historic Herbert Woods boat yard. Among the museum's many intriguing exhibits are the only concrete dinghy ever constructed, an ice yacht, tools from traditional Broads industries such as eel catching, gun punts for duck-shooting (complete with incredibly long guns), and a display featuring one of Broadland's most destructive pests, the coypu.

A pleasant excursion from Potter Heigham is a visit to **Horsey Mere**, about six miles to the east, and **Horsey Windpump** (both National Trust).

SANDRINGHAM

A couple of miles north of Castle Rising is the entrance to **Sandringham Country Park** and **Sandringham House**, the royal family's country retreat. Unlike the State Rooms at Windsor Castle and Buckingham Palace, where visitors marvel at the awesome trappings of majesty, at Sandringham they can savour the atmosphere of a family home. The rooms the visitor sees at Sandringham are those used by the royal family when in residence, complete with family

Sandringham House

North Norfolk Railway, Sheringham

Just to the west of the town, at Upper Sheringham, footpaths lead to the lovely grounds of **Sheringham Park** (National Trust). The Park was landscaped by Humphry Repton, who declared it to be his 'favourite and darling child in Norfolk'.

portraits and photographs, and comfy armchairs. Successive royal owners have furnished the house with an intriguing medley of the grand, the domestic and the unusual, and there are some splendid royal vehicles on show, including the first car bought by a member of the royal family - a 1900 Daimler.

SHERINGHAM

Like so many other former fishing villages in England, Sheringham owes its transformation into a resort to the arrival of the railway. During the Edwardian peak years of rail travel, some 64 trains a day steamed into the station but the line became yet another victim of the Beeching closures of the 1960s. Devotees of steam trains joined together and, by dint of great effort and enthusiasm, managed to re-open the line in 1975 as the **North Norfolk Railway**, better known as **The Poppy Line**.

SNETTISHAM

Snettisham is best known nowadays for its spacious, sandy beaches and the **RSPB Bird Sanctuary**, both about two miles west of the village itself. But for centuries Snettisham was much more famous as a prime quarry for carrstone, an attractive soft-red building-block that provided the 'light relief' for the walls of thousands of Georgian houses around the country, and for nearby Sandringham House. In the British Museum is Snettisham's greatest gift to the national heritage: an opulent collection of gold and silver ornaments from the 1st century AD, the largest hoard of treasure ever found in Britain, discovered here in 1991.

SOUTH WALSHAM

This small village is notable for having two parish churches built within yards of each other. Just to the north of the village is the **Fairhaven Woodland and Water Garden**, an expanse of delightful water gardens lying beside the private **South Walsham Inner Broad**. Its centrepiece is the 900-year-old King Oak, lording it over the surrounding displays of rare shrubs and plants, native wild flowers, rhododendrons and giant lilies.

The best way to see the remains of **St Benet's Abbey** is from a boat along the River Bure (indeed, it's quite difficult to reach it any other way). Rebuilt in 1020 by King Canute, after the Vikings had destroyed an earlier Saxon building, St Benet's became one of the richest abbeys in East Anglia.

SWAFFHAM

Swaffham's one-time claim to be the 'Montpellier of England' was justified by the abundance of handsome Georgian houses that used to surround the large, wedge-shaped market place. A good number still survive, along with the **Assembly Room** of 1817 where the quality would foregather for concerts, balls and soirees. The central focus of the market square is the elegant **Butter Cross**, presented to the town by the Earl of Orford in 1783. It's not a cross at all, but a classical lead-covered dome standing on eight columns and surmounted by a life-size statue of Ceres, the Roman goddess of agriculture - an appropriate symbol for this busy market town, from which ten roads radiate out across the county.

From the market place an avenue of limes leads to the quite outstanding Church of **St Peter & St Paul**, a 15th century masterpiece with one of the very best double hammerbeam roofs in the county, strikingly embellished with a host of angels, their wings widespread. **Swaffham Museum** in the Town Hall is the setting for the story of the town's past. Visitors can follow Howard Carter's road to the Valley of the Kings, see the Symonds Collection of handmade figurines, and admire the Sporle collection of locally-found artefacts.

A more recent addition to Swaffham's attractions is the **EcoTech Discovery Centre**, opened in 1998.

TERRINGTON ST CLEMENT

Terrington St Clement is a sizable village notable for the **'Cathedral of the Marshland'**, a 14th century Gothic masterwork more properly known as St Clement's church, and for the **African Violet Centre**, where some quarter of a million violets are grown each year, in a wide range of colour and species.

THETFORD

Some 2,000 years ago, Thetford may well have been the site of **Boudicca's Palace**. In the 1980s, excavations for building development at Gallows Hill, north of the town, revealed an Iron Age enclosure. It is so extensive it may well have been the capital of the Iceni tribe which gave the Romans so much trouble. Certainly, the town's strategic location at the meeting of the Rivers Thet and

St Peters Church, Thetford

Thetford Treasure, a 4th century hoard of gold and silver jewellery discovered as recently as 1979 by an amateur archaeologist with a metal detector.

Even older than the Ancient House is the 12th century **Cluniac Priory** (English Heritage), now mostly in ruins but with an impressive 14th century gatehouse still standing. During the Middle Ages, Thetford could boast 24 churches; today, only three remain.

Thetford's industrial heritage is vividly displayed in the **Burrell Steam Museum**, in Minstergate, which has full-size steam engines regularly 'in steam', re-created workshops and many examples of vintage agricultural machinery. The Museum tells the story of the Burrell Steam Company, which formed the backbone of the town's industry from the late 18th to the early 20th centuries, their sturdy machines famous around the world.

To the west of the town stretch the 90 square miles of **Thetford Forest**, the most extensive lowland forest in Britain. The Forestry Commission began planting in 1922, and although the woodland is largely given over to conifers, with Scots and Corsican Pine and Douglas Fir predominating, oak, sycamore and beech can also be seen throughout. There is a particularly varied trail leading from the Forestry Commission Information Centre which has detailed information about this and other walks through the area.

On the edge of the forest, about two

Little Ouse made it an important settlement for centuries. At the time of the *Domesday Book*, 1086, Thetford was the sixth-largest town in the country and the seat of the Bishop of East Anglia, with its own castle, mint and pottery.

Of the **Castle**, only the 80-foot motte remains, but it's worth climbing to the top of this mighty mound for the views across the town. Perhaps the most striking of the town's many fine old buildings is the **Ancient House** Museum in White Hart Street, a magnificent 15th century timber-framed house with superb carved oak ceilings. It houses the Tourist Information Centre and a museum where some of the most interesting exhibits are replicas of the miles west of Thetford, are the ruins of **Thetford Warren Lodge**, built around 1400. At that time a huge area here was preserved for farming rabbits, a major element of the medieval diet. The vast warren was owned by the Abbot of Thetford Priory, and it was he who built the Lodge for his gamekeeper.

Still in the forest, reached by a footpath from the village of Santon Downham, are **Grimes Graves**, the earliest major industrial site to be discovered in Europe. At these unique Neolithic flint mines, Stone Age labourers extracted the materials for their sharp-edged axes and knives. It's a strange experience entering these 4,000 year old shafts which descend some 30 feet to an underground chamber. (The experience is even better if you bring your own high-powered torch.)

WELLS-NEXT-THE-SEA

There's no doubt about the appeal of Wells' picturesque quayside, narrow streets and ancient houses. Wells has been a working port since at least the 13th century, but over the years the town's full name of Wells-next-the-Sea has become increasingly inapt - its harbour now stands more than a mile from the sea. In 1859, to prevent the harbour silting up altogether, Lord Leicester of Holkham Hall built an Embankment cutting off some 600 acres of marshland. This now provides a pleasant walk down to the sea.

Running alongside the Embankment is the **Harbour Railway**, which trundles from the small museum on the quay to the lifeboat station by the beach. This narrow-gauge railway is operated by the same company as the **Wells— Walsingham Light Railway** which carries passengers on a particularly lovely ride along the route of the former Great Eastern Railway to Little Walsingham.

WEST RUNTON

The parish of West Runton can boast that within its boundaries lies the highest point in Norfolk - **Beacon Hill**. This eminence is 330 feet high, so you won't be needing any oxygen equipment to reach the summit, but there are some excellent views.

West Runton's major tourist attraction is undoubtedly the **Norfolk Shire Horse Centre** where twice a day, during the season, these noble beasts are harnessed up and give a half-hour demonstration of the important role they played in agricultural life right up until the 1930s. Several other heavy breeds, such as the Suffolk Punch, Clydesdale and Percheron, also have their home here, along with no fewer than nine different breeds of pony.

WYMONDHAM

The exterior of **Wymondham Abbey** presents one of the oddest ecclesiastical buildings in the county; the interior reveals one of the most glorious. The Abbey was founded in 1107 by the Benedictines - or Black Monks, as they were known because of the colour of

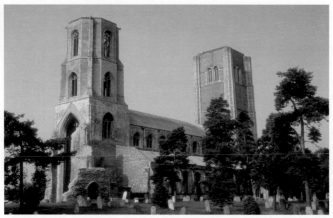

Wymondham Abbey

century tomb, of the last Abbot, in delicate terracotta work, and a striking modern memorial to the local men who lost their lives in the First World War.

Railway buffs will also want to visit the historic their habits. Step inside and you find a **Railway Station**, built in 1845 on the magnificent Norman nave, 112 feet long. Great Eastern's Norwich-Ely line. At its (It was originally twice as long, but the peak, the station and its section eastern end, along with most of the employed over 100 people. Still Abbey buildings, was demolished after providing a rail link to Norwich, London the Dissolution of the Monasteries.) and the Midlands, the station has been The superb hammerbeam roof is restored, and its buildings house a supported by 76 beautifully carved railway museum, restaurant and tea angels. There's also an interesting 16th room, and a piano showroom.

THE ARK ROYAL

FREEMAN STREET, WELLS-NEXT-THE-SEA, NORFOLK NR23 1BQ
TEL: 01328 710478

Norfolk

Directions: Wells-next-the-Sea lies on the A149 about halfway between
Hunstanton and Sheringham.

Wells-next-the-Sea is not quite so close to the sea as it once was, and its harbour now stands more than a mile from the sea. The Embankment that runs from the town to the sea provides a pleasant walk, but for visitors in search of friendly hospitality, good food and drink, the walk to the **Ark Royal** is the route to choose.

Set well back from the road, with plenty of picnic benches at the front, this substantial 1960s pub is run by Shirley Thake with the help of her daughter. Inside, there's plenty of space and comfort for drinkers and diners, and a separate room opposite the main bar where children keep themselves amused. Four cask ales head a long list of beers, lagers and wines available throughout

the day, and traditional pub dishes are prepared by Shirley and her staff, served every lunchtime and evening.

Everyone is welcome at the Ark Royal's quiz nights, which are the last Wednesday of each month (excluding July & August). The picturesque quayside, the narrow streets and the ancient houses make Wells a very pleasant place to explore, and the beach is one of the best in the country. It's a good place for railway enthusiasts, with a little railway running from the museum on the quay to the lifeboat station, and the same company's light railway running through lovely countryside on the former Great Eastern tracks between Wells and Little Walsingham. This is also great walking country, and Wells is on the Norfolk Coast Path that runs from Hunstanton to Cromer.

- 🕐 11-11 (Sun 12-10.30)
- 🍴 Traditional pub snacks and meals
- 💷 Major cards accepted
- 🅿 Car park, children's play room
- 🎵 Quiz last Wed of month
- ❓ Pleasant walk to the sea, Holkham Hall 3 miles

THE BELL INN

3 LOWER STREET, SALHOUSE, NR NORWICH, NORFOLK NR13 6RW
TEL/FAX: 01603 721141

> **Directions:** Leave Norwich on the Salhouse Road. At Salhouse turn left at the roundabout intersecting with the Plumstead to Wroxham road.

On the edge of the Broads and an easy drive out of Norwich, **The Bell** has been dispensing hospitality since about 1650, when it was built as an ale house. Joanna Nash has a long connection with this splendid inn, first as a chef, then as a manager, and since August 2004 as the owner. She remains firmly in charge of the cooking, which is a major attraction at The Bell. Locally sourced produce features strongly on the menus, which include bar snacks – sandwiches, jacket potatoes, honey-roast ham, all-day breakfast – and the full choice. Popular main courses include delicious steak & kidney pie, lasagne and a hearty lamb shank, all homemade, and there's an impressive selection of vegetarian main courses typified by mushroom stroganoff, red Thai curry and broccoli and cheese

pasta bake. Traditional roasts feature on Sunday, and the interesting list of specials regularly includes fresh fish from Lowestoft, and a variety of homemade meat and vegetarian dishes, and seasonal game supplied by a local gamekeeper.

Diners can choose between the lounge bar and the restaurant with its pristine linen and sparkling table settings. Food theme nights feature different national cuisines, and Joanna also pushes the boat out for special occasions such as Burns Night, St George's Day and St Patrick's Day. The Bell is not just a magnet for food-lovers, it's also a delight for cask ale connoisseurs, and in the beamed bar small local breweries such as Wolf, Buffy's and Humpty Dumpty are regularly featured alongside the bigger boys. The inn has an extensive lawned garden with a paved patio area, and the added attraction of a bowling green that is used by village team.

- Winter: 11-3.30 & 5.30-11 (Sun 12-10.30). Summer: open all day every day
- Bar and restaurant menus
- Not Amex
- Car park, garden, bowling green
- Quiz & Jazz nights in winter, darts
- Parish Walk 4 to 5 miles; Woodbastwick Estate Village 1 mile, Wroxham 2 miles, Broadlands Conservation Centre 2 miles, Norwich 5 miles

THE BLACK SWAN

THE STREET, LITTLE DUNHAM, NR SWAFFHAM, NORFOLK PE32 2DG
TEL: 01760 722200 FAX: 01760 336330

Directions: Little Dunham lies 5 miles northeast of Swaffham off the A47.

On a bend in the centre of the Norfolk village of Little Dunham, the **Black Swan** is a fine old coaching inn dating back to the mid-17th century. Christine Bowen and Paul Tucker are maintaining this long tradition of hospitality, and the quaint, cosy bar is a favourite meeting place for the local customers, who come for a chat and a glass or two of the several cask ales that are always kept in perfect condition. Paul is in charge behind the bar, while Christine looks after the food side of the business. The original barns and stables from coaching days have been sympathetically converted into a charming, comfortable restaurant, where the menu offers a good choice of wholesome, freshly prepared dishes. Fish & chips is the Friday speciality, and there's always a good choice for vegetarians.

Food is served Tuesday to Friday lunchtime and evening and all day Saturday and Sunday. Pool, darts and cribbage are the favourite games played in the bar, and the first and third Sundays of every month are quiz nights. This is excellent walking country, and golf and trout fishing are available nearby. Among the places of interest within a short drive are the imposing ruins of Castle Acre Priory, the village museum at Litcham and the museums and the marvellous 15th century Church of St Peter & St Paul in Swaffham.

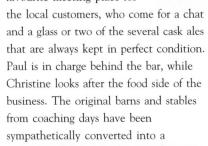

- 12-3 & 7-11 (Sat & Sun all day; closed Mon lunchtime)
- Traditional home cooking (no food Mon evening)
- Major cards accepted
- Car park, patio
- Quiz 1st and 3rd Sunday each month
- e-mail: chris-paul@supanet.com
- Castle Acre 3 miles, Litcham 4 miles, Swaffham 5 miles, Dereham 8 miles

THE BLUE LION

HOUGHTON LANE, NORTH PICKENHAM, NR SWAFFHAM,
NORFOLK PE37 8LF
TEL: 01760 440289

Directions: The inn stands on a corner site in North Pickenham, which lies on a minor road 3 miles east of Swaffham.

The Blue Lion occupies a prominent corner site in the village of North Pickenham, accessible from the A47 or the B1077. This centuries-old pub, its cream-painted exterior adorned with hanging baskets, came into the care of Mick and Caron Lee in September 2004, and these go-ahead licensees immediately set about restoring the old place to its pristine state. A big open fire warms the beamed bar, where the inviting traditional look is being retained and enhanced in the restoration programme. Caron is 're-inventing' the kitchen, and is offering visitors a range of straightforward snacks and pub dishes, along with a traditional Sunday lunch with a choice of roast meats as the centrepiece. The Lees' longer-term plans include bringing on stream some letting bedrooms, which will make the Blue

Lion an even more attractive proposition for visitors touring the region.

North Pickenham stands on the long established 50-mile Peddar's Way footpath, which runs from the Little Ouse River east of Thetford up to Holme next the Sea, where it joins the Norfolk Coast Path. This facility attracts walkers in their droves, and the Blue Lion is more than ready to take on thirsts and appetites sharpened by a few hours' walking. The nearest town to the Blue Lion is Swaffham, which is well worth taking time to explore. It has a large number of imposing Georgian houses, the magnificent 15th century Church of St Peter & St Paul with one of the finest hammerbeam roofs in the county, and the excellent Swaffham Museum housed in the handsome redbrick Town Hall.

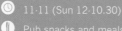

🕐 11-11 (Sun 12-10.30)

🍴 Pub snacks and meals

🛏 Planned

🅿 Car park, beer garden

@ e-mail: mickncaron@btinternet.com

❓ Swaffham 3 miles

THE BOAR INN

STATION ROAD, GREAT RYBURGH, NORFOLK NR21 0DX
TEL: 01328 829212 FAX: 01328 829421

Norfolk

Directions: Great Ryburgh is located 4 miles southeast of Fakenham between the
A1067 Fakenham-Norwich road and the B1146 Fakenham-Dereham road. The inn
stands opposite the church at the junction of Station Road and Bridge Road.

The Boar Inn stands on a corner site in
the centre of the village of Great
Ryburgh, opposite the round-towered
Saxon church. The inn's long black-and-
white frontage is adorned in spring and
summer with a pretty row of flower tubs
and hanging baskets, and the look inside
is cosy and inviting. The bar area sports
a log-burning fire in a large inglenook,
and there's another open fire in the 50-
cover non-smoking restaurant, which has
a suntrap patio. The tables are pine, and
some of the chairs came from the chapel,
their hymnbook pockets still in place.
Meals are served every lunchtime and
every evening in both the bar and the
restaurant. The bar menu offers
sandwiches with hot or cold fillings,
jacket potatoes, ploughman's platters and
basket meals, and the full menu includes

grills, fish and chicken dishes, Eastern
favourites, vegetarian main courses and
classics such as steak & ale, cottage and
fish pies, chilli and lasagne. Sunday
lunch brings traditional roasts.

The Boar Inn is well placed for a
number of places of interest and has five
comfortably appointed en suite letting
rooms with television and tea/coffee
facilities. The inn is run by Julie Sadler,
and Julie and her staff are always happy
to help with their local knowledge.
Among the main attractions in the area
is Fakenham, with its racecourse,
markets and Museum of Gas and Local
History and, just a mile away is
Pensthorpe Park Nature Reserve, home
to Europe's best collection of rare, exotic
and endangered water birds. The Boar's
owner, John Frankland, also owns The
Bull, a 17th century inn at Litcham.

- 🕐 11-2.30 & 6.30 –11 (Sun 12-2 & 7-10.30)
- 🍽 Restaurant and bar menus
- 💷 Not Amex
- 🛏 5 en suite rooms
- 🅿 Parking, small front garden
- 🎵 Games room
- ❓ Pensthorpe Park 1 mile, Fakenham 4 miles, Raynham Hall 4 miles

THE BRIDGE INN

LENWADE, NR NORWICH, NORFOLK NR9 5SE
TEL: 01603 872248 FAX: 01603 870826

Directions: Lenwade lies on the A1067 about 10 miles west of Norwich.

The partnership of Peter and Vicki Forder and Patrick Perry brought many years experience in the licensed trade when they took over the running of **The Bridge Inn** in September 2004. Their 17th century roadside inn is a place of wide appeal, offering a warm welcome, a civilised, relaxed ambience, a fine range of drinks, outstanding food and

comfortable accommodation. Two very talented chefs put the best and freshest local produce to excellent use in their dishes, which are served every day in the lounge bar or in the separate restaurant every lunchtime and every evening. The

- 🕐 11-11
- 🍴 Bar and restaurant meals
- 💷 Major cards accepted
- 🛏 4 bedrooms with shared facilities
- Ⓟ Car park, gardens, own fishing lakes
- @ e-mail: pmforder@hotmail.com
- ❓ Norfolk Wildlife Centre & Country Park 1 mile, Dinosaur Adventure Park 1 mile, Swannington Manor 3

guest accommodation comprises four bedrooms with televisions and tea/coffee-making facilities, and The Bridge offers a very unusual amenity in the shape of its own fishing lakes in the extensive grounds behind the building – anglers can fish in the lakes for just £5 a day.

The inn is a popular venue for wedding receptions and other special occasions; a marquee is available attached to the side of the inn, and a resident goat makes sure that the grass is always well tended. This is great walking country, and one of the many lovely walks takes in Alderford Common, a haven for wildlife, and Swannington Manor, whose gardens are famous for the 300-year-old yew and box topiary hedges. Other places well worth a visit and very close to The Bridge include the Norfolk Wildlife Centre & Country Park at Great Witchingham and the Dinosaur Adventure Park with its life-size models, children's activity centre and many other attractions for all the family.

THE BRISLEY BELL INN

THE GREEN, BRISLEY, NORFOLK NR20 5DW
TEL: 01362 668686

> **Directions:** The inn lies at the heart of the village of Brisley, 7 miles north of Dereham on the B1145.

Roger and Jean Greer and their son and son-in-law make an excellent team at the **Brisley Bell Inn**, a handsome redbrick hostelry overlooking the village green. The interior has a traditional look in keeping with the building's 16th century origins, and the oak-beamed bar is a perfect spot to relax with a glass or two from the great selection of beers and lagers that are always available. Jean is a very talented cook, and a blackboard announces the day's choice, which includes time-honoured pub classics and much more besides.

Food is served every lunchtime and evening except Monday, and booking is strongly recommended at the weekend. Brisley is a village with a long and fascinating history, and the Brisley Inn is just one of several distinguished buildings.

The moated house at Old Hall Farm stands in another corner of the Green, and the village is dominated by the Church of St Bartholomew has many interesting features, including a three-decker pulpit, box pews and benches and a crypt below the chancel where prisoners on their way to Norwich prison were kept overnight.

Brisley is also well known to local historians and naturalists for its huge expanse of heathland, the best example of unspoilt common in Norfolk. Walking is naturally a popular activity here, and the Brisley Bell is the ideal place for satisfying a fresh-air thirst and appetite. The Greers plan to open a campsite adjacent to the inn for the 2005 season.

- 🕐 11-3 & 6-11 (Sat & Sun all day)
- 🍴 Home cooking
- 💷 Major cards accepted
- 🅿 Car park, beer garden
- ❓ Brisley's Church of St Bartholomew; North Elmham 2 miles, Gressenhall 4 miles, Dereham 7 miles, Fakenham 8 miles

Norfolk

THE CHERRY TREE

HIGH STREET, WICKLEWOOD, NR WYMONDHAM, NORFOLK NR18 9QA
TEL: 01379 676523

Directions: From the A11 at Wymondham take the B1135 Dereham road for
about 2 miles, then left on to minor road marked Wicklewood.

Built in the middle of the 19th century, **The Cherry Tree** is a prominent landmark in the village of Wicklewood. Behind its distinctive pastel-pink frontage, this popular award-winning pub (Morning Advertiser Village Pub of the Year Central Region 2004) has two bars, a small one for smokers and the much larger non-smoking bar with leather sofas, a curved solid oak counter top and a wonderful maple floor that was once the base of a squash court. The inn is owned and run by Roger Abrahams and Julie Savory and serves as the tap room for Buffy's Brewery. The brewery, at nearby Tivetshall St Margaret, was founded by Roger and Julie and since 1993 has been supplying the local pub trade and other selected outlets. Buffy's brews range from Norwich terrier (3.6% ABV) to the richly flavoured dark amber Festival 9X at 9.0% ABV, brewed just once a year.

The Cherry Tree always has several Buffy's on tap, along with ales from other small local breweries, the local Banham cider and a good selection of wines. In the dining area (also non-smoking), a good choice of freshly prepared, mainly organic food is served, from sandwiches, ploughman's platters and omelettes to the speciality home-produced pies made with 'proper' shortcrust pastry. Senior citizens can take advantage of a special menu available lunchtime Monday to Friday. The Cherry Tree hosts regular food theme evenings such as steak & wine or featured national cuisines; there are also monthly jazz or folk music evenings and a quiz once a month on a Wednesday. The inn has ample off-road parking and an enclosed garden where children can play in safety.

- 🕐 12-3 & 6-11 (Sat 12-12, Sun 12-10.30)
- 🍴 Home cooking · light bites and full menu
- 💷 Not Amex
- 🅿 Car park, garden
- @ e-mail: buffysbrewery@evemail.net website: www.buffys.co.uk
- ❓ Wymondham Abbey, Wymondham-Dereham Railway 2 miles

THE STREET, DILHAM, NR NORTH WALSHAM, NORFOLK NR28 9PS
TEL: 01692 536398

Directions: The inn is located on the main street of Dilham, which lies just off the A149 about 6 miles southeast of North Walsham.

On the main street running through a pleasant Norfolk village, **The Cross Keys** presents a very inviting sight with its long white-painted frontage and red-tiled roof. At one end are two traditional village essentials, a letter box in the wall and a red telephone box. The promise of the outside is more than fulfilled within, where visitors can choose between the public bar with pool, darts and television, and the lounge with a log-burning stove and seats for up to 30. Adnams Bitter and Broadside and Greene King IPA are always available, as well as the usual range of other beers, lagers and ciders. Food is served every lunchtime and evening, offering sandwiches, burgers, omelettes and salads for lighter snacks, along with tagliatelle with a choice of four sauces, broccoli and

brie rosti, cod, scampi, garlic tiger prawns, beef & Guinness pie, chicken, leek and stilton pie, chilli con carne and giant Yorkshire pudding filled with bangers and mash. Weekly specials add to the choice, and traditional roasts are the centrepiece of Sunday lunch.

The Cross Keys is run by Sheila and Trevor Hardingham, who took over in February 2003 and have built up a strong local following; it's a very popular spot for a function or special celebration. It's a great place to visit at any time of the year, but it really comes into its own in the summer, when full use is made of the beer garden and the patio that overlooks the pub's bowling greens. The four greens are used by local teams, and sipping a glass of ale to the satisfying clunk of wood on wood is a wonderful way of passing an hour or two.

- 12-3 & 6-11 (Sun 12-3 & 7-10.30)
- Snacks and full menu
- Ample parking, patio garden
- Pool, darts, bowls
- The Broads; Sutton Windmill 3 miles, Wroxham 5 miles, North Walsham 6 miles

THE CROWN

LYNN ROAD, GAYTON, NR KING'S LYNN, NORFOLK PE32 1PA
TEL/FAX: 01553 636252

Directions: Gayton is situated on the B1145 about 4 miles east of King's Lynn.

Since taking over the reins of **The Crown** in 1999 Felicity Atherton has not looked back. Felicity is a regional winner of the Greene King licensee of the Year 2004 and the inn is the winner of the West Norfolk Camra Pub of the Year 2004. The building dates from the 13th century and first served as a home for stonemasons working on the village church; it later became a stopping place on the King's Lynn-Norwich coaching run. Set back from the road its cheerful green and white frontage adorned with flowers, the inn is immensely appealing both outside (there's a large garden) and within. The bars and restaurant have the look and charm of the quintessential English village inn, with beams, open fires, candlelight, old photographs and a

collection of china plates.

The bar snack menu, available every lunchtime and evening, offers soup, bloomer-bread sandwiches and all-time favourites like scampi, ham & eggs and home-made steak & kidney pie. There's also a popular lunchtime speciality buffet, and in the evening the menu provides a mouthwatering choice that varies according to the seasons and what's best in the markets. Dishes range from classics such as garlic mushrooms and steaks to seasonal game and more exotic offerings, and Christmas pudding is usually available whatever the time of year. The Crown is also a magnet for connoisseurs of real ales. A holder of the Cask Marque Award, it always has a wide choice of well-kept ales including Greene King XX Mild and IPA, Abbot and Old Speckled Hen, and guest ales that are changed every quarter. Entertainment at The Crown includes jazz and folk music evenings and regular quizzes.

12-2.30 & 6-11 (Fri, Sat & Sun open all day)

Bar snacks and evening menu

Not Amex

Car park, garden, disabled facilities including toilet

Folk music 1st Sun of month, jazz 3rd Sun of month, regular quizzes

e-mail: crownath2wf@supanet.com

King's Lynn 4 miles, West Acre open-air theatre 8 miles, Castle Acre Priory 8 miles, Sandringham 5 miles.

THE DUKE OF EDINBURGH

COAST ROAD, BACTON, NORFOLK NR12 0EU
TEL: 01692 650280 FAX: 01692 652153

> **Directions:** The inn lies on the B1159 coast road midway between Happisburgh and Mundesley.

On the coast road at Bacton, between Happisburgh and Mundesley, **The Duke of Edinburgh** is a handsome redbrick building with a unique pub sign. Owner Jackie Landamore designed and installed the sign, a big blow-up photograph of the Duke surrounded by a royal crest. Inside, the pub has been smartly refurbished and sympathetically modernised, and the bar is a great place to enjoy a drink (Greene King, Adnams and Woodforde cask ales), a chat and perhaps a game of pool or darts. In the glass-sided non-smoking dining area food is served throughout the day, ranging from sandwiches and jacket potatoes to burgers, steaks, cod, plaice and popular home-made classics including chilli, lasagne, beef curry and

steak & kidney pie. Friday is cod and chips day, and on Sunday the crowds come for the eat-as-much-as-you-like carvery with a choice of three roast meats.

This is a very family-friendly place, and well-behaved children are welcome in the lounge bar and restaurant. Live music evenings with a barbecue are a great draw on Wednesdays in July and August, and at the weekend out of high season. Bacton is right on the coast, the beach being nearby, and the coast road (B1159) provides easy access to many of the county's main attractions. The Duke of Edinburgh is an excellent family base for discovering these delights, and the five non-smoking en suite guest bedrooms offer a very comfortable night's rest before (and after) a day's exploring in the bracing Norfolk air. Alternatively, the pub has a camping and caravan site with electric hook-ups on a large site at the rear.

- 11-midnight (Sun from 12)
- Snack and full menus
- Not Amex
- 5 en suite rooms
- Ample parking, adventue playground
- Live music Wednesdays in July & August, weekends other months, pool, tv, gaming machines
- e-mail: thedukeph@aol.com website: www.thedukeatbacton.co.uk
- Paston (tithe barn) 1 mile, Happisburgh 3 miles, Mundesley 3 miles, North Walsham 4 miles

THE EELS FOOT INN

ORMESBY BROAD, ORMESBY ST MICHAEL, NR GREAT YARMOUTH,
NORFOLK NR29 3LP
TEL: 01493 730342

Directions: Ormesby St Michael is located just off the A149 three miles west of Caister.

A splendid location right by the beautiful Trinity Broads is just one of the many attractions of the **Eels Foot Inn**. Open seven days a week throughout the year, it has a spacious, airy bar overlooking the Broad, large gardens with plenty of seating, and two non-smoking restaurants. The inn is run by Angela Fell and her family, who have a warm welcome for visitors of all ages. The choice of food is very wide, from sandwiches and jacket potatoes to pizzas, seafood, liver & bacon, chicken tikka masala, steaks, a whole rack of ribs, home-made pies and the popular Sunday carvery with a choice of four meats. Vegetarians are not forgotten with tasty main dishes such as brie and redcurrant tart or three cheese pasta broccoli bake. Food is

served very lunchtime and evening, and all day during the school summer holidays.

Children are very well catered for with a junior brunch menu, a play area with swings and climbers - and a bouncy castle every Sunday and every day during school holidays. Other entertainment is provided by a pool table, and there's live music most Friday and Saturday nights and some Sunday afternoons. The inn is a great place to come for a meal, for a drink (Greene King IPA, Adnams Broadside and Bitter and Wells Bombardier on tap) or for celebrating a special occasion, and the function room, which can accommodate up to 150, has its own bar facilities. The Eels Foot Inn can offer great fishing on Trinity Broad, and rowing boats can be hired. The very unusual name comes from the fact that eels used to swim up to here from the sea, and a map of Trinity Broad shows that it resembles the shape of a foot!

- 11·11 (Sun 12·10.30)
- Bar and restaurant menus
- Not Amex
- Car park, garden, children's play area, moorings, rowing boats for hire, fishing
- Live music most Fridays & Saturdays and some Sundays
- Trinity Broads (Ormesby Broad) on doorstep; Caister 3 miles, Potter Heigham 4 miles, Great Yarmouth 6 miles

THE FOX & HOUNDS

THRIGBY ROAD, FILBY, NR GREAT YARMOUTH, NORFOLK NR29 3HJ
TEL: 01493 369255

> **Directions:** Filby lies about 3 miles west of Caister on the A1064. The inn is located close to the centre of the village on the way south to Thrigby.

The Fox & Hounds is a sturdy redbrick building dating back about 100 years. The century-long tradition of hospitality is now carried on by Rebecca Payne, her partner Tom and their friendly dog Sam, the delightful offspring of a Jack Russell and a question mark. Rebecca, Norfolk born and raised, takes care of culinary matters, while Tom looks after the drinks side of the business. Adnams Broadside and Best Bitter are always available, along with the usual range of draught and bottle beers, lagers and ciders, and wine is dispensed in handy third of a bottle size. Food is served every lunchtime and evening, and from 12 to 6 On Sunday, when there's a choice of two roasts and two vegetarian main courses, as well as children's portions of roasts. The weekday menu spans sandwiches, jacket potatoes, burgers, salads, BBQ chicken, lasagne, steak & kidney pie, cod

and scampi. There's always a good choice of vegetarian main courses such as red bean and chickpea curry, and a children's menu.

Traditional diversions in the bar include pool, darts, dominoes and cribbage, and St Patrick's Day is always celebrated with an evening of live music. Outside is a large tree-shaded grassed area with plenty of picnic tables, and the inn has ample off-road parking. There are many nearby walking, boating and sightseeing opportunities for working up a thirst and appetite, and among the numerous local attractions are Thrigby Hall Gardens with their unique collection of Asian mammals, reptiles and birds. Filby itself puts on a great floral display every year, with every house, shop, garden and lamp post a riot of colour.

- 🕐 12-11 (Sun to 10.30)
- 🍴 Snacks and full menu
- Ⓟ Ample parking, large garden
- 🎵 Live music St Patrick's night, traditional pub games
- ❓ Thrigby Hall ½ mile, Caister 3 miles, Great Yarmouth 6 miles

THE GEMINI PUB & RESTAURANT

Norfolk

SANDY LANE, DEREHAM, NORFOLK NR19 2EA
TEL: 01362 698841 FAX: 01362 699543

Directions: Close to the centre of Dereham on the old A47 Norwich road.

The Gemini Pub & Restaurant is a modern building with wheelchair access to the bar by way of a gentle ramp. It was built in 1965 and took its name from the Gemini spacecraft launched in that year. Like its namesake, the inn was an immediately success, which continues today in the care of Bron, Andy, Georgia and their staff, with the help of Sheba the German Shepherd and Judge the Doberman. Interesting features inside include sporting cartoons and a collection of over 200 original autographs on the walls. All the food here is freshly prepared and home-cooked, with as much local produce as

possible. The menus and daily specials feature classics such as prawn cocktail, lasagne, liver & bacon, chilli con carne and steak & kidney pudding. Pizzas cooked in the wood-fired oven are also very popular. Head chef Gavin Barron is a local celebrity, with recipes in the local press, and he and his team are happy to cater for functions and special occasions.

Real ales on tap include Greene King IPA and regularly changing guests such as St Austells Tribute and Highgate Brewery's Black Pig; there's also Budweiser on draught, and plenty of bottled beers and lagers, wines, spirits and soft drinks. The pub's grounds include a barbecue area and plenty of space for children to romp in safety. Live entertainment is laid on every Friday evening, and the inn fields three pool teams in the local leagues. The licensees have just expanded the dining area, and they plan to bring eight en suite guest bedrooms on stream in late summer 2005.

- 🕐 12-11, Sun to 10.30
- 🍴 Traditional pub dishes served all day
- 💷 All the major cards accepted
- 🛏 8 en suite rooms planned for Aug/Sept 2005
- 🅿 Car park
- 🎵 Live entertainment Fridays, pool, sky tv
- @ e-mail: thegeminipub@aol.com
- ❓ In Dereham: the Church of St Nicholas (Seven Sacrament Font, tomb of William Cowper); Gressenhall Rural Life Museum 3 miles

THE GREYHOUND

Norfolk

THE STREET, TIBENHAM, NR NORWICH, NORFOLK NR16 1PZ
TEL: 01379 677676   FAX: 01379 677887

Directions: Coming from the south on the A140 about 8 miles north of Diss, turn left on to the B1134 at Tivetshall St Margaret, then third right on to minor road signposted Tibenham

David and Colleen Hughes have created a relaxed, welcoming atmosphere at the **Greyhound**, which lies in a quiet, prosperous village reached down country lanes north of Diss. The premises date back to 1731, and behind the smartly modernised redbrick exterior the two bars are ideal spots to relax and unwind with good conversation and a glass or two of beer – there's always a choice of four real ales including an Adnams, Greene King IPA and two regularly changing guest beers. Straightforward classic pub food is served in the bars and restaurant at lunchtime on Saturday and Sunday and in the evening from Wednesday to Sunday; the pub is closed Monday during

the day and all Tuesday.

The Greyhound has a games room, but it's only the oldest regulars who can recall the times when the actor James Stewart used to play darts here when stationed at the nearby American Air Force base. The pub has ample off-road parking and a beer garden, and visitors wanting a stop-off for the night can make use of the small caravan and camping site that belongs to the pub. Strolls around the village and the surrounding countryside are good ways to generate a thirst, while a little further afield the local attractions include Banham Zoo, home to some of the world's rarest wildlife, and the pleasant market town of Attleborough, best known for the beautiful Church of St Mary.

- 🕐 6.30-11 Mon, Wed, Thurs, Fri; 12-11 Sat & Sun; closed Tuesday
- 🍴 Classic pub dishes
- 🚐 a small caravan site is adjacent
- 🅿 Car park, beer garden
- 🎵 Occasional live music
- @ e-mail: mail@thetibenhamgreyhound.co.uk
- ❓ Banham 4 miles, Attleborough 8 miles

THE GRIFFIN HOTEL

CHURCH ROAD, ATTLEBOROUGH, NORFOLK NR17 2AH
TEL: 01953 452149

Directions: The Griffin stands by the A11 about halfway between Thetford and Norwich.

Opposite the Town Hall in the centre of the pleasant market town of Attleborough, **The Griffin Hotel** is a handsome old building with a black-and-white frontage topped by a red-tiled roof. Inside, some very ancient, close-set wooden pillars testify to the building's 16th century origins, and another striking feature is the bar counter with its ornate stone work and Tudor-style canopy. A full range of drinks includes five cask ales (three permanent and two guests) and straightforward, satisfying cooking offers anything from a light snack to a three-course meal. Landlord Richard Ashbourne has been keeping his customers happy since arriving here in 1987, and the excellent hospitality offered at his versatile establishment extends to overnight accommodation.

Seven guest bedrooms, two of them with en suite facilities, are popular with both business and leisure visitors, offering good value for money and a convenient base for exploring the town and the surrounding area.

The inn has a pleasant beer garden that overlooks the town's undoubted glory, the splendid Church of St Mary. The chief treasure is a massive vaulted chancel screen with paintings of the saints and embellished with the arms of the 24 bishoprics into which the country was divided in the 15th century. Two miles to the west is a popular family attraction in the shape of the Tropical Butterfly Gardens and Bird Park, and the B1077 leads south from the town to Banham Zoo, home to a large collection of rare animals from around the world. The Griffin is a popular choice with motor racing enthusiasts, as the Snetterton circuit is just five miles down the A11.

- 10.30-3.30 & 5.30-11 (Fri, Sat & Sun all day)
- Snack and à la carte menus
- Major cards accepted
- 7 rooms (2 en suite)
- Car park, beer garden
- e-mail: griffinattleboro@aol.com
- Church of St Mary in Attleborough; Tropical Butterfly Gardens and Bird Park 2 miles, Banham 5 miles, Snetterton 5 miles, Wymondham 6 miles

THE HILL HOUSE

HAPPISBURGH, NORFOLK NR12 0PW
TEL/FAX: 01692 650004

> **Directions:** From the A149 Great Yarmouth-North Walsham road, turn off at Stalham on to the B1159 and follow signs for Happisburgh (about 4 miles).

On a site close to the rugged Norfolk shoreline, **The Hill House** has a church and a lighthouse for neighbours. This family-friendly 16th century coaching inn is run by Sue and Clive Stockton, who are the most welcoming and attentive of hosts. Equally friendly are their two dogs – Major, a Belgian Shepherd, and Cocoa, a delightful mix. The inn offers an excellent range of food and drink that visitors can enjoy in the beamed bar with its woodburning stove and pictures of bygone days, in the restaurant, in the family room or out in the lovely beer garden. The bar and restaurant menus provide an impressive choice of dishes to suit all tastes and appetites, from sandwiches, burgers and omelettes to steaks, savoury pies, salmon and lobster.

There are plenty of vegetarian main courses, and some scrumptious sweets to round off a meal.

The theme nights, held every other Friday from October to March and featuring a different world cuisine, are always very popular occasions. Six cask ales are on tap, including Adnams Best, Shepherd Neame Spitfire and Buffy's Elementary Ale brewed specially for the pub. Every summer solstice the pub hosts a marvellous beer festival, with at least 40 real ales and ciders, live music and other entertainment – the date for 2005 is 16th to 20th June. The Hill House was a favourite haunt of Sir Arthur Conan Doyle, who wrote *The Dancing Men* while staying here in 1903. Happisburgh nearly had a railway then; the tracks did not get as far as Happisburgh before the Company involved folded but the old signal box still stands in the pub's garden. It now houses one of the letting bedrooms, and there are two further comfortable, spacious rooms in the main building.

- Winter: Mon-Wed 12-3 & 7-11, Thurs-Sat 12-11, Sun 12-10.30. Summer open all day every day
- Bar and restaurant menus
- All the major cards
- 3 guest rooms
- Ample parking, garden
- Pool, darts, annual beer festival
- email: clive.stockton@btinternet.com
- Happisburgh's Church of St Mary; North Walsham 4 miles, Sutton Windmill 4 miles

THE JOHN H STRACEY

WEST END, BRISTON, NR MELTON CONSTABLE, NORFOLK NR24 2JA
TEL: 01263 860891 FAX: 01263 862984

Directions: The inn lies on the B1354 Aylsham-Fakenham road south of Holt.

Easy to find on the B1354 Aylsham-Fakenham road in Briston, **The John H Stracey** is a lively, popular pub named after the renowned British boxer. He officially re-opened the inn about 30 years ago, as the owner at the time was his sparring partner. The inn started life as long ago as the 16th century and became an important stop on the Wells to Norwich coaching route. The present owners Ray and Hilary Fox, here for 20 years, continue the long tradition of hospitality, ably assisted by their son Rupert and twin daughters Alison and Clarissa. The bar is full of old-world character, with heavy black beams and a log fire with a splendid copper canopy enhanced by a display of various copper pieces. Ruddles County is a regular among the cask ales, and the frequently changing guests might include Old Speckled Hen, Woodforde's Wherry and Reepham Rapier. Regular customers

come from miles around to enjoy the food, and the long and varied menus are available lunchtime and evening. Among the perennial favourites are home-cooked ham, steaks, spaghetti Bolognese, curries, the Sunday roasts and Stracey's famous homemade steak & ale pie.

Tuesday and Friday are fish & chips nights, and on Wednesday Italian specials are added to the menu. In the 'posh nosh' section the likes of asparagus soup, filler steak Rossini, salmon poached in white wine and roast duckling with a choice of sauces. The inn is a popular venue for functions, parties and other celebrations. It's also a great place to stay, and the three bedrooms – a double en suite, a double and a twin – all have television, tea trays and lovely views of the countryside. The coast at Sheringham is not far away, and Blakeney, Holt and the National Trust's Blickling Hall are among the many local attractions.

- ○ 1-2.30 & 6.30-11 (Sun 12-2.30 & 6.30-10.30)
- ❙ Traditional home cooking
- £ Not Amex
- ⊟ 3 rooms (1 en suite)
- Ⓟ Car park, side garden
- ❓ Holt 4 miles, Mannington Gardens 6 miles, Blakeney 8 miles, Blickling Hall 8 miles

BURNHAM ROAD, NORTH CREAKE, NORFOLK NR21 9JW
TEL: 01328 738185

Directions: North Creake is on the B1355 Fakenham-Burnham Market road.

The bright sunny yellow exterior of **The Jolly Farmers** and the two smiling framers on the sign are a promise of the warm welcome and fine hospitality that awaits inside. Dating from the early part of the 19th century, this traditional inn on the B1355 has a warm, homely feel assisted by mellow woods, enormous open hearths and the way the inn is divided into small rooms with bookshelves and intimate corners. The main bar area has walls painted a pale yellow, a large open fire, wooden bar counter, quarry-tiled floor and scrubbed pine tables. There's also a smaller bar area with pool table, log-burning stove and pew-style benches. Food is a very important part of business at The Jolly Farmers, and visitors can eat anywhere, but the main dining area is the non-smoking 'red room' with its vivid red walls. The inn is run by Adrian Allen and his wife Heather, and it is Heather who is the creative force behind most of the delicious food that has earned the inn such a fine reputation.

The menu and specials board offer an impressive choice that caters for all tastes and appetites and runs from sandwiches and salads to steak & ale pie, plain and sauced meat and fish dishes, seasonal game, curries and vegetarian dishes. The drinks are also taken seriously here, and real ales include Adnams Best Bitter and Broadside served straight from the cask. When the weather is kind the handsome beer garden is the perfect place to enjoy the excellent food and drink on offer. The area round the inn is popular with walkers and cyclists, and tourists will find many places of interest in the vicinity, including Creake Abbey, the churches at North Creake and South Creake, the majestic Holkham Hall and the village of Burnham Thorpe with its Lord Nelson connection.

- Wed-Sat 12-2.30 Sun 12-3; Tues-Sat 7-11 Sun 7-10.30
- Home cooking
- Not Amex
- Car park, beer garden
- Occasional Medieval and Irish music, darts, pool
- e-mail:sandersadrn@aol.com website: www.jolly-farmers.com
- Walking, cycling; Creake Abbey 1 mile, Burnham Thorpe (Nelson connection) 3 miles, Houghton Hall 4 miles, Holkham Hall 6 miles

Norfolk

THE JOLLY FARMERS

NORTH WALSHAM ROAD, SWANTON ABBOTT, NR NORWICH,
NORFOLK NR10 5DW
TEL/FAX: 01692 538542

Directions: The inn is located in the village of Swanton Abbott, just off the B1150 Norwich-North Walsham road.

In a pleasant rural setting just off the B1150 Norwich-North Walsham road, **The Jolly Farmers** is very much at the heart of village life. The 300-year-old building is distinguished by a splendid brick and flint frontage and a steep tiled roof. Inside, the bar area, with cask ale mats adorning the beams, has a tile-floored eating area with seats for 40, and the separate bright, airy restaurant has French doors that open on to a courtyard garden (there's another, larger beer garden at the back of the inn). Welcoming hosts Sue and Peter Callaway provide connoisseurs of cask ales with a frequently changing and always interesting selection at this free house, including varieties from the Nethergate, Woodforde and Wolf breweries. Nethergate also supplies Peter

with beer infused with coriander, ginger and other flavours.

Food is also a very important part of business at The Jolly Farmers, and the menu offers hearty home cooking using local supplies whenever possible. Mega mixed grill, roast chicken, ribs with BBQ sauce and steak & kidney pudding are among the favourites, along with liver, bacon and onions, chicken curry and chilli con carne. There are fish dishes, pasta dishes, vegetarian main courses and children's choices, with sandwiches, jacket potatoes and snacks for lighter or quicker alternatives. The Jolly Farmers is the village's social centre, with live music at the weekend, pool, darts, a tug of war team and an annual beer festival in August. Attached to the pub is a general store (the only one in the village) run by Peter and Sue.

- 11-2.30 & 6-11, open all day Sat & Sun
- Snack and à la carte menus
- Not Amex
- Ample parking, beer and courtyard gardens, general store
- Live music Saturday, karaoke, annual beer festival
- Bure Valley Railway 3 miles, North Walsham 3 miles, Wroxham ('Capital of the Broads') 5 miles

THE KINGS HEAD

MARKET PLACE, NEW BUCKENHAM, NORFOLK NR16 2AN
TEL: 01953 860487

> **Directions:** New Buckenham stands at the junction of the B1077 and B1113 5 miles southwest of Attleborough.

Overlooking the green in the village of New Buckenham, **The Kings Head** is a delightful country pub with a black-and-white frontage and a history that goes back at least as a far as 1645. The oldest records show that it was a stopover on the London to Norwich coaching run, and today it remains a haven of hospitality with an excellent licensee in Jackie Watts. Here since 1996, Jackie takes care of every aspect of running the pub, and she makes sure that her customers never go hungry or thirsty. Adnams heads the list of well-kept cask ales, and Jackie's home cooking is guaranteed both to please and to satisfy. Traditional favourites include a super steak & kidney pudding, and baguettes and sandwiches make tasty lighter snacks. Some of the regulars are ace cribbage players, and the pub has carried off many prizes in local competitions.

Plans for overnight accommodation at the Kings Head have been shelved, but there are many places of interest in the locality that can fit in well with a trip to this splendid old inn. The Buckenhams, Old and New, have some very attractive cottages and houses, and the Church of St Mary in nearby Attleborough is one of the very finest in the county, with some beautiful vaulting and paintings of saints. Diss, about eight miles away, is a particularly attractive old market town, and the village of Bressingham has lovely gardens and a steam railway and museum. Even closer is Banham Zoo, home to a large collection of some of the world's rarest animals.

- 🕐 12-2 (Fri to 3.30) & 7-11
- 🍴 Home cooked snacks and meals
- Ⓟ Patio
- ❓ Banham Zoo 2 miles, Attleborough 5 miles, Bressingham 6 miles, Diss 8 miles

THE LOBSTER & THE

13 HIGH STREET, SHERINGHAM, NORFOLK NR26 8JP
TEL: 01263 822716   FAX: 01263 824560

Directions: The Lobster lies 50 yards from the sea in the centre of town.

The Lobster is not just *in* the very centre of Sheringham, it's also *at* the very centre of the town's social life. Fifty yards from the beach, it was built as a coaching inn in the 1800s, and it remains a busy, lively place that appeals both to the locals and holidaymakers. It's a home from home for the lifeboat crew, and the walls in the bar are adorned with photographs of the lifeboats and Air Sea Rescue, along with ship's lanterns, lobster pots and other maritime paraphernalia. The inn has a comfortable beamed lounge area and a public bar where pool, darts and dominoes are played. The main bar area and the attractive gardens are accessible to wheelchairs, as is the non-smoking

Stables Restaurant . Proprietor Alistair Deans, his family and his team of chefs have put The Lobster is one of the best eating places in the region, and the traditional English cuisine makes excellent use of the finest produce from award-winning local suppliers. The menu runs from sandwiches and ploughman's lunches to salads and a wide variety of seafood, meat, poultry and vegetarian dishes.

Complementing the food are cask-conditioned ales (the inn is a CAMRA member and is featured in The Good Beer Guide) including Greene King IPA, Abbot Ale and guest beers from smaller local breweries, and wines from around the world. The outside areas are a blaze of colour in the summer, when the Sunday hog roast barbecues are guaranteed to bring in the crowds. Beer festivals are held several times a year, and the whole of Sheringham joins in the fun of the inn's Lobster Potty Festival . Plans are in hand for the addition of six letting bedrooms.

- 🕐 11.30-11 (Sat from 11, Sun 12-10.30)
- 🍴 Full bar menu
- 💷 Not Amex
- 🛏 6 rooms planned
- Ⓟ Two garden areas
- 🎵 Pool, darts, dominoes, beer festivals, Lobster Potty Festival, Folk Festival
- @ e-mail: alistairdeans@tesco.net website: www.the-lobster.com
- ❓ Beach 50 yards, Sheringham Museum, North Norfolk Railway (Poppy Line), Sheringham Park NT 1 mile, Cromer 5 miles

VIA GUN STREET, SHERINGHAM, NORFOLK NR26 8JP
TEL: 01263 822716 FAX: 01263 824560

Directions: The restaurant is situated at the back of The Lobster reached via Gun Street.

The Stables is the non-smoking restaurant of The Lobster public house, offering a selection of mouthwatering dishes based on the very best local produce from land and sea prepared by a team of expert chefs. The old stables behind the pub have been converted to a very stylish restaurant open every evening from 6 o'clock until late. The atmosphere is comfortable and relaxing, and many original features of the old stables have been retained. The bistro menu is served Monday to Thursday, the fine dining menu Friday to Sunday, and a two-or three-course pre-theatre menu is available every night between 6 and 7. For anyone wanting to push the boat out, it just has to be lobster: these are still caught in the little fishing boats that ply their trade from the beach (Sheringham never had a harbour), and this traditional industry is commemorated in the golden lobster that forms part of the town's coat of arms.

Locally caught crab is also very popular, and among the many dishes highlighting the wonderful local fish are Cley hot-smoked eel, lemon sole and pasta marinara with seafood from Sheringham, Wells and Morston. Meat-eaters and vegetarians also have an excellent choice, and it's refreshing to see a very 'grown-up' children's menu with dishes such as garlicky king prawns, steak strips with mushroom and onion gravy, roasted Mediterranean vegetables and a choice of pizzas and pasta. Home-made desserts round things off in style, and the well-chosen wine list includes several house wines available by glass (two sizes) and bottle. There's plenty to see in and around Sheringham, including the Museum, the National Trust's Sheringham Park with its superb Humphry Repton gardens, and the steamed hauled North Norfolk Railway that runs to Holt.

- 🕐 6 to late
- 🍴 Bistro, fine dining and pre-theatre menus
- 💷 Not Amex
- 🛏 6 rooms planned at The Lobster
- ❓ The Beach 50 yards, Sheringham Museum, Sheringham Park NT, North Norfolk Railway to Holt

THE MARSHLAND ARMS

47 SCHOOL ROAD, MARSHLAND ST JAMES, NR WISBECH,
CAMBRIDGESHIRE PE14 8EY
TEL: 01945 430319 FAX: 01945 430838

Directions: Marshland St James lies on a minor road off the A47 4 miles east of Wisbech.

Friendly smiles, a relaxed, inviting ambience, a good pint and tasty home cooking are among the chief assets of the **Marshland Arms**, which stands in the village of Marshland St James at the northern end of the Fens. When closure threatened some ten years ago, this 200-year-old inn was

rescued by Steve Woolner, who runs a local haulage company, and since taking over he and his family have invested great effort and expense in bringing the place back to its best. A full range of cask ales, beers, lagers and wines is served in the bar, and the chef is really putting the inn on the local gastronomic map with an excellent variety of dishes that take their inspiration from England,

the Med and the world at large. Food is served in the bar (separate bar meals) or in the 30-cover non-smoking restaurant, which is closed on Monday evening in addition to the pub closures of Monday and Tuesday lunchtimes.

The Marshland Arms has one room available for overnight accommodation (no children, pets or smoking). Marshland is very close to Wisbech, one of the largest of the Fenland towns, and one with many attractions for the visitor; among the most notable are the National Trust's Peckover House, the fine Church of St Peter & St Paul, the house where Octavia Hill, co-founder of the National Trust, was born, the fascinating Wisbech & Fenland Museum, and last, but by no means least, Elgood's Brewery and Brewing Museum.

- 12·2 & 7·11 (Fri 12·2 & 5.30·11; Sat 12.30·11, Sun 12·10.30); closed Mon & Tues lunchtimes
- Home cooking
- Major cards accepted
- 1 double en suite room
- Car park, beer garden
- website: www.marshlandarms.co.uk
- Wisbech 2 miles, Kings Lynn 12 miles, 25 miles from Norfolk Coast.

NORWICH ROAD, ROUGHTON, NORFOLK NR11 8SJ
TEL: 01263 761389 FAX: 01263 768868

> **Directions:** The inn is on the A140 3 miles south of Cromer.

The New Inn is a substantial 18th century building that's easy to find on the A140 3 miles south of Cromer. It offers a very pleasant, relaxed and traditional ambience in which to enjoy a glass of ale in the public bar or a leisurely meal in the comfortable dining area. The affable hosts are Sean Crampsie, who hails from County Donegal, and his wife Tina; both are excellent cooks, and their respective Irish and Eastern origins enable them to offer a particularly interesting choice of food. Traditionalists will opt for the simple pub classics, while the more adventurous can try something more exotic from Tina's repertoire.

Food is served lunchtime and evening seven days a week, and all day in summer, and the restaurant includes a non-smoking section. From 5 o'clock until 11 every evening except Monday the very extensive choice of Chinese dishes can be ordered (in person or by telephone) to take away. The list runs to about 140 items, with set meals for 2 or more in addition. A full range of draught and bottled beers, lagers and wine is available in the bar, and when the sun shines visitors can enjoy an alfresco drink or meal in the garden. The New Inn no longer offers guest accommodation, but the ambience and the food make a visit very worthwhile, and there are many places of interest within a short drive. The seaside town of Cromer, complete with a traditional pier, is just a few minutes' drive away, and even closer is the National Trust's Fellbrigg Hall, one of Norfolk's grandest houses.

- 🕐 12-3 & 5-11 (all day Sat & Sun and in summer)
- 🍴 English and Chinese cooking
- 💷 Major cards accepted
- 🅿 Car park, beer garden
- 🎵 Quiz nights
- @ e-mail: crampsie@aol.com
- ❓ Cromer 4 miles, Felbrigg Hall 3 miles

THE OLD RED LION

THE GREEN, ALDBOROUGH, NORFOLK NR11 7AA
TEL: 01263 761451

Directions: The inn is in the centre of Aldborough, west of the A140 about midway between Aylsham and Cromer.

The **Old Red Lion** is a handsome listed 16th century building covered in red and green ivy, overlooking the huge village green at the end of a stunning little row of cottages. The promise of the exterior is more than fulfilled inside this grand old inn, where old floor tiles, sturdy old tables and chairs, pictures, fresh flowers, pretty curtains, oak and brass create a delightfully traditional, homely ambience. There is a real log fire, lit every day in winter. Licensee Trudy Johnson, who took over the reins in 2001, has the place just as she wants it, and just as her customers want it; she is a serious and very talented cook (she has worked in leading Norfolk hotels as a chef), and anyone wanting to eat is advised to book, as she cooks only as much as she's happy to serve.

To accompany the fine food, or to enjoy on their own, are some excellent cask ales,

including one brewed locally especially for the Old Red Lion. Allan who handles the bar and is a real ale expert. He is only too happy to chat to customers about ales and answer any questions they may have. In the summer, the Old Red Lion also functions as a tea room, a delightful place to take a break when touring the area or watching cricket on the adjacent village green. The inn has ample off-road parking, a patio and a beer garden. There's live music most weekends, and each July on the green, there is a traditional fair and classic car rally. Two en suite guest bedrooms at the inn provide a comfortable, civilised base from which to explore the local places of interest, which include the National Trust's Blickling Hall, one of England's greatest Jacobean houses, Manningham Hall, a medieval moated manor house, and Wolterton Park, an 18th century mansion set in grounds designed by Humphry Repton. The nearby A140 offers easy access to these attractions and to the charming seaside town of Cromer.

- 🕐 11-11 (from 12 in winter)
- 🍴 Home cooking, real ales & Tap room
- 🛏 2 en suite rooms
- Ⓟ Car park, patio, garden
- 🎵 Live music most weekends
- ❓ Blickling Hall 5 miles, Aylsham (Bure Valley Railway) 6 miles, Manningham Hall 4 miles, Wolterton Hall 4 miles. Short distance from Norfolk Coast, including Sheringham & Cromer

STATION RD, NORTH ELMHAM, NR DEREHAM, NORFOLK NR20 5HH
TEL: 01362 668300

Directions: The inn is located at North Elmham, 6 miles north of Dereham on the B1145.

In the historic village of North Elmham, on the B1145 north of Dereham, the **Railway Freehouse** provides excellent hospitality throughout the day. The roadside inn comprises two adjacent mid-Victorian buildings, and behind the red brick and flint frontages the bars are cosy and homely, with heavy wooden tables and plenty of comfortable sofas to sink into and unwind with a drink by the roaring log fire. The informal ambience has been created by proprietors Colin and Julie Smith, who have been here for 44 years and are two of the most respected landlords in Norfolk. They are justly proud of their pub, and know exactly what their customers want. They keep their regulars happy with a selection of five real ales, draught and bottled beers, lagers and ciders. In the immaculate little restaurant generously served traditional pub dishes are offered, from the traditional menu or changing specials board, which put the emphasis on good honest flavours and value for money.

North Elmham was the seat of the Bishops of East Anglia until 1071 – it was then moved to Thetford and later to Norwich – and the substantial remains of the Saxon Cathedral can still be seen. Also worth a visit is the Church of St Mary, with a stone-dressed flint tower and some notable screen panel paintings depicting the Saints. The church is a particularly pretty sight when decked out with flowers for the village flower festival over the August Bank holiday, which coincides with the annual 'Railway Beer Festival'.

- 11-11
- Home cooking
- Major cards accepted
- Car park, Basic camping facilities available during the summer months
- e-mail: julie@therailway96.freeserve.co.uk
- Brisley 2 miles, Dereham 6 miles, Fakenham 10 miles

THE RED LION

CHURCH STREET, COLTISHALL, NORFOLK NR12 7DW
TEL: 01603 737402

Directions: Coltishall lies about 7 miles north of Norwich at the junction of the B1130 and B1354.

The Red Lion is a 17th century coaching inn standing virtually in the shadow of the even older parish church. Licensees Melanie and Peter Lamb share the main duties at this welcoming hostelry, with Melanie in charge of the kitchen and Peter quenching local thirsts behind the bar. Adnams and other cask ales head the list of liquid refreshment, while Melanie produces good honest pub food in generous portions at very kind prices; the choice runs from quick snacks and light bites to full meals and is available every lunchtime and evening and all day on Saturday and Sunday. The pub has ample space for cars, and the beer garden is a popular spot in fine weather.

The charming village of Coltishall is

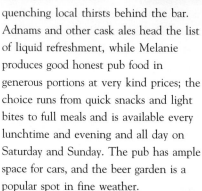
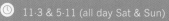

🕐 11-3 & 5-11 (all day Sat & Sun)

🍴 Traditional home-cooked pub food

💷 Major cards accepted

Ⓟ Car park, beer garden

🎵 Occasional live music

❓ Redwings Horse Sanctuary 1 mile, Wroxham (Bure Valley Railway) 3 miles, Norwich 10 miles

sometimes known as the 'Gateway to Broadland' as it lies at the start of the navigable section of the River Bure. The 220 square miles of the Norfolk Broads, providing some 120 miles of navigable waterways, bring visitors in their thousands but they are by no means the only attraction hereabouts. In Coltishall itself, the Ancient Lime Kiln is a monument to Norfolk's industrial heritage – and home to a colony of bats who have acquired squatters' rights. A short distance south, on the B1150, is another animal refuge, the Redwings Horse Sanctuary, founded in 1984 and home at any one time to more than 1,000 horses, ponies, donkeys and mules. Anyone who's bats about old railways will head for nearby Wroxham, the southern terminus of the narrow-gauge Bure Valley Railway.

THE RED LION

NEEDHAM, HARLESTON, NORFOLK IP20 9LG
TEL: 01379 853930 FAX: 01379 853639

Directions: Needham lies about 5 miles east of Diss on the A143 towards Bungay
and Great Yarmouth.

A few miles east of Diss, in the heart of
the beautiful Waveney Valley, **The Red
Lion** has earned a well-deserved
reputation as one of the very best food
pubs in the whole county. It is owned
and run by Lebanon-born 'Jovial' Jess
Issa, his wife Amanda (Mandy) and her
father Ralph, who together with mum
Daphne came here in 1985. The whole
place is kept in immaculate order,
winning Gold Top Spot environmental
awards for the past ten years. Outside the
attractive white-painted pub, a
handsome red lion in a chef's hat holds a
board with the invitation to 'stop for a
bite'. And food is what this place is all
about, ranging from simple bar snacks to
what must be the most extensive à la
carte menu of any pub in East Anglia.
The choice in the non-smoking
restaurant runs from a snack menu with

jacket potatoes and burgers to an
impressive selection of meat, poultry,
fish and vegetarian dishes, some of them
classics such as steak & kidney pie or
battered cod, others more unusual, like
braised venison or matloubi, a Lebanese
dish of diced rumpsteak, cauliflower,
aubergine, tomatoes and rice.

Adnams and Greene King cask ales are
always on tap in the cosy bar, and there's
a world-wide wine list. As well as being a
fine place for a meal, the Red Lion is
also a popular village local. Pool and
darts are played in the bar, and the
spacious gardens are great for families.
Fishing, sailing and windsurfing on the
adjacent lake or a walk along the banks
of the Waveney are all guaranteed to
work up an appetite, and there's
definitely no better place to satisfy a
fresh-air appetite than the Red Lion.
The owners plan to bring three self-
catering chalets on stream for the 2005
season.

12-3 & 6-11

Extensive bar and à la carte menus

All major credit cards accepted

Self-catering accommodation
planned for 2005

Garden

e-mail: needhamredlion@aol.com
website: www.needhamredlion.co.uk

Diss 5 miles, 100th Bomb Group
Memorial Museum 4 miles

THE SCOLE INN

SCOLE, NR DISS, NORFOLK IP21 4DR
TEL: 01379 740481 FAX: 01379 740762

Norfolk

> **Directions:** Scole is on the A140 bypass 2 miles east of Diss.

The Scole Inn is one of the best-known and best-loved hostelries in the region, with a reputation for hospitality, service and quality food and drink that has been built up over many years. And it's also one of the most recognisable buildings in the county with its splendid Dutch-influenced gables and tall chimneys. The interior retains many of its original 17th century features, including the main staircase and vast fireplaces, two of which are said to be the largest in East Anglia. In the beamed bar, well-kept cask ales accompany a menu of traditional pub favourites, and in the restaurant fresh seasonal produce is used to excellent effect in dishes that are complemented by a fine selection of wines. Traditional Sunday lunch, with a choice of three roasts, is a regular feature in many a local diary. The inn is open for coffee, pastries and the popular 'breakfast butties' throughout the day, so no one visiting the Scole Inn should stay hungry for long. A private dining room has seats for 30, and the inn holds a

licence to conduct civil wedding ceremonies, catering for wedding parties of up to 50.

The overnight accommodation is divided between the main building, each room with its own fireplace and many with four-poster beds, and the converted Georgian stables. All rooms are splendidly equipped, with private facilities, telephone, television, trouser press and hairdryer. Booking can be made on a Bed & Breakfast or Dinner Bed & Breakfast basis, and the inn is open all year round. The Scole Inn is the most eminent landmark in the village close to the border with Suffolk from which it takes its name. Now by-passed by the busy A140, and consequently more tranquil, it is within a short drive of many places of interest; closest is the pretty market town of Diss, which Sir John Betjeman declared to be his favourite Norfolk town.

- 🕐 12-3 & 6-11
- 🍴 Bar and restaurant menus
- 💷 All major cards
- 🅿 Car park
- ❓ Diss 2 miles

BEACH ROAD, MUNDESLEY, NR CROMER, NORFOLK NR11 8BQ
TEL: 01263 720448 FAX: 01263 722771

> **Directions:** Mundesley is located on the B1159 7 miles southeast of Cromer;
> from the south, leave the A149 and take the B1159 at Stalham.

It was the railways that first brought visitors to Mundesley to enjoy the bracing sea air and the superb sandy beach. The railway has long gone, but the visitors still make the journey by car or coach to this delightful place, and those in the know head for the seafront and **The Ship Inn**. At this fine-looking flint-faced redbrick building dating from the mid-18th century they can expect the warmest of welcomes from the Fowler family and a winning combination of good food, good ale and good fun. A full range of drinks is served in the cosy public bar, and in the dining area the big blackboard menu lists a wide selection of dishes to cater for appetites large and small.

Sandwiches or rustic rolls come with generous fillings such as bacon & melted brie or steak & fried onions, and other typical favourites are roast chicken with a perky BBQ sauce, cod in ale batter and a tasty plate of ham, eggs and chips. The Sunday lunchtime carvery is particularly popular, and the Fowlers are happy to provide hot and cold buffets for functions, parties, wedding receptions and other special occasions. Christine Fowler also finds time to run a small catering company specialising in cakes. One of the Ship's prize assets is the large garden directly overlooking the beach, which many consider to be the finest in Norfolk. The family's plans include bringing on stream nine guest bedrooms, which will provide a perfect base for a beach holiday.

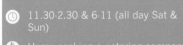

- 🕐 11.30-2.30 & 6-11 (all day Sat & Sun)
- 🍴 Home cooking + catering company
- 💷 Major cards accepted
- 🛏 Planned
- 🅿 Car park, garden with sea views
- 🎵 Live music Sat night
- ❓ Walks in the bracing sea air, North Walsham 4 miles, Cromer 7 miles

THE SWAN

3 DEREHAM ROAD, MATTISHALL, NR DEREHAM, NORFOLK NR20 3QB
TEL: 01362 850305

Norfolk

Directions: Mattishall lies 3 miles east of Dereham off the A47 or B1135.

Standing opposite the parish church in the quiet, attractive Norfolk village of Mattishall, **The Swan** is a superbly maintained inn offering real hospitality throughout the day. The smartly informal central bar, with its pink-washed walls and open fires, is the hub of village life, and hosts Liz Crosby and Tony Norris have an equally warm welcome for regular customers and visitors to this very pleasant part of the world. Several monthly changing cask ales supplement the permanent Websters brew, and food is an increasingly popular part of the business. The best of familiar traditional English fare is served throughout opening hours, along with curries and other adopted pub classics, with a variety of snacks for lighter appetites.

Twice a month, The Swan hosts live Friday music sessions, and the bar has a pool table. There's ample off-road parking, and the beer garden has an area for children to play. This civilised pub in a civilised village is a delight to visit at any time of day, and an excellent place to seek out for refreshment while touring the region. Walking and golf are popular activities hereabouts, and railway enthusiasts will head for one of the stations on the Mid-Norfolk Railway that runs between Wymondham and Dereham. The latter is one of the most ancient towns in the county, and its attractions include the splendid Church of St Nicholas, the second largest in Norfolk.

- 🕐 12-11
- 🍴 Traditional pub dishes served all day
- 💷 Major cards accepted
- 🅿 Car park, beer garden, children's play area
- 🎵 Live music Friday twice monthly
- ❓ Dereham 3 miles, Mid-Norfolk Railway 4 miles

LYNN ROAD, ROYDON, NR KINGS LYNN, NORFOLK PE32 1AQ

TEL:01485 600362

Norfolk

> **Directions:** From Kings Lynn take the A149 to the roundabout with the A148, then on to a minor road eastwards for about 2 miles.

The area in and around the village of Roydon has plenty to interest the visitor, but for a warm welcome and great hospitality **The Three Horseshoes** is definitely the place to head for. Dating from the first years of the 18th century, this fine old redbrick inn with a red-tiled roof is superbly

maintained outside and in, a great credit to licensee Alec Jackson, who took over here in January 2004. The decor in the public rooms is cosy and homely, the perfect spot for enjoying a drink and a chat. The Greene King IPA is in excellent condition, and there's a good selection of other draught and bottled beers, lagers and wine.

Good honest food is available every lunchtime and evening, and in warm weather a drink and a meal can be enjoyed at picnic tables at the front of the pub.

There's a pool table in the separaet games room and regular entertainment includes quiz nights on the first Wednesday of the month and karaoke sessions on the third Saturday of the month. This excellent walking country, and the town of King's Lynn is steeped in history, with numerous fine old buildings, museums and churches to visit. Also close by is the pretty village of Castle Rising, where the church and the formidable 12th century Keep attract many visitors. A couple of miles north of Castle Rising is the royal residence of Sandringham.

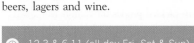

- (clock) 12-3 & 6-11 (all day Fri, Sat & Sun)
- Snacks and full menu
- (£) Major cards accepted
- (P) Car park, beer garden
- (♪) Quiz 1st Wed of month, karaoke 3rd Sat of month, pool table
- (@) e-mail: jacksonalec@aol.com
- (?) Castle Rising 4 miles, Kings Lynn 5 miles

THE WALPOLE ARMS

THE COMMON, ITTERINGHAM, NR NORWICH, NORFOLK NR11 7AR
TEL: 01263 587258   FAX: 01263 587074

Norfolk

Directions: Itteringham lies 6 miles northwest of Aylsham. Take the B1354 out of Aylsham and turn right about 1mile after Blickling Hall on to a minor road signposted Itteringham.

Well hidden it may be – tucked away down the little lanes of North Norfolk – but if ever a pub was worth tracking down, it is surely the **Walpole Arms**. This traditional village pub, built in the 17th century as a farmhouse, is owned and run by Richard Bryan and Keith Reeves, both long-term Norfolk residents; the former is a prolific writer and broadcaster who for ten years produced the popular television programme Masterchef, the latter a well respected wine merchant. Their passion for food and drink, combined with the impressive talents of head chef Andy Parle and his team, has made this the leading pub-restaurant in the region, winner of numerous and recognised by leading food guides: Michelin 2004 *Bib Gourmand*, Country Pub of the year in

the Norfolk Food Awards, East Anglia Dining Pub of the Year with Les Routiers. Norfolk produces outstanding fruit and vegetables as well as the best seafood and game in the land, and nothing but the best will do for Andy, whose previous posts have included Adlard's in Norwich and Le Pont de la Tour in London. The mussels are the finest from Morston and the game is reared, killed and hung at Gunton Hall. Typical dishes on the mouthwatering main menu run from paprika sardine fillets and terrine maison with pickled prunes for starters to braised lamb shanks, sea bass with saffron mash, paella for 2 and the Italian dish *suppli* – tomato and mozzarella rice cakes.

The Walpole Arms is also very much a village local, with a cosy, characterful oak-beamed public bar serving a wide selection of beers and wines and excellent bar snacks and a pleasant garden for alfresco sipping in fine weather.

- 🕐 12·3 & 6·11 (Sun 12·3 & 7·10.30)
- 🍽 A la carte and bar snacks
- 💷 Major cards accepted
- 🛏 Planned
- 🅿 Car park, beer garden
- @ e-mail: goodfood@thewalpolearms.co.uk web: www.thewalpolearms.co.uk
- ❓ Mannington Hall 1 mile, Blickling Hall 4 miles, Bure Valley Railway 6 miles

THE WHITE HORSE

KIRKGATE STREET, HOLME BY THE SEA, NR HUNSTANTON,
NORFOLK PE36 6LH
TEL: 01485 525512

> **Directions:** Holme by the Sea lies 3 miles northeast of Hunstanton off the A149.

The delights of the countryside and the coast are equally accessible at the **White Horse**, a cream-painted mid-Victorian stone building surrounded by attractive old outbuildings. The licensee is Glynis Thomson, who took over the reins in 2002 and has been making changes to get the inn looking just as she wants it. Open fires warm the public areas, where a full range of draught and bottle beers and lagers is on hand to quench fresh-air thirsts. Food is a very important part of the pub's business, and word of the skills in the kitchen has spread throughout the surrounding area and beyond. In the spacious, comfortable restaurant the frequently changing menu offers an unusually wide and interesting range of dishes to suit all tastes. Typical starters

from a choice of about a dozen might be home-made mackerel pâté with lime marmalade and melba toast or wild mushroom and coriander risotto, while among the main courses could be grilled lemon or Dover sole, ribeye steak with Lyonnaise potatoes, and pan-fried medallions of pork fillet with a rich red wine sauce.

The fine food is accompanied by a good selection of wines. The White Horse is very much at the social hub of the village, and regular events include blues nights on Tuesday and on Sunday in winter. Walking is a popular pastime at Holme, which is the point where the long-established 50-mile Peddar's Way meets the Norfolk Coast Path. The area is also popular with birdwatchers and nature lovers, and Holme is famous as the site of 'Sea Henge', a Bronze Age tree circle that was discovered on the beach.

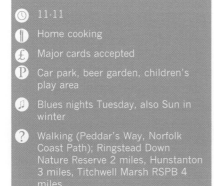

- 🕐 11-11
- 🍴 Home cooking
- 💷 Major cards accepted
- 🅿 Car park, beer garden, children's play area
- 🎵 Blues nights Tuesday, also Sun in winter
- ❓ Walking (Peddar's Way, Norfolk Coast Path); Ringstead Down Nature Reserve 2 miles, Hunstanton 3 miles, Titchwell Marsh RSPB 4 miles

THE WHITE HORSE AT LONGHAM

Norfolk

WENDLING ROAD, NR DEREHAM, NORFOLK NR19 2RD
TEL: 01362 687464   FAX: 01362 687484

> **Directions:** Turn off the A47 Swaffham-Dereham road for Wendling and Longham. First left to Bittering, follow the road for about 2½ miles to the sign for Longham.

Outstanding hospitality and service, excellent food and drink and superb accommodation are among the many reasons for visiting **The White Horse at Longham**. For more than 350 years this redbrick village pub has been welcoming visitors from near and far, and that tradition of hospitality is as strong as ever under Barry White, Chrissie Sandford and their staff. This quintessentially English country inn has all the features that make for a memorable visit: comfortable seating in the spacious lounge bar or beer garden, a handsome wood and brick bar with a wood-burning stove to keep things cosy, a fine range of drinks and splendid food. Real ales on tap include Woodforde's brews and two changing guest ales, and there's a good selection of other beers,

lagers, scrumpy cider, wines, spirits and soft drinks.

In the non-smoking restaurant areas, one of them a delightful conservatory overlooking the garden, the chefs produce a mouthwatering variety of dishes, from prawn cocktail, garlic mushrooms and goujons of sole for starters to daily fish specials, filled giant Yorkshire puddings, braised lamb shank, chilli con carne and super pies (steak & kidney, steak & Guinness, chicken and mushroom). The enjoyment level stays high right to the end with scrumptious desserts such as fruit pies and lemon brûlée. Sandwiches and snacks are available on the bar menu. With five very comfortable, well-equipped guest bedrooms, all with en suite facilities, The White Horse is a great base to enjoy this beautiful area.

- 🕐 12-2.30 & 6.30-11 (closed Monday lunchtime)
- 🍴 A la carte and bar menus
- 💷 Not Amex
- 🛏 5 en suite rooms
- 🅿 Car park, lawned garden
- ❓ Gressenhall (Norfolk Rural Life Museum) 3 miles, Dereham 4 miles, Swaffham 10 miles

THE WOOLPACK

MAIN ROAD, TERRINGTON ST JOHN, NR KING'S LYNN,
NORFOLK PE14 7RR   TEL: 01945 881097

Directions: Terrington St John lies just off the A47 about 5 miles east of Wisbech
and 6 miles west of King's Lynn.

The Woolpack is a handsome three-storey
building dating back to the late 1800s. It
retains all the charm and character of a
traditional village inn, yet decorated
uniquely. The new, **non-smoking** dining
area (55 covers) has strong 'art deco' tones,
with big geometric abstract prints by 'Piet
Mondrian' (1922). The high ceiling sports
a similar 'Lincrusta' frieze with black
banding and a specially commissioned 7
glass panel, depicting 'The Ribbon of Life'
(**everyone** has hiccups in their life: can
you spot them in the stained glass
windows?). Exclusively designed felt wall
hangings - based on Picasso's work of the
1920's - hang amongst 'Georgia O'Keefe's'
big, throbbing, flower paintings. Here is
proof that pub architecture does not have
to be fake beams, horse-brasses and a faded
'Haywain'! The Ladies Room is sassy, with
shocking pink walls, multi-coloured toilet
seats and Andy Warhol prints of Marilyn
Monroe.

The Woolpack, now a special pub, has
become a **destination restaurant** wildly
popular with a big reputation. From the
everyday pub favourites and home-made
pies to daily wet fish specials such as
scallops or local, line-caught bass! Priding
themselves on quality fresh ingredients to
produce exciting and innovative menu
selections, **with notice** the head chef
boasts - *"challenge me to make you authentic
dishes from anywhere in the world (subject to
availability!)"*. Food is served every
lunchtime and evening every day - but
arrive hungry 'cos you can't miss out on an
inspirational selection of home-made
sweets (yum yum). This cheerful freehouse
admirably fulfils its time honoured role of
lively local, a perfect spot to relax over a
glass of ale (Greene King IPA and Charles
Wells Eagle are the regular cask ales) and a
weekly guest ale - its a CAMRA
recognised pub.

The Woolpack has ample parking front
and rear of the building, one overlooking
the large beer garden with an abundance of
herbs, flowers and shrubs. The enthusiastic
and award-winning owners, Lucille and
Barry Carter and their staff offer a warm
welcome and hospitality second to none.

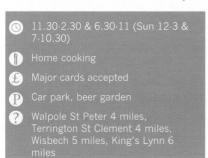

- 11.30-2.30 & 6.30-11 (Sun 12-3 &
  7-10.30)
- Home cooking
- Major cards accepted
- Car park, beer garden
- Walpole St Peter 4 miles,
  Terrington St Clement 4 miles,
  Wisbech 5 miles, King's Lynn 6
  miles

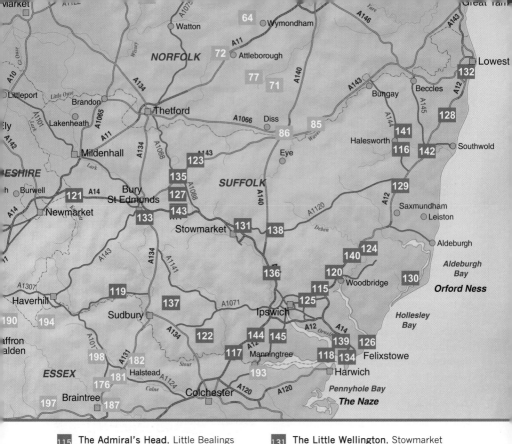

115	The Admiral's Head, Little Bealings	131	The Little Wellington, Stowmarket
116	The Angel Hotel, Halesworth	132	The Morning Star, Lowestoft
117	The Black Horse, Stratford St Mary	133	The Old Cannon Brewery, Bury St Edmunds
118	The Bristol Arms, Shotley Gate, Ipswich	134	The Ordnance Hotel, Felixstowe
119	The Bull Inn, Cavendish	135	The Pykkerell, Ixworth, Bury St Edmunds
120	The Cherry Tree Inn, Woodbridge	136	The Sorrel Horse Inn, Barham, Ipswich
121	The Cock Inn, Kentford, Newmarket	137	The Swan Inn, Little Waldingfield
122	The Cock Inn, Polstead	138	The Ten Bells, Stonham Aspal
123	The Cock Inn, Stanton	139	The Three Mariners, Trimley St Mary
124	The Dog & Duck, Campsea Ashe	140	The Three Tuns Coaching Inn, Pettistree
125	The Falcon, Rushmere St Andrew	141	The Triple Plea, Broadway, Halesworth
126	The Ferry Boat Inn, Felixstowe	142	The White Hart Inn, Blythburgh
127	The Fox, Pakenham	143	The White Horse, Beyton
128	The Horse & Groom, Wrentham	144	The White Horse Inn, Capel St Mary
129	The Kings Head, Yoxford	145	The White Horse Inn, Tattingstone
130	The Kings Head Inn, Orford		

Please note all cross references refer to page numbers

SUFFOLK

Suffolk is very much a maritime county, with over 50 miles of coastline. The whole coast is a conservation area, which the 50-mile Suffolk Coastal Path makes walkable throughout. With all the miles of meandering rivers and superb stretches of coastline, it is only natural that watery pursuits are a popular pastime, and everything from sailing to scuba diving, angling to powerboat racing, is available. Many of the local museums also have a nautical theme, and the Suffolk coast has been a source of inspiration for many of the nation's most distinguished artists, writers and composers.

The sea brings its own dangers, sometimes in human form, and it was against the threat of a Napoleonic invasion that Martello Towers were built in southeastern Suffolk, in the tradition of Saxon and Tudor forts and the precursors of concrete pillboxes. Aldeburgh's at Slaughden is the most northerly (and the largest), while the tower at Shoreham in Sussex is the southernmost.

Inland Suffolk has few peers in terms of picturesque countryside and villages, and the area of central Suffolk between the heathland and the coast is a delightful place for getting away from it all to the real countryside, with unchanged ancient villages, gently flowing rivers and rich farm land. The Rivers Deben and Gipping run through much of the region, which also boasts its fair share of churches, museums, markets, fairs and festivals. The little market towns

PLACES OF INTEREST

Aldeburgh 97	Lavenham 107
Beccles 98	Leiston 108
Blythburgh 98	Long Melford
Brandon 99	108
Bury St Edmunds	Lowestoft 109
100	Mildenhall 109
Carlton Colville 101	Newmarket 110
Cavendish 102	Orford 110
Clare 102	Pakenham 111
Dunwich 102	Shotley 111
Earsham 103	Somerleyton 111
East Bergholt 103	Southwold 112
Felixstowe 103	Stonham Aspal
Flixton 104	112
Framlingham 104	Stowmarket 112
Hadleigh 104	Stratford St Mary
Haverhll 105	113
Horringer 105	Sudbury 113
Ipswich 105	Thorpeness 113
Kersey 106	Woodbridge 113
Kessingland 106	

Abbey Gateway, Bury St Edmunds

of Stowmarket and Needham Market are full of interest, and in this part of Suffolk some of the best-preserved windmills and watermills are to be found. The relative flatness of Suffolk gives every encouragement for motorists to leave their machines, and the peninsula, still relatively peaceful, is ideal for a spot of walking or cycling, or even boating. Southeast of Ipswich, the peninsula created by the River Deben and the River Orwell is one of the prettiest areas in Suffolk, its winding lanes leading through a delightful series of quiet rural villages and colourful riverside communities.

John Constable, England's greatest landscape painter, was born at East Bergholt in 1776 and remained at heart a Suffolk man throughout his life. He was later to declare *'I associate my careless boyhood with all that lies on the banks of the Stour. Those scenes made me a painter and I am grateful.'* The Suffolk tradition of painting continues to this day, with many artists drawn particularly to Walberswick and what is known as 'Constable country'.

Cambridgeshire, Norfolk, the A134 and the A14 frame the northern part of West Suffolk, which includes Bury St Edmunds, a pivotal player in the country's religious history, and Newmarket, one of the major centres of the horseracing world. Between and above them are picturesque villages, bustling market towns, rich farming countryside, the fens, and the expanse of sandy heath and pine forest that is Breckland. The area south and west of Bury towards the Essex border contains some of Suffolk's most attractive and peaceful countryside. The visitor will come upon a succession of picturesque villages, historic churches, remarkable stately homes, heritage centres and nature reserves. In the south, along the River Stour, stand the historic wool towns of Long Melford, Cavendish and Clare.

ALDEBURGH

Aldeburgh is another coastal town that once prospered as a port with major fishing and shipbuilding industries. Drake's *Greyhound* and *Pelican* were built at Slaughden, now taken by the sea, and during the 16th century some 1,500 people were engaged in fishing.

Aldeburgh is perhaps best known now for the **Aldeburgh Festival**, started in 1948 by Benjamin Britten and others; the festival's main venue is Snape Maltings, but many performances take place in Aldeburgh itself.

The town's maritime connections remain very strong. There has been a lifeboat here since 1851, and down the years many acts of great heroism have been recorded. The very modern lifeboat station is one of the town's chief attractions for visitors, and there are regular practice launches from the shingle beach. A handful of fishermen still put out to sea from the beach, selling their catch from their little wooden huts, while a thriving yacht club is the base for sailing on the Orde and, sometimes, on the sea.

At the very southern tip of the town, the Martello tower serves as a reminder of the power of the sea: old pictures show it standing well back from the waves, but now the seaward side of the moat has disappeared and the shingle is constantly being shored up to protect it. Beyond it, a long strip of marsh and shingle stretches right down to the mouth of the river at Shingle Street. On the beach at the other end of town is a great metal structure in the shape of a seashell, a tribute to Benjamin Britten devised by the renowned artist Maggie Hambling.

Back in town there are several interesting buildings, notably the **Moot Hall** and the parish church of **St Peter and St Paul**. The Moot Hall is a 16th century timber-framed building that was built in what was once the centre of town. It hasn't moved, but the sea long ago took away several houses and streets. Inside the Hall is a museum of town history and finds from the nearby Snape burial ship. Britten set the first scene of Peter Grimes in the Moot Hall. A sundial on the south face of the Hall proclaims, in Latin, that it only tells the time when the sun shines.

The church, which stands above the town as a very visible landmark for mariners, contains a memorial to the poet George Crabbe and a

Beach at Aldeburgh

Yacht Club, Aldeburgh

beautiful stained-glass window, the work of John Piper, depicting three Britten parables: *Curlew River*, *The Burning Fiery Furnace* and *The Prodigal Son*. Britten and his companion Peter Pears are buried in the churchyard, part of which is set aside for the benefit of wildlife.

BECCLES

The largest town in the Waveney district at the southernmost point of the Broads, Beccles has in its time been home to Saxons and Vikings, and at one time the market here was a major supplier of herring (up to 60,000 a year) to the Abbey at Bury St Edmunds. The parish church of **St Michael** was built in the second half of the 14th century by the Abbot of Bury. Its tower stands separate, built in the 16th century, rising almost 100 feet and containing a peal of bells. An unusual feature at the north facade is an outside pulpit taking the form of a small balcony. The priest could enter the pulpit from inside the church and preach to lepers, who were not allowed inside.

Another building with Dutch-style gables houses the **Beccles and District Museum**, whose contents include 19th century toys and costume, farm implements, items from the old town gaol and memorabilia from the sailing wherries, including a wealth of old photographs. Beccles is an old printing town, and has the **William Clowes Museum of Print** on the site of the Newgate works of the famed printer. Here the visitor will learn about the history of printing since the 1800s, with woodcuts, books and machinery; tours of the factory are also available.

BLYTHBURGH

Blythburgh's church of **Holy Trinity** is one of the wonders of Suffolk, a stirring sight as it rises from the reed beds, visible for miles around and floodlit at night to spectacular effect. This 'Cathedral of the Marshes' reflects the days when Blythburgh was a prosperous port with a bustling quayside wool trade. With the silting up of the river, trade rapidly fell off and the church fell into decay. In 1577 the steeple of the 14th century tower was struck by lightning in a severe storm; it fell into the nave, shattering the font and taking two lives. The scorch marks visible to this day on the north door are said to be the claw marks of the Devil in the guise of hellhound Black Shuck, left as he sped towards Bungay to terrify the congregation of **St Mary's**.

Disaster struck again in 1644, when Dowsing and his men smashed windows, ornaments and statues, blasted the wooden angels in the roof with hundreds of bullets and used the nave as a stable, with tethering rings screwed into the pillars of the nave. Luckily, the bench-end carvings escaped the desecration, not being labelled idolatrous. These depict the Labours of the Months, and the Seven Deadly Sins. Blythburgh also has a Jack o'the Clock, a brother of the figure at Southwold, and the priest's chamber over the south porch has been lovingly restored complete with an altar made with wood from *HMS Victory*. The angels may have survived, but the font was defaced to remove the signs of the sacraments.

A mile south, at the junction of the A12 and the Walberswick road, **Toby's Walks** is an ideal place for a picnic and, like so many places in Suffolk, has its own ghost story. This concerns Tobias Gill, a dragoon drummer who murdered a local girl and was hanged here after a trial at Ipswich. His ghost is said to haunt the heath, but this should not deter picnic-makers.

The Norman Gwatkin Nature Reserve is an area of marsh and fen with two hides, walkways and a willow coppice.

BRANDON

On the edge of **Thetford Forest** by the Little Ouse, Brandon was long ago a thriving port, but flint is what really put it on the map. The town itself is built mainly of flint, and flint was mined from early Neolithic times to make arrowheads and other implements and weapons of war. The gun flint industry brought with it substantial wealth, and a good flint-knapper could produce up to 300 gun flints in an hour. The invention of the percussion cap killed off much of the need for this type of work, however, so they turned to shaping flints for church buildings and ornamental purposes. **Brandon Heritage Centre**, in a former fire station in George Street, provides visitors with a splendid insight into this industry, while for an even more tangible feel, a visit to **Grime's Graves**, just over the Norfolk border, reveals an amazing site covering 35 acres and 300 pits (one of the shafts is open to visitors). With the close proximity of numerous warrens and their rabbit population, the fur trade also flourished here, and that, too, along with forestry, is brought to life in the Heritage Centre.

The whole of this northwestern corner of Suffolk, known as **Breckland**, offers almost unlimited opportunities for touring by car, cycling or walking. A mile south of town on the B1106 is **Brandon Country Park**, a 30-acre landscaped site with a tree trail, forest walks, a walled garden and a visitor centre. There's also an orienteering route leading on into Thetford Forest, Britain's largest lowland pine forest. The **High Lodge Forest Centre**, near Santon Downham (off the B1107), also attracts with walks, cycle trails and adventure facilities.

Suffolk

BURY ST EDMUNDS

A gem among Suffolk towns, rich in archaeological treasures and places of religious and historical interest, Bury St Edmunds takes its name from St Edmund, who was born in Nuremberg in AD841 and came here as a teenager to become the last King of East Anglia. A staunch Christian, he was tortured and killed by the Danes in 870. A shrine built in his honour was incorporated into the Norman Abbey Church, and town soon became a place of pilgrimage. For many years St Edmund was the patron saint of England, until replaced by St George. Growing rapidly around the great abbey, which became one of the largest and most influential in the land, Bury prospered as a centre of trade and commerce, thanks notably to the cloth industry.

Rebuilt in the 15th century, the Abbey was largely dismantled after its Dissolution by Henry VIII, but imposing ruins remain in the colourful Abbey Gardens beyond the splendid Abbey Gate and Norman Tower. **St Edmundsbury Cathedral** was originally the Church of St James, built in the 15th/16th century and accorded cathedral status (alone in Suffolk) in 1914. The original building has been much extended over the years (notably when being adapted for its role as a cathedral) and outstanding features include a magnificent hammerbeam roof, whose 38 beams are decorated with angels bearing the emblems of St James, St Edmund and St George.

St Mary's Church, in the same complex, is also well worth a visit: an equally impressive hammerbeam roof, the detached tower standing much as Abbot Anselm built it in the 12th century, and several interesting monuments, the most important commemorating Mary Tudor, sister of Henry VIII, Queen of France and Duchess of Suffolk. The **Abbey Gardens,** laid out in 1831, have as their central feature a great circle of flower beds following the pattern of the Royal Botanical Gardens in Brussels. Bury is also full of fine non-ecclesiastical buildings, many with Georgian frontages concealing medieval interiors. Among the most interesting are the handsome **Manor House Museum** with its collection of clocks, paintings, furniture, costumes and objets d'art; the **Victorian Corn Exchange** with its imposing colonnade;

House in Bury St Edmunds

Bury St Edmunds

storyboards, artefacts, illustrations and audio displays bring the history and art of brewing to life. Brewery tours include a look round the museum and beer-tasting. The shop sells a variety of memorabilia, souvenirs, gifts and clothing – as well, of course, as bottles and cans of the frothy stuff.

The **Bury St Edmunds Art Gallery** is housed in one of Bury's noblest buildings, built to a Robert Adam design in 1774.

Perhaps the most fascinating building of all is **Moyse's Hall Museum**, located at one end of the Buttermarket. Built of flint and limestone about 1180, it has claims to being the oldest stone domestic building in England. Originally a rich man's residence, it later saw service as a tavern, gaol, police station and railway parcels office, but since 1899 it has been a museum, and now houses some 10,000 items, including many important archaeological collections, from a Bronze Age hoard, Roman pottery and Anglo-Saxon jewellery to a 19th century doll's house and some grisly relics of the notorious Red Barn murder. A new wing contains the Suffolk Regiment collection and education room.

the Athenaeum, hub of social life since Regency times and scene of Charles Dickens's public readings; **Cupola House**, where Daniel Defoe once stayed; the **Angel Hotel**, where Dickens and his marvellous creation Mr Pickwick stayed; and the **Nutshell**, owned by Greene King Brewery and probably the smallest pub in the country. The **Theatre Royal**, now in the care of the National Trust, was built in 1819 by William Wilkins, who was also responsible for the National Gallery in London. It once staged the premiere of *Charley's Aunt*, and still operates as a working theatre.

One of Bury's oldest residents and newest attractions is the **Greene King Brewery Museum and Shop**. Greene King has been brewed here in Bury since 1799; the museum's informative

CARLTON COLVILLE

Many a transport enthusiast has enjoyed a grand day out at the **East Anglia Transport Museum**, where children young and old can climb aboard to enjoy rides on buses, trams and trolleybuses (one of the resident trolleybuses was built at the Garrett works in Leiston).

Suffolk

CAVENDISH

Cavendish is splendidly traditional, with its church, thatched cottages, almshouses, Nether Hall and the **Sue Ryder Foundation Museum** spread around the green. The last, in a 16th century rectory by the pond, illustrates the work of the Sue Ryder Foundation, and was formally opened by Queen Elizabeth II in 1979. Once a refuge for concentration camp victims, it houses abundant war photographs and memorabilia. Nether Hall is a well-restored 16th century building and the headquarters of **Cavendish Vineyards**.

Cottages at Cavendish

CLARE

A medieval wool town of great importance, Clare repays a visit today with its fine old buildings and some distinguished old ruins. Perhaps the most renowned tourist attraction is **Ancient House**, a timber-framed building dated 1473 and remarkable for its pargeting, the decorative treatment of external plasterwork, usually by dividing the surface into rectangles and decorating each panel. It was very much a Suffolk speciality, particularly in the 16th and 17th centuries, with some examples also being found in Cambridgeshire and Essex. The decoration could be simple brushes of a comb, scrolls or squiggles, or more elaborate, with religious motifs, guild signs or family crests. Some pargeting is incised, but the best is in relief – pressing moulds into wet plaster or shaping it by hand. Ancient House sports some splendid entwined flowers and branches, and a representation of two figures holding a shield. The best-known workers in this unique skill had their own distinctive styles, and the expert eye could spot the particular 'trademarks' of each man (the same is the case with the master thatchers). Ancient House is now a museum.

DUNWICH

Surely the hidden place of all hidden places, Dunwich was once the capital of East Anglia, but the sea took its toll down the centuries and all that now remains of ancient Dunwich are the ruins of a Norman leper hospital, the archways of a medieval friary and a buttress of one of the nine churches that once served the community.

Today's village comprises a 19th century church and a row of Victorian cottages, one of which houses the

Dunwich Museum.

Dunwich Forest, immediately inland from the village, is one of three – the others are further south at Tunstall and Rendlesham – named by the Forestry Commission as Aldewood Forest. Work started on these in 1920 with the planting of Scots pine, Corsican pine and some Douglas fir; oak and poplar were tried but did not thrive in the sandy soil. The three forests, which between them cover nearly 9,000 acres, were almost completely devastated in the hurricane of October 1987, Rendlesham alone losing more than a million trees; the replanting will take many years to be fully established.

South of the village lies **Dunwich Heath**, one of Suffolk's most important conservation areas. The nearby village of **Westleton** is the main route of access to the RSPB-managed **Minsmere Bird Sanctuary**, the most important sanctuary for wading birds in eastern England.

Dunwich Heath (National Trust)

walks by the lakes and river.

EAST BERGHOLT

Narrow lanes lead to this picturesque and much-visited little village, birthplace of the painter John Constable. The **Constable Country Trail** starts here and passes through Flatford Mill and on to Dedham in Essex. **St Mary's**, one of the many grand churches built with the wealth brought by the wool trade, is naturally something of a shrine to Constable, his family and his friends, including Willy Lott, whose cottage is featured in *The Hay Wain*.

EARSHAM

All Saints Church and Earsham Hall are well worth a visit, but what brings most people here is the **Otter Trust**, on the banks of the Waveney, where the largest collection of otters in natural enclosures are bred for re-introduction into the wild. Waterfowl, herons and deer are also kept here, and there are some lovely

FELIXSTOWE

Popular with holidaymakers, Felixstowe is also one of Europe's busiest container ports. The resort is strung out round a wide, gently curving bay, where the long seafront road is made even prettier with trim lawns and gardens.

The Martello tower is a noted landmark, as is the **Pier**, which was once long enough to merit an electric tramway. It was shortened as a security measure during the Second World War. All kinds of attractions are provided for holidaymakers, including one very unusual one. This is the **Felixstowe Water Clock**, a curious piece assembled from dozens of industrial bits and pieces.

Church at Framlingham

The original fishing hamlet from which the Victorian resort was developed lies beyond a golf course north of the town. This is **Felixstowe Ferry**, a cluster of holiday homes, an inn, a boatyard, a sailing club, fishing sheds and a Martello tower. A ferry takes foot passengers (plus bicycles) across to Bawdsey.

At the southernmost tip of the peninsula is **Landguard Point**, where a nature reserve supports rare plants and migrating birds.

Just north on this shingle bank is **Landguard Fort**, built in 1718 (replacing an earlier construction) to protect Harwich harbour and now home to **Felixstowe Museum**.

FLIXTON

Javelin, Meteor, Sea Vixen, Westland Whirlwind: names that evoke earlier days of flying, and just four of the 20 aircraft on show at The **Norfolk and Suffolk Aviation Museum**, on the site of a WW2 USAAF Liberator base.

FRAMLINGHAM

The marvellous **Castle**, brooding on a hilltop, dominates this agreeable market town, as it has since Roger Bigod, 2nd Earl of Norfolk, built it in the 12th century. The castle is in remarkably good condition, partly because it was rarely attacked – though King John put it under siege in 1215. Its most famous occupant was Mary Tudor, who was in residence when proclaimed Queen in 1553. Nine of the castle's 13 towers are accessible - the climb up the spiral staircase and the walk round the battlements are well worth the effort. In the north wing is the **Lanman Museum**, devoted to agricultural, craftsman's tools and domestic memorabilia.

HADLEIGH

The old and not-so-old blend harmoniously in a variety of architectural styles in Hadleigh. Timber-framed buildings, often with elaborate plasterwork, stand in the long main street as a reminder of the prosperity generated by the wool trade in the 14th to 16th centuries, and there are also some fine houses from the Regency and Victorian periods. The 15th century **Guildhall** has two overhanging storeys, and together with the Deanery Tower and the church makes for a magnificent trio of huge appeal and contrasting construction – timber for the Guildhall, brick for the tower and flint for the church.

HAVERHILL

Notable for its fine Victorian architecture, Haverhill also boasts one fine Tudor gem. Although many of Haverhill's buildings were destroyed by fire in 1665, the **Anne of Cleves House** was restored and is well worth a visit. Anne was the fourth wife of Henry VIII and, after a brief political marriage, she was given an allowance and spent the remainder of her days at Haverhill and Richmond. **Haverhill Local History Centre**, in the Town Hall, has an interesting collection of memorabilia, photographs and archive material.

HORRINGER

Horringer's village green is dominated by the flintstone Church of St Leonard, and beside the church are the gates of one of the country's most extraordinary and fascinating houses. **Ickworth House** was the brainchild of the eccentric 4th Earl of Bristol and Bishop of Derry, a collector of art treasures and an inveterate traveller (witness the many

Bristol Hotels scattered around Europe). His inspiration was Belle Isle, a house built on an island in Lake Windermere, and the massive structure is a central rotunda linking two semi-circular wings. Its chief glories are some marvellous paintings by Titian, Gainsborough, Hogarth, Velasquez, Reynolds and Kauffman, but there's a great deal more to enthral the visitor: late Regency and 18th century French furniture, a notable collection of Georgian silver, friezes and sculptures by John Flaxman, frescoes copied from wall paintings discovered at the Villa Negroni in Rome in 1777. The Italian garden, where Mediterranean species have been bred to withstand a distinctly non-Mediterranean climate, should not be missed, with its hidden glades, orangery and temple rose garden, and in the park landscaped by Capability Brown there are designated walks and cycle routes, bird hides, a deer enclosure and play areas. More recent attractions include the vineyard and plant centre.

IPSWICH

History highlights Ipswich as the birthplace of Cardinal Wolsey, but the story of Suffolk's county town starts very much earlier than that. It has been a port since the time of the Roman occupation, and by the 7th century the Anglo-Saxons had expanded it into the largest port in the country. At the beginning of the 19th century the risk from silting was becoming acute at a time when trade was improving and industries were springing up. The Wet

Christchurch Mansion and Museum, Ipswich

Dock, constructed in 1842, solved the silting problem and, with the railway arriving shortly after, Ipswich could once more look forward to a safe future. The Victorians were responsible for considerable development: symbols of their civic pride include the handsome **Old Custom House** by the Wet Dock, the Town Hall, and the splendid **Tolly Cobbold** brewery, rebuilt at the end of the 19th century, 150 years after brewing started on the site. Victorian enterprise depleted some of the older buildings, but a number survive, notably the house where Wolsey was born, the Ancient House with its wonderful pargeting, and the fine former Tudor merchants' houses which grace the town's historic waterfront. A dozen medieval churches remain, of which St Margaret's is the finest, boasting some very splendid flintwork and a double hammerbeam roof. Another, St Stephen's, today houses the town's Tourist Information Centre.

Christchurch Mansion is a beautiful Tudor home standing in 65 acres of attractive parkland, a short walk from the town centre. Furnished as an English country house, it contains a major collection of works by Constable and Gainsborough, as well as many other paintings, prints and sculptures by Suffolk artists from the 17th century onwards. **Ipswich Museum** is in a Victorian building in the High Street, while in a former trolleybus depot on Cobham Road is the **Ipswich Transport Museum**, a fascinating collection of vehicles, from prams to fire engines, all made or used around Ipswich.

On the outskirts of town, signposted from Nacton Road, is **Orwell Country Park**, a 150-acre site of wood, heath and reedbeds by the Orwell estuary.

KERSEY

The ultimate Suffolk picture-postcard village, Kersey boasts a wonderful collection of timbered merchants' houses and weavers' cottages with paint and thatch. The main street has a **Water Splash**, which, along with the 700-year-old Bell Inn, has featured in many films and travelogues. The Church of St Mary, which overlooks the village from its hilltop position, is of massive proportions, testimony to the wealth that came with the wool and cloth industry.

KESSINGLAND

The village's major tourist attraction is the **Suffolk Wildlife Park**, 100 acres of

Kersey

hall house with a superb crown post roof. It was restored by the Gayer Anderson brothers, and has a fine collection of their furniture. The **Church of St Peter and St Paul** dominates the town from its elevated position. It's a building of great distinction, perhaps the greatest of all the 'wool churches' and declared by the 19th century architect August Pugin to be the finest example of Late Perpendicular style in the world.

The Priory originated in the 13th century as a home for Benedictine monks, and the present timber-framed house on the site dates from about 1600. In the original hall, at the centre of the building, is an important collection of paintings and stained glass.

coastal parkland that are home to a wide range of wild animals, from aardvarks to zebras by way of bats, flamingos, giraffes, meerkats and sitatunga. The flamingos have their own enclosure. Burmese pythons are used for snake-handling sessions – an experience that's definitely not for everyone!

LAVENHAM

An absolute gem of a town, the most complete and original of the medieval 'wool towns', with crooked timbered and whitewashed buildings lining the narrow streets.

More than 300 of Lavenham's buildings are officially listed as being of architectural and historical interest, and none of them is finer than the superb 16th century **Guildhall**. **Little Hall** is hardly less remarkable, a 15th century

Lavenham

LEISTON

For 200 years the biggest name in Leiston was that of Richard Garrett, who founded an engineering works here in 1778 after starting a business in Woodbridge. The Garrett works are now the **Long Shop Museum**, the factory buildings having been lovingly restored, and many of the Garrett machines are now on display, including traction engines, a steam-driven tractor and a road roller. The Garrett works closed in 1980, but what could have been a disastrous unemployment situation was alleviated to some extent by the nuclear power station at **Sizewell**, on the coast near Leiston.

LONG MELFORD

Long Melford's long main street is filled with antiques shops, book shops and art galleries, and is a favourite place for collectors and browsers. Some of the houses are washed in the characteristic Suffolk pink, which might originally have been achieved by mixing ox blood or sloe juice into the plaster.

Holy Trinity Church is big enough to be a cathedral, but served (and still serves) comparatively few parishioners. This magnificent Perpendicular-style edifice has a 180-foot nave and chancel and half timbers, flint 'flushwork' (stonework) of the highest quality, and 100 large windows to give a marvellous sense of light and space.

Melford Hall, east of town beyond an imposing 16th century gateway, has

Long Melford

rooms in various styles, some with ornate walnut furniture, and there's a notable collection of Chinese porcelain on show. Most delightful of all is the Beatrix Potter room, with some of her watercolours, first editions of her books and, among the toys, the original of Jemima Puddleduck.

Kentwell Hall is a red-brick Tudor moated mansion approached by a long avenue of limes. Its grounds include a unique Tudor rose maze, and are set out to illustrate and re-create Tudor times, with a walled garden, a bakery, a dairy and several varieties of rare-breed farm animals. The Hall was the setting for a film version of *Toad of Toad Hall*.

The most easterly town in Britain is a fishing port and also a popular holiday resort, the star attraction being the lovely South Beach with its golden sands, safe swimming, two piers and all the expected seaside amusements and entertainment. **Claremont Pier**, over 600 feet in length, was built in 1902, ready to receive day-trippers on the famous Belle steamers. The buildings in this part of town were developed in mid-Victorian times by the company of Sir Samuel Morton Peto, also responsible for Nelson's Column, the statues in the Houses of Parliament, the Reform Club and Somerleyton Hall.

At the heart of the town is the old harbour, home to the **Royal Norfolk & Suffolk Yacht Club** and the **Lifeboat Station**. Further upriver is the commercial part of the port, used chiefly by ships carrying grain and timber. The history of Lowestoft is naturally tied up with the sea, and much of that history is recorded in fascinating detail in the **Lowestoft & East Suffolk Maritime Museum** with model boats, fishing gear, a lifeboat cockpit, paintings and shipwrights' tools. The setting is a flint-built fisherman's cottage in Sparrow's Nest Gardens. The **Royal Naval Patrol Museum** nearby remembers the minesweeping service in models, photographs, documents and uniforms.

Oulton Broad, on the western edge of Lowestoft, is a major centre of amusements afloat, with boats for hire and cruises on the Waveney. It also attracts visitors to Nicholas Everitt Park to look around **Lowestoft Museum**, housed in historic Broad House.

Lowestoft's **ISCA Maritime Museum** has a unique collection of ethnic working boats, including coracles, gondolas, junks, dhows, sampans and proas.

MILDENHALL

Mildenhall was once a port for the hinterlands of West Suffolk, and most of its heritage is recorded in the excellent **Mildenhall & District Museum** in King Street. Here will be found exhibits of local history (including the distinguished RAF and USAAF base), crafts and domestic skills, the natural history of the Fens and Breckland and, perhaps most famously, the chronicle of the 'Mildenhall Treasure'. This was a cache of 34 pieces of 4th century Roman silverware - dishes, goblets and spoons - found by a ploughman in 1946 at Thistley Green and now on display in the British Museum in London, while a replica makes its home here where it was found. The parish of Mildenhall is the largest in Suffolk, so it is perhaps fitting that it should boast so magnificent a parish church as **St Mary's**, built of Barnack stone; it dominates the heart of the town and indeed its west tower commands the flat surrounding countryside.

NEWMARKET

On the western edge of Suffolk, the historic centre of British racing lives and breathes horses, with 60 training establishments, 50 stud farms, the top annual thoroughbred sales and two racecourses (the only two in Suffolk). Thousands of the population are involved in the trade, and racing art and artefacts fill the shops, galleries and museums. In 1605, James I paused on a journey northwards to enjoy a spot of hare coursing. He enjoyed the place and said he would be back. By moving the royal court to his Newmarket headquarters, he began the royal patronage which has remained strong throughout the years.

The visitor to Newmarket can learn almost all there is to know about flat racing and the royal connection: **The Jockey Club**; the **National Horseracing Museum**; **Palace House**, which contains the remains of Charles II's palace; **Nell Gwynn's House**, which some say was connected by an underground passage beneath the street to the palace; **Tattersalls**, where leading thoroughbred sales take place from April to December; the **British Racing School**, where top jockeys are taught the ropes; the **National Stud**; and the **Animal Health Trust**.

ORFORD

The ruins of one of the most important castles in medieval England are a most impressive sight, even though the keep is all that remains of the original building commissioned by Henry II in 1165.

St Bartholomew's Church was built at the same time, though the present church dates from the 14th century. A wonderful sight at night when floodlit, the church is regularly used for the performance of concerts and recitals, and many of Benjamin Britten's works were first heard here. Orford was once a thriving port, but the steadily growing shingle bank of Orford Ness gradually cut it off from the sea, and down the years its appeal has changed. The sea may have gone but the river is still there, and in summer the quayside is alive with yachts and pleasure craft. On the other side of the river is **Orford Ness**, the largest vegetated shingle spit in England which is home to a variety of rare flora and fauna. Access to the spit is in the hands of the National Trust, is by

Horse Racing at Newmarket

ferry from Orford quay; boats also leave the quay for the RSPB reserve at **Havergate Island**.

PAKENHAM

Pakenham is home to the 17th century **Nether Hall** and **Newe House**, a handsome Jacobean building with Dutch gables and a two-storey porch. The Church of St Mary has an impressive carved Perpendicular font, and in its adjacent vicarage is the famous Whistler Window - a painting by Rex Whistler of an 18th century parish priest. The fens were an important source of reeds, and many of Pakenham's buildings show off the thatcher's art.

Pakenham's current unique claim to fame is in being the last parish in England to have a working watermill *and* windmill, a fact proclaimed on the village sign.

SHOTLEY

Right at the end of a peninsula, with the Orwell on one side and the Stour on the other, Shotley is best known as the home of *HMS Ganges*, where generations of sailors received their training. The main feature is the 142-foot mast, up which trainees would shin at the passing-out ceremony. A small museum records the history of the establishment from 1905 to 1976, when it became a police academy. At the very tip of the peninsula is a large marina where a classic boat festival is an annual occasion.

SOMERLEYTON

Somerleyton Hall, one of the grandest and most distinctive of stately homes, is a splendid Victorian mansion built in Anglo-Italian style by Samuel Morton Peto. Its lavish architectural features are complemented by fine state rooms, magnificent wood carvings (some by Grinling Gibbons) and notable paintings. The grounds include a renowned yew-hedge maze, where people have been going round in circles since 1846, walled and sunken gardens, and a 300-foot pergola. There's also a sweet little miniature railway, and **Fritton Lake Countryworld**, part of the Somerleyton Estate, is a 10-minute drive away.

Somerleyton Hall

SOUTHWOLD

A town full of character
and interest for the
holidaymaker and for the
historian. Though one of
the most popular resorts on
the east coast, Southwold
has very little of the kiss-
me-quick commercialism
that spoils so many seaside
towns. Among buildings
that represent many styles,
shapes and sizes, William

Southwold Beach

Denny's **Buckenham House** is among
the most elegant and interesting. On the
face of it a classic Georgian town house,
it's actually much older, dating probably
from the middle of the 16th century.

Southwold's maritime past is recorded
in the **Museum** set in a Dutch-style
cottage in Victoria Street. The
Southwold Sailors' Reading Room
contains pictures, ship models and other
items, and at Gun Hill the **Southwold
Lifeboat Museum** has a small collection
of RNLI-related material with particular
reference to Southwold.

No visitor to Southwold should leave
without spending some time in the
splendid church of **St Edmund King and
Martyr**, which emerged relatively
unscathed from the ravages of the
Commonwealth.

STONHAM ASPAL

At Stonham Barns, the **British Birds of
Prey and Nature Centre** is home to
every species of British owl, together

with raptors from Britain and around the
world. These wonderful birds flap their
wings in regular flying displays, and in
the Pets Paradise area children can meet
and greet hamsters and horses, mice and
meerkats, parrots and piglets.

STOWMARKET

Much of Stowmarket's history and legacy
are brought vividly to life in the splendid
Museum of East Anglian Life, situated
in the centre of town to the west of the
marketplace (where markets are held
twice a week), in a 70-acre meadowland
site on the old Abbot's Hall Estate. Part
of the open-air section features several
historic buildings that have been moved
from elsewhere in the region and
carefully re-erected on site, and there's
also a collection of working steam
engines, farm animals and year-round
demonstrations of all manner of local
arts and crafts, from coopering to
chandlery, from sheep shearing to
saddlery. Serious scenic walkers should

make for the **Gipping Valley River Park** walk, which follows the former towpath all the way to Ipswich.

STRATFORD ST MARY

One of John Constable's favourite locations, Stratford St Mary is the most southerly village in Suffolk. *The Young Waltonians* and *A House in Water Lane* (the house still stands today) are the best known of his works set in this picturesque spot. The village church is typically large and imposing, with parts dating back to 1200. At the top of the village are two splendid half-timbered cottages called the **Ancient House** and the **Priest's House**.

SUDBURY

Sudbury is the largest of the 'wool towns' and still home to a number of weaving

Gainsborough Statue, Sudbury

concerns. The town Sudbury boasts three medieval churches, but what most visitors make a beeline for is **Gainsborough's House** on Gainsborough Street. The painter Thomas Gainsborough was born here in 1727 in the house built by his father John. More of the artist's work is displayed in this Georgian-fronted house than in any other gallery, and there is also assorted 18th century memorabilia and furnishings.

THORPENESS

Thorpeness is a unique seaside village with a charm all of its own. Buying up a considerable packet of land called the Sizewell estate in 1910, the architect, barrister and playwright Glencairn Stuart Ogilvie created what he hoped would be a fashionable resort with cottages, some larger houses and an atmospheric and lovely 65-acre boating and pleasure lake.

The 85-foot water tower, built to aid in the lake's construction, looked out of place, so Ogilvie disguised it as a house. Known ever since as the **House in the Clouds**, it is now available to rent as a holiday home. The neighbouring mill, moved lock, stock and millstones from Aldringham, stopped pumping in 1940 but has been restored and now houses a visitor centre.

WOODBRIDGE

Standing at the head of the Deben estuary, Woodbridge is a place of

House in the Clouds, Thorpeness

considerable charm with a wealth of handsome buildings and a considerable sense of history, as both a market town and a port. The shipbuilding and allied industries flourished here, as at most towns on the Suffolk coast, and there's still plenty of activity on and by the river, though nowadays it is all leisure-orientated. The town's greatest benefactor was Thomas Seckford, who rebuilt the abbey, paid for the chapel in the north aisle of St Mary's Church and founded the original almshouses in Seckford Street. In 1575 he gave the town the splendid Shire Hall on Market Hill. Originally used as a corn exchange, it now houses the **Suffolk Punch Heavy Horse Museum**, with an exhibition devoted to the Suffolk Punch breed of heavy working horse, the oldest such breed in the world. Opposite the Shire

Hall is **Woodbridge Museum**, a treasure trove of information on the history of the town and its more notable residents. Woodbridge has two marvellous mills, both in working order, and both great attractions for the visitor. The **Tide Mill** has been meticulously restored and the waterwheel still turns, fed by a pond which replaced the original huge mill pond when it was turned into a marina. **Buttrum's Mill**, named after the last miller, is a tower mill standing six storeys high a mile west of the town centre. A marvellous sight, its six storeys make it the tallest surviving tower mill in Suffolk.

A mile or so east of Woodbridge on the opposite bank of the Deben is **Sutton Hoo**, a group of a dozen grassy barrows containing an Anglo-Saxon ship and one of the greatest hoards of treasure ever unearthed in Britain. The permanent display in the special exhibition hall reveals how Anglo-Saxon nobles lived, went to war and founded a kingdom in East Anglia.

Woodbridge Harbour and Tide Mill

THE ADMIRAL'S HEAD

SANDY LANE, LITTLE BEALINGS, NR WOODBRIDGE,
SUFFOLK IP13 6LW
TEL: 01473 625912   FAX: 01473 611275

> **Directions:** Little Bealings is located on a minor road west of the A12 about 3 miles southwest of Woodbridge.

The Admiral's Head has been a pub for more than 200 years, and when it was rebuilt virtually from scratch in 1980 it retained a Georgian look and some of the original features, including beams in the bar that came from a 17th century barn in Newmarket.

Other eyecatching features include a variety of sturdy wooden furniture, a slate floor and an ornate brick front to the serving area. Since the spring of 2004 the Admiral's Head has been in the capable hands of Jazmine and Rosario, who have given the pub a big boost by introducing traditional Italian specialities on to the menu. Lasagne, penne pasta with sausages and salami, mushroom risotto and ravioli with spinach and ricotta are the specialities of the house, while other favourites include sizzling prawns, chargrilled tuna steak and the international Suffolk chicken breast stuffed with creamy Italian taleggio cheese and wrapped in pancetta. Three cask ales are always on tap, and there's a good list of Old and New World wines to accompany the fine food. Two rooms are available for private dinners, one with seats for up to 12, the other catering for up to 40. The Admiral's Head, which is closed on Sunday evening and all day Monday, is an easy drive from the charming town of Woodbridge and the Sutton Hoo Anglo-Saxon burial site, one of the most important archaeological sites ever unearthed in Britain.

- 🕐 11.30-2.30 & 6-11, Sun 11.30-4; closed Sunday evening and all Monday
- 🍴 A la carte menus L & D
- £ Major cards accepted
- Ⓟ Car park, patio garden
- @ e-mail: theadmiralshead@btinternet.com website: www.theadmiralshead.co.uk
- ❓ Martlesham 2 miles, Woodbridge 3 miles, Sutton Hoo 4 miles, Ipswich 4 miles

THE ANGEL HOTEL

THE THOROUGHFARE, HALESWORTH, SUFFOLK IP19 8AH
TEL: 01986 873365 FAX: 01986 874891

Directions: The Angel Hotel is located centrally in Halesworth. From the A12 between Yoxford and Blythburgh, take the A144 into Halesworth. From the A143 Diss-Bungay road take the B1123 just north of Needham.

With two bars, a delightful central courtyard, a 55-seater restaurant and seven comfortable bedrooms, **The Angel Hotel** is an excellent choice for a drink, a snack, a meal or an overnight or extended stay. This characterful old inn dating back to the 16th century stands at the top of the town's pedestrianised thoroughfare and has long been a popular meeting place for the residents of Halesworth. Richard Rhodes and his staff are carrying on the tradition of hospitality in fine style, and the welcome they offer is equally warm for their many regular patrons and for new faces.

The bars and the glass-roofed courtyard are open all day for Adnams and guest cask ales, other drinks and home-cooked snacks

and meals, whilst Cleone's Italian restaurant serves classic and contemporary dishes every lunchtime and evening. The printed menu is supplemented by daily specials such as grilled red snapper marinated in marjoram, basil, parsley and garlic or pan-fried sirloin steak with a gorgonzola butter.

An eye-catching feature in the courtyard is a tavern clock made in 1780 by George Suggate, a renowned clockmaker who was a native of Halesworth. The first-floor bedrooms (four doubles, three twins) are individual in style but all have bath and shower en suite, television, radio-alarm, hairdryer and tea/coffee facilities. Breakfast is served in the restaurant at a time to suit guests. Smoking is permitted in one of the two bars but not in the restaurant or the bedrooms. Halesworth has much to interest the visitor, including many fine old buildings and the Halesworth & District Museum.

- 🕐 11-11
- 🍴 Bar and Restaurant menus
- 💷 All the major cards
- 🛏 7 en suite rooms
- 🅿 Car park, courtyard
- @ e-mail: hotel@angel-halesworth.co.uk
  web: www.angel-halesworth.co.uk
- ❓ Cycle and walking paths nearby; golf courses; Halesworth & District Museum; Blythburgh 6 miles, Southwold 8 miles, Dunwich 10 miles

THE BLACK HORSE

LOWER STREET, STRATFORD ST MARY, SUFFOLK CO7 6JS
TEL: 01206 323112

Suffolk

> **Directions:** Stratford St Mary lies just off the A12 4 miles north of Colchester.

Visitors to this fine old inn on the edge of the village are greeted by a smart newly painted pink frontage, just one of many enhancements recently made by the owning brewery and tenants Pat and James Sandle. Inside, **The Black Horse** sports splendid old beams and pillars and gleaming horse brasses, setting a traditional tone in the bar and creating a friendly, relaxing ambience in which to enjoy a glass of one of the several cask ales that are always available. Pat's cooking is a major attraction, served all day and offering something for everyone. The choice in the non-smoking restaurant includes classics such as ham, eggs and chips, lasagne, steak & kidney pie and the Sunday roasts to scrumptious desserts such as apple crumble or spotted dick. Bar snacks – baguettes and jacket potatoes – make satisfying lunchtime meals for those with less time to spare.

The Black Horse has a large garden with a children's play area, and next to the inn is a useful camping and caravanning facilities.

This is very much a pub for all the family (including the dog), and on the social side there are regular live music and karaoke evenings and annual rock and blues festivals. The village of Stratford St Mary, the most southerly in Suffolk, was a great favourite with the painter John Constable, and two well-known paintings, *The Young Waltonians* and *A House in Water Lane*, are set here. That house still stands, and there are several other places to interest the visitor, including an imposing 12th century church and two fine old half-timbered buildings, the Ancient House and Priest's House. All the famous landmarks of Constable Country are within very easy reach, and with the A12 close by it's an easy drive to Colchester.

- ◷ 12-11 (Sun to 10.30)
- ▯ Home cooking
- £ All the major cards
- Ⓟ Car park
- ♫ Regular live bands, rock & blues festivals, karaoke
- ? Dedham 2 miles, East Bergholt 3 miles, Colchester 4 miles, Ipswich 10 miles

THE BRISTOL ARMS

BRISTOL HILL, SHOTLEY GATE, IPSWICH, SUFFOLK IP9 1PU
TEL: 01473 787200 FAX: 01473 788686

Directions: Eight miles southeast of Ipswich. Take the A137 to the southern edge of Ipswich, then turn left on to the B1456 through Woolverstone, Chelmondiston and Shotley Street to Shotley Gate.

San Remo-born Nando Sappia, his wife Pauline and their sons Scott and Barry are the welcoming hosts at the **Bristol Arms**, which enjoys a superb setting by the River Stour, with splendid views of the river and over to the port of Harwich. Dating back in part to the 12th century and once the haunt of smugglers, the inn has a particularly warm and friendly atmosphere. Behind the smart bay-windowed frontage is a perfect spot to relax over a pint of Adnams Bitter or Broadside, a glass of wine or a glass of freshly squeezed orange juice. The decor has an appropriately nautical theme, with effective use of wood, and the theme continues through to the menu, which offers a regularly changing selection of seafood dishes, including Cromer crab, fish pie and traditional fish & chips. The

fish is always top quality, much of it coming fresh from the trawlers at Lowestoft. Meat lovers are equally well catered for with classics such as lasagne (cooked to Nando's secret recipe!), toad in the hole and excellent pies topped with puff pastry, suet pastry or mashed potato. Both Scott and Barry are accomplished chefs, and Scott worked for a time with Delia Smith at Norwich football club. The non-smoking restaurant can seat 80 in comfort, and when the sun shines the patio garden, with seats for 60, is in great demand. Food is served every lunchtime and evening. Children are welcome, and the inn is a popular venue for parties and special celebrations.

Close to the inn is a marina where an annual classic boat festival brings in the crowds. Shotley village, a short walk up the road, is the home of *HMS Ganges*, where generations of sailors received their training.

- 🕐 11-2.30 & 5.30 –11, Saturday 11-11, Sun 12-10.30
- 🍴 A la carte menu
- 💷 All the major cards
- 🅿 Car park, wheelchair access to public areas and toilets
- 🎵 Occasional live music and karaoke
- @ e-mail: bristolarms@aol.com
- ❓ Shotley village (*HMS Ganges*), Ipswich 8 miles

THE BULL INN

HIGH STREET, CAVENDISH, SUFFOLK CO10 8AX

TEL/FAX: 01787 280245

Directions: The inn is situated in the centre of Cavendish, 3 miles west of Long Melford on the A1092.

On the main street of Cavendish, **The Bull Inn** is a very handsome redbrick building adorned by hanging baskets, flower tubs and a fine covering of creeper. Inside, the look is delightfully traditional, with gnarled uprights and ceiling beams, open fireplaces and rustic furniture including some splendid pew-style benches. At the back is a spacious patio area that adjoins the greens of Cavendish Bowls Club. The hosts at this outstanding 16th century inn are Paul and Julie Drawwater, who have three grown-up children and a gorgeous lapsu called Tia. Paul and Julie are both talented trained chefs, and their menus of traditional dishes feature many seafood specialities, from Cromer crabs to salmon, sea bass, cod, plaice and skate. A separate blackboard announces Julie's delectable desserts, which might include raspberry meringue, bread and butter pudding with apricot sauce or crème brûlée – a super way to end a meal, and very hard to resist! Fans of cask ales also have an excellent choice featuring several permanent and seasonal brews from Adnams (Broadside, Best Bitter, Jubilee, Explorer, Regatta etc).

Cavendish and the surrounding villages, towns and countryside are full of interest for the tourist, and The Bull is an ideal base from which to plan excursions and explorations. The two recently refurbished guest bedrooms are both en suite, with all the expected facilities, and the day gets off to a fine start with a full English breakfast served in the dining room. The main attractions in Cavendish itself are the Sue Ryder Museum and the Parish Church of St Mary, whose treasures include two handsome lecterns and some fine Flemish and Italian statues.

- 🕐 11-3 & 6-11 (Sat:11-3 & 6-11, Sun 12-4 & 7-10.30)
- 🍴 Traditional home cooking with seafood specialities
- 💷 Not Amex
- 🛏 2 en suite rooms
- 🅿 Car park, patio garden
- ❓ Sue Ryder Museum, Nether Hall (Cavendish Vineyards), Clare 3 miles, Long Melford 3 miles

THE CHERRY TREE INN

CUMBERLAND STREET, WOODBRIDGE, SUFFOLK IP12 4AG
TEL: 01394 384627

Suffolk

Directions: The inn lies 1½ miles off the A12 at the southern Woodbridge roundabout, opposite Notcutts Garden centre.

Since taking over as tenants of the **Cherry Tree Inn** in January 2001, Geoff and Sheila Ford have established themselves as very popular and successful hosts. Their efforts have been rewarded with a number of accolades, including nomination for Community Pub of the Year and a winner in the Woodbridge in Bloom competition. The 17th century building has a charming old-world interior with wood panelling, twisting oak beams, low ceilings and real coal fires, creating an inviting ambience in which to enjoy a glass or two of Adnams or a guest cask ale – all kept in tip-top condition and earning a Cask Marque Award and an entry in the Good Beer Guide. This is also an excellent place for food, and the chefs set great store by local produce on menus that range from light snacks to a full menu supplemented by daily specials such as filo prawns, chicken & vegetable pie and pork schnitzel; there's a choice of traditional roasts for Sunday lunch, and home-made puddings make a delicious end to a meal.

As well as being well known for good food, the Cherry Tree is also a popular 'local' with a thriving social side that offers something for all the family. There are swings and other amusements for children and picnic tables for everyone in the garden, while in the bars most of the classic pub games are played; Thursday is quiz night, with free chips to assist the thought processes, and Friday evenings swing to live music and dancing. The garden is partly shaded by a Grade II listed barn, where the go-ahead tenants have just created three letting rooms for Bed & Breakfast. All three have en suite facilities, one has wheelchair access and all share a decked patio area.

- ○ 11-3 & 5-11 (Sat & Sun all day)
- ❚ A la carte
- £ Major cards accepted
- ⊟ 3 rooms in a converted barn
- Ⓟ Car park, patio garden, children's play area, boules
- ♫ Quiz Thursday, live music and dancing Friday
- @ e-mail: info@thecherrytreepub.co.uk web: www.thecherrytreepub.co.uk
- ❓ Woodbridge town centre ¼ mile, River Deben ¼ mile, Sutton Hoo 3 miles, Rendlesham Forest 5 miles, Butley Priory 5 miles, Ipswich 6 miles

THE COCK INN

BURY ROAD, KENTFORD. NR NEWMARKET, SUFFOLK CB8 7PR
TEL/FAX: 01638 750360

Directions: Kentford lies about 4 miles east of Newmarket on the B1506, very close to junction 39 of the A14.

Dubliner Francis O'Brien brought many years experience in the licensed trade when he took over the reins of **The Cock Inn** in the summer of 2004. The two adjoining properties in the heart of the village of Kentford date back many centuries, and careful refurbishment has updated the comfort and amenities while retraining the delightful old-world atmosphere. The small, traditional public bar is a favourite spot for the local residents to meet for a chat over a glass of excellent ale, and both the locals and visitors from further afield sing the praises of the Cock Inn's cooking. The 40-cover restaurant, resplendent with dark oak, specialises in home-cooked dishes, all freshly prepared using the best seasonal produce, and the printed menu is supplemented by daily specials. Food is served every lunchtime and evening.

This fine country pub has a long and interesting history, the oldest parts dating from the 13th century. Ancient beams are still very much in evidence, some with intricate carvings, and in the 1960s a priest hole was discovered behind a fireplace. The restaurant was originally the stable block and coach house. This is racing country, and many of the regulars are avid followers of the turf. Francis plans to bring some letting bedrooms on stream for 2005, which will make the inn an ideal base of operations for racegoers. A much visited curiosity at a crossroad close to the inn is the Gypsy Boy's Grave, the grave of a young lad who hanged himself after being accused of sheep-stealing. Flowers are still sometimes laid at the site, occasionally by punters hoping for good luck at the races.

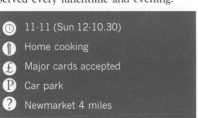

- 🕐 11-11 (Sun 12-10.30)
- 🍴 Home cooking
- 💷 Major cards accepted
- 🅿 Car park
- ❓ Newmarket 4 miles

Suffolk

THE COCK INN

THE GREEN, POLSTEAD, SUFFOLK CO6 5AL
TEL/FAX: 01206 263150

Directions: Polstead is 11 miles southwest of Ipswich (A12 then B1068); or the A1071 beyond Hadleigh on to minor road marked Polstead. From Colchester take the A134 to Nayland, then B1087 to Stoke-by-Nayland and minor road to Polstead.

The Cock Inn is a pretty pink-washed public house on the equally pretty green in the village of Polstead. The main part of the building dates from the 17th century, while the restaurant is housed in the Victorian extension. The inn is run by sisters Jo and Karen Leafe, who came here in 1999 and continue to gain new friends. Both are excellent chefs, and their prowess has earned wide recognition, including AA rosettes for their culinary skills. Visitors come from near and far to enjoy the super food on offer, which includes all-time favourites salmon fishcakes and a great steak & kidney suet pudding. Other typical choices run from lemon sole, cod and bream to chilli con carne, liver & bacon and succulent steaks. Thursday is curry night and Friday is steak night, and there

are always plenty of options for vegetarians. Seniors' lunches at bargain prices are a weekday feature and for a tasty, satisfying lunchtime snack there is the Suffolk huffer, a large white bap with a wide selection of fillings, from simple cheese or ham to chargrilled sausage, goat's cheese & honey and lamb with a mint dressing.

The choice of drinks is equally diverse, from Greene King IPA, Adnams Bitter and guest cask ales to good house wines and an impressive list of over 30 malt whiskies. The pleasure of a meal at this delightful inn is enhanced by the decor and furnishings in the restaurant, including exposed brickwork, beams and an open fire. There are plenty more seats in the bar, and on fine days the picnic benches on the front lawn soon fill up. Families are very welcome, and children have a play area where they can romp in safety.

🕐 11-3 & 6-11 (open all day at weekends in summer; closed Monday all year except Bank Holidays)

🍽 A la carte and bar menus

£ Major cards accepted

Ⓟ Car park, children's play area

@ website: www.geocities.com/cockatpolstead

❓ Stoke-by-Nayland 2 miles, Hadleigh 5 miles, Ipswich 11 miles

THE COCK INN

THE STREET, STANTON, NR BURY ST EDMUNDS, SUFFOLK IP31 2BP
TEL: 01359 250230

Suffolk

> **Directions:** From Bury St Edmunds take the A143 towards Diss. Turn right at the sign to Stanton, and right at the war memorial. The inn is 200 yards on.

The Cock Inn is a handsome cream-painted building with a long history of hospitality. Now Grade II listed, it was built in 1564 and became an important stop on the Bury-Norwich coaching run. Today, it attracts customers from the surrounding area and is also a favourite stopping place for tourists exploring the Suffolk countryside. With Nigel and Christine ruling the roost since 1997, The Cock Inn is firmly established as a great place for a drink and a meal. A Free House, and a regular winner in regional Best Kept Cellar and Cask Ale Quality Awards, it keeps Greene King IPA in prime condition as well as a guest ale, often from a small local brewery, such as Ridleys or St Peters in Bungay. Nigel and his staff produce a wide variety of dishes

on both bar and restaurant menus. Sandwiches, hot baguettes, jacket potatoes, burgers and pub classics such as lasagne, gammon and egg and steak & vegetable pie make up the bar menu, while the restaurant menu typically includes curries, steaks, grills and hearty pork casserole or beef bourguignon. There's also an excellent choice for vegetarians and a separate children's menu. The non-smoking dining area features beams, rafters, brass and copper ornaments, neatly laid pink-clothed tables and a big brick hearth that houses a tank of tropical fish. The inn is a paid-up member of the Clean Air Charter, and filter machines create a comfortable ambience throughout. The roomy lounge bar is the social hub of the inn, with a bank of three dart boards, a quiz machine, juke box, wide-screen television, and a stage where discos, karaoke, quizzes and regular live music sessions are held.

- 🕐 Mon-Thurs 11.30-3; Mon & Tues 7-11; Wed & Thurs 6-11; open all day Fri, Sat & Sun
- 🍴 A la carte and bar menus
- £ All majors except Amex
- 🅿 Car park, patio
- 🎵 Monthly disco, monthly karaoke, quiz last Sun of month, regular live music sessions
- @ email: djdanny2001@hotmail.com
- ❓ St John's Church 1 mile, Wyken Vineyards 1 mile, Pakenham (Nether Hall, Mill and Watermill) 3 miles, Bury St Edmunds 8 miles

THE DOG & DUCK

CAMPSEA ASHE, NR WOODBRIDGE, SUFFOLK IP13 0PT
TEL: 01728 748439

Directions: From the A12 Ipswich-Lowestoft road take the B1078 2½ miles to Campsea Ashe. The inn is on the left in the centre of the village, opposite Wickham Market station.

The Dog & Duck is an early 19th century inn, roomy and inviting, with a friendly, mellow ambience generated by hosts Terry and Barbara Burgess. They have built up a strong local following not just for their hospitality but also for the good range of drinks served in the bar and for Barbara's excellent home cooking. Hearty traditional pub classics are her speciality, and in the three dining areas (one non-smoking) her steak & kidneys are always in demand. Woodforde's Wherry and Adnams brews are always on tap, and there's a wide choice of other beers and lagers, wines, spirits and soft drinks. Pool, darts and boules are all played enthusiastically at the Dog & Duck, which attracts a broad spectrum of patrons – locals, walkers,

cyclists, coach parties – there's even a hitching post for the convenience of the occasional visitor arriving on horseback!

Motorists on the nearby A12 take a break from their journey to enjoy the hospitality, and the Dog & Duck is also an ideal base for touring the Suffolk countryside and coast. The Bed & Breakfast guest accommodation comprises five chalets, all with en suite facilities, and two suitable for families. One of the chalets is accessible to guests in wheelchairs. Children and pets are welcome, and the pub has ample off-road parking space. In Campsea Ashe itself, the Church of St John is well worth a visit, and among many nearby places of interest are the towns of Woodbridge and Aldeburgh, Tunstall Forest, the Anglo-Saxon burial site at Sutton Hoo, Butley Priory and the charming village of Orford with its Castle, Church and quayside on the River Orde.

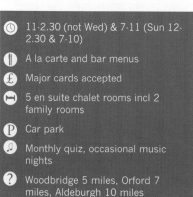

- 🕐 11-2.30 (not Wed) & 7-11 (Sun 12-2.30 & 7-10)
- 🍴 A la carte and bar menus
- £ Major cards accepted
- 🛏 5 en suite chalet rooms incl 2 family rooms
- Ⓟ Car park
- 🎵 Monthly quiz, occasional music nights
- ❓ Woodbridge 5 miles, Orford 7 miles, Aldeburgh 10 miles

THE FALCON

165 PLAYFORD RD, RUSHMERE ST ANDREW, NR IPSWICH,
SUFFOLK IP5 1DD
TEL: 01473 622338

Directions: Rushmere St Andrew lies just north of the A1214 east of Ipswich towards the A12.

A short drive from Ipswich, in a country lane off the A1214, **The Falcon** is well worth tracking down for the excellent hospitality offered by experienced licensee Cynthia Nolan and her son Mark. The public rooms provide a choice of mood and ambience: the carpeted bar, with its brick features, copper and brass ornaments and pictures of local scenes, a quiet, inviting spot to relax over a glass of Adnams and a chat, while the more gregarious will make for the games room, where darts, pool, cribbage, dominoes and a juke box keep things on the go. In fine weather, families make a beeline for the lawned beer garden, where there's a slide to keep the little ones happy.

A loyal band of regular customers can testify to the quality of Cynthia's cooking, which is served Tues-Sun inc, lunchtime and evening. Dishes on her menu cater for a variety of tastes and appetites, and include steak and kidney pie and fresh fish. Her subtle skills with herbs and spices are shown in enjoyably different dishes such as chicken with a Chinese-style marinade or tuna with Cajun spices. The area round The Falcon has plenty of interesting, scenic walks, and a nearby B&B provides a comfortable and convenient base for business in Ipswich or touring the Suffolk countryside and coast. There are many attractions within an easy drive, including Martlesham; Waldringfield, on a beautiful stretch of the Deben estuary; the delightful town of Woodbridge at the head of the estuary; and the remarkable Anglo-Saxon burial site of Sutton Hoo.

- 🕐 11.30-3 & 6-11 (Sun 7-10.30)
- 🍴 Home cooking
- 💷 Not Amex
- 🅿 Car park
- 🎵 Monthly quiz, games room
- ❓ Ipswich 3 miles, Martlesham 3 miles, Woodbridge 5 miles, Sutton Hoo 6 miles

THE FERRY BOAT INN

FELIXSTOWE FERRY, NR FELIXSTOWE, SUFFOLK IP11 9RZ
TEL: 01394 284203

Directions: On the Deben Estuary side of Felixstowe (north) follow signs to the golf club and keep going to the end of the road to the ferry.

The Ferry Boat Inn is truly a destination pub – and a really delightful one well worth the short drive up from Felixstowe. It stands north of the town at the end of the road that runs past the golf club, stopping by the ferry that plies across the Deben Estuary to Bawdsey. The inn dates back to the 15th century, and the attractive main bar has a splendidly traditional look with a polished flagstone floor, beams, handsome wood panelling, a wood-burning stove and sturdy country furniture. There are also pictures and paintings of the locality, which is closely linked with the sea and maritime history. Greene King IPA, Adnams Bitter and Old Speckled Hen are always available, and Landlord Robert Ward has the services of a top-class chef.

The blackboard menu offers a mouthwatering choice that includes seafood dishes from the local catch and elsewhere, and among the many excellent choice are salmon fishcakes, sea bass, cod, haddock, crab and mussels. The choice for meat-eaters is almost as diverse, with typical dishes like chargrilled steaks, chicken curry and steak & Guinness pie. The over-60s lunchtime cod or haddock, chips and peas is a popular lunchtime option. The Ferry Boat Inn shares its end-of-road setting with a sailing club and one of the many Martello towers built to defend the coast against an attack by Napoleon. There are some bracing walks and splendid sea views, and those with time to spare can take a trip on the ferry across the estuary to Bawdsey and the Manor (now a leisure centre), one of the secret stations where radar was developed.

🕐 11-3 & 5-30.11, July till end September 11-11

🍴 Home cooking 12-2 & 6.30-9, Sun 12-2 & 6-8.30

💷 Most cards accepted

🅿 Car park

@ website: www.ferryboatinn.com

❓ Ferry to Bawdsey, sailing club, golf club in walking distance; Felixstowe town centre 1 mile, Ipswich 12 miles

THE FOX

PAKENHAM, SUFFOLK IP31 2 JU

TEL: 01359 230347

> **Directions:** Pakenham lies about 5 miles east of Bury St Edmunds – turn right off the A143 past Great Barton.

This eighteenth century Greene King Pub has been carefully restored to its former glory, thanks to the hard work of Landlords Barbara and Peter Kingston. Set right in the centre of the village of Pakenham, the Fox is a truly traditional pub and restaurant. Barbara's extensive menu of traditional home cooked lunches and evening meals is complimented by the pub's quality, cask conditioned beers and fine wines. Served in either the bar and adjacent dining room or in the 'reading room' non-smoking restaurant. The Fox has also extensive landscaped gardens with large patio area overlooking a river, pond and waterfall feature and, during the summer months, becomes a sun trap and peaceful haven for all to enjoy. But above all, the welcome you'll receive at the Fox is not only warm and friendly but interesting too! Peter is an ex-animation television director and writer and illustrator of some forty five

children's books and both he and Barbara lived and worked in California U.S.A. for several years. Whilst Peter worked with studios like Hanna Barbera, MGM and Universal Pictures, Barbara designed, built and opened an English Pub/ Restaurant in the centre of California's Canyon Country! Quite a unique couple with quite a unique village pub!

The village sign at Pakenham, which lies in a triangle formed by the A14, the A143 and the A1088, proclaims the fact that Pakenham is the last village in England to have a working watermill and a working windmill. Both still stand, both produce freshly ground flour for sale, and both are among the many places of interest that can be visited on the village's circular walks. Also in the village or nearby are the 17th century Nether Hall, the Jacobean Newe House with Dutch gables and a two-storey porch, and the Church of St Mary with its impressive carved font and the famous Whistler Window – a painting by Rex Whistler of an 18th century parish priest.

- 🕐 12-3 & 6-11
- 🍴 Lunch and Evening meals
- 💷 Major cards accepted
- 🅿 Car park, garden, children's play area
- @ e-mail: peterkingston1@aol.com
- ❓ Watermill and windmill; Ixworth 2 miles, Bury St Edmunds 5 miles

THE HORSE & GROOM

1 LONDON ROAD, WRENTHAM, SUFFOLK NR34 7HJ
TEL: 01502 675279

Directions: The inn lies on the A12 about 7 miles south of Lowestoft.

The Horse & Groom is an 18th century roadhouse situated on a busy stretch of the A12 about 7 miles south of Lowestoft. Hosts Mary Anne Stewart and Roger Trigg, experienced publicans and members of the Institute of Innkeepers, set very high standards here, as in their previous pubs, in terms of both the welcome and the hospitality extended to visitors, whether familiar faces or first-timers. Old beams and a slatted wooden bar front take the eye in the bar, where the cask ales are always in top condition (barley Mow and Broadside are among the favourite brews), and the whole place is kept in apple pie order, from the pewter mugs

above the bar and the gleaming horse brasses to the spotless toilets.

Outside, there's ample off-road parking, a lawned garden with picnic benches, and a marquee at one end of the garden that is available for functions. Home-cooked food is served every lunchtime and evening, and on Tuesday and Thursday lunchtimes senior citizens can enjoy a bargain lunch. The pub has a pool table, and the first Sunday of every month is quiz night. The Horse & Groom is an excellent place to seek out or to pause on a journey along the A12. There are all sorts of interesting things to see and do in the vicinity, including walks and wildlife on the Suffolk Heritage Coast, the Suffolk Wildlife Park at Kessingland, the 'church within a church' at Covehithe and the towns of Lowestoft and Southwold.

- 🕐 11-3 & 6-11 (all day Sat & Sun)
- 🍴 Home cooking
- 🅿 Car park, garden, marquee
- 🎵 Quiz first Sunday of the month; pool table
- @ e-mail: roger.trigg@genie.co.uk
- ❓ Covehithe 2 miles, Wansford 4 miles, Kessingland 4 miles, Southwold 6 miles, Lowestoft 7 miles

THE KINGS HEAD

BROOK STREET, YOXFORD, SUFFOLK IP17 3EX
TEL/FAX: 01728 668008

> **Directions:** The inn is situated at the junction of the A12 and A1120 in Yoxford, 4 miles north of Saxmundham, 10 miles south of Southwold.

Occupying a strategic position at the junction of the A12 and A1120, **The Kings Head** announces itself as Suffolk's first Non-Smoking Freehouse. A go-ahead new owner Ben Heslop arrived in April 2004 with the firm intention of extending still further the wide-reaching reputation the pub has gained not only as a perfect spot to break a journey along the busy A12 but also as a much sought after destination restaurant. The dining area, recently redecorated and furnished with plenty of smart pine tables and new chairs, is a very popular place to sit down to anything from a light snack to a three-course feast. Lunchtime snacks include traditional favourites such as baguettes, ploughman's platters and filled Yorkshire puddings, while the full menu offers a splendid choice of dishes based on the very best ingredients, locally sourced as far as possible. Cod, haddock, plaice and

sole arrive fresh from the boats at Lowestoft. Much of the meat, including outstanding steaks comes from a renowned butcher in nearby Peasenhall and the sausages from a local organic farm.

Well-chosen, well-priced wines accompany the fine food, and connoisseurs of cask ales can choose between several local ales including Adnams and Woodfords, there are also guest ales too. Erdinger wheat beer from Germany is sold on draught which is very rare and more than worth travelling for. With easy access from all directions, the Kings Head takes its regular custom from a wide catchment area, and for many tourists and holidaymakers it is as important a part of their itinerary as nearby attractions such as Dunwich, Minsmere, Sibton Abbey and Blythburgh's wonderful Church of the Holy Trinity.

- 🕐 11.30-3 & 5.30-11 (closed Sun eve)
- 🍴 Home cooked bar snacks and full menu
- 💷 Major cards accepted
- 🅿 Car park
- ❓ Sibton Abbey & Church of St Peter 2 miles, Saxmundham 4 miles, Dunwich 5 miles, Blythburgh 8 miles, Southwold 10 miles

Suffolk

THE KINGS HEAD INN

ORFORD, SUFFOLK IP12 2LW
TEL: 01394 450271 FAX: 01394 459157

Directions: Orford lies 12 miles east of Woodbridge at the end of the B1084. The Kings Head is in the centre, by the market square.

Orford is without doubt one of the most charming and most interesting of all the places in Suffolk, with something to please everyone. Anyone looking for traditional hospitality combined with bags of atmosphere, good food and good drink. Dating back as far as the 13th century, and once a haunt of smugglers, the inn has a great host in Ian Thornton, in charge since 2000 and always terrific company. Log fires keep the bars cosy, and on the walls are photographs and historical facts about Orford in days gone by. Adnams Ales head the list of drinks, and there's a good choice of wines to enjoy either on their own or to accompany the excellent food served in the bar and non-smoking restaurant.

Orford is famous for its seafood,

especially its oysters and smoked fish, and these always feature prominently on the appealing and varied menu. For diners wanting to push the boat out, the seafood platter is just the thing, with smoked mackerel, scampi, cod, salmon, tiger prawns and mussels. There's plenty for meat-eaters as well, and the blackboard lists further choices that might include farmhouse vegetable soup, pork steaks with a mustard sauce and a super chicken pie. The Kings Head also offers characterful guest accommodation in three en suite bedrooms with their own separate entrance. The fine Church of St Bartholomew, where concerts and recitals take place regularly, stands just behind the inn, and Orford Castle is a short walk away. Down the road is Orford Quay, from where boat trips leave for Orford Ness and the RSPB Reserve of Havergate Island.

🕐 11.30-3 & 6-11 (Sun 12-4 & 7-10.30)

🍴 Bar snacks and à la carte menu

£ Not Amex

🛏 3 en suite rooms with separate entrance

🅿 Car park at rear

@ e-mail: ian_thornton@talk21.com
website: www.kingshead-orford-suffolk.co.uk

❓ In Orford: St Bartholomew's Church, Orford Castle, ferry to Orford Ness and Havergate Island.

THE LITTLE WELLINGTON

12 STOWUPLAND ROAD, STOWMARKET, SUFFOLK IP14 5AG
TEL: 01449 612276

> **Directions:** Stowmarket stands on the A14 Ipswich to Bury St Edmunds road. The inn is a two-minute walk from the railway station.

Stowmarket, the largest town in the heart of Suffolk, enjoyed periods of growth when the River Gipping was still navigable to Ipswich and when the London-Norwich railway arrived. It was to cater with the increased number of visitors arriving by train that the **Little Wellington** was built in the mid-19th century, and it has been dispensing hospitality and quenching thirsts ever since. It seems that it acquired its name because there was another inn, called the Duke of Wellington, opposite. The Little Wellington's pub sign is a version of the famous caricature portrait of the Duke as a Wellington boot. With Karina and Trevor Theobald at the helm, this is a very popular local meeting place, and also a welcome place to pause for motorists on the busy A14. A central wooden serving area is flanked by two spotless bar areas with wooden floors, polished pine furniture and photographs

of old Stowmarket – a very comfortable and convivial spot for enjoying a glass of cask ale; Greene King IPA, Abbot Ale and Speckled Hen are always on tap, along with a good selection of draught and bottled beers, lagers and wines.

Outside is a large lawned beer garden with a children's play area. Functions can be catered for in the garden, and a marquee is available for larger groups. Barbecues are held on Sundays, weather permitting, and the licensees plan to introduce a bar menu by the end of 2004. The Little Wellington hosts live music sessions most Saturday nights and fields teams of darts, crib and pool in the local leagues. It also holds regular charity events raising money for good causes, notably St Elizabeth's Hospice in Ipswich.

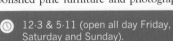

🕐 12-3 & 5-11 (open all day Friday, Saturday and Sunday).

🍴 Planned for end 2004

🅿 Ample parking at rear

🎵 Live music Saturday, charity events

❓ In Stowmarket: Museum of East Anglian Life and Gipping Valley River Park Walk; Stonham Aspal (Birds of Prey Centre) 7 miles

THE MORNING STAR

CARLTON ROAD, LOWESTOFT, SUFFOLK NR23 0ND
TEL: 01502 573727

Directions: The Morning Star lies off the link road close to the centre of town.

The **Morning Star** is a big, bold 1930s redbrick pub located on a corner site in a mainly residential area close to the town centre and the many amenities and attractions of Britain's most easterly town.

Licensees Gordon and Lynn have a welcome for one and all, and there's plenty of space in the large bar for enjoying a chat and a drink: six cask ales, including three regularly rotating guests, are always on tap, and straightforward, well-priced pub food is served every lunchtime, with a traditional roast on Sunday. The pub, which is open all day, every day, has plenty of off-road parking and a beer garden.

Friday night is music night at the Morning Star, and there's a guaranteed full house; but this is a popular place at any time, and its long opening hours are a bonus not just for the local residents but also for the many tourists and holidaymakers who flock to the Suffolk coast or pass through the town throughout the year.

Lowestoft has a wide variety of attractions to interest the visitor, including excellent shops, its lovely South Beach and two museums associated with its maritime heritage. And many an old bus-spotter has shed a nostalgic tear when visiting the East Anglia Transport Museum at Carlton Colville, where children and the young at heart can climb aboard and ride on old buses, trams and trolleybuses.

- 11-11 Mon - Sat, 12 - 10.30 Sun.
- Pub snacks and meals served lunchtime
- Car park, beer garden
- Live music Friday
- All the attractions of Lowestoft are nearby; Carlton Colville 2 miles

86 CANNON STREET, BURY ST EDMUNDS, SUFFOLK IP33 1JR
TEL: 01284 768769 FAX: 01284 701137

Directions: From the A14 Bury exit head for the centre. Turn left at the roundabout into Northgate Street, then immediately right at Cadney Lane and left into Cannon Street.

The Old Cannon Brewery, which started life as an ale house in 1845, is a handsome sight with its Suffolk white-brick facade topped by a slate roof. Inside, the scene is set by bare wooden floors, wooden tables and a galleried area above the bar. But what immediately takes the eye is a pair of vast, gleaming stainless steel brewing kettles. Co-owner and chief brewer Richard Eyton-Jones has many years' experience in the brewing business, and was responsible for building the renowned St Peter's Brewery in Bungay. His partner Carole Locker also has a background in public house management. Here in Bury, a town with a long tradition of brewing, they produce a superb variety of beers, including Best

Bitter (3.8°), Blonde Bombshell (4.2), and Gunners Daughter (5.5) and seasonal specials. They also stock wheat beers, continental beers and lagers and the excellent local Aspall cider. This is also a great place for food, and the menu takes its inspiration from home and overseas with dishes such as Thai spiced potted seafood, lamb's liver & Suffolk Black bacon, smoked haddock topped with Welsh rarebit, and sesame & honey roasted duck breast. Bury is a place that needs plenty of time to explore, and the Old Cannon Brewery is an ideal base, with five very smart and comfortable en suite bedrooms; a good breakfast is served in the dining area. The inn has a pleasant courtyard with a patio area, tables and chairs and attractive flower tubs.

- 🕐 12-3 & 6-11
- 🍴 Home cooking on à la carte menus lunch and dinner
- 💷 All except Amex
- 🛏 5 en suite rooms
- 🅿 Parking at rear
- @ website:
  www.oldcannonbrewery.co.uk
- ❓ In Bury: St Edmundsbury Cathedral, Abbey Gardens, Greene King Brewery museum and shop, Moyses Hall

THE ORDNANCE HOTEL

1 UNDERCLIFFE ROAD WEST, FELIXSTOWE, SUFFOLK IP11 2AN
TEL: 01394 273427 FAX: 01394 282513

Directions: The Ordnance Hotel is located 200 yards from the beach in Felixstowe.

Purpose-built in 1888, the **Ordnance Hotel** stands a short walk from the seafront, set well back from the road and shaded by attractive trees. It takes its name from the army quarters and stables that once stood on the site. The day rooms comprise a large and comfortable carpeted bar furnished in traditional style, an equally roomy residents' lounge, a games room with pool and darts and a restaurant with seats for 100. The function room is also of generous proportions, holding 100 seated or 150 standing, making the Ordnance a popular venue for wedding receptions, family parties and other special occasions. The bar stocks a weekly changing selection of cask ales, and the food choice runs from

bar snacks and light meals to classic pub dishes and meals with transatlantic inspiration served in the restaurant, newly transformed into the Route 66 American diner. The food is complemented by a very good wine list.

This is a very sociable place, and entertainment includes regular quiz, live music and karaoke nights. For visitors staying overnight or enjoying a longer break, Manager Neil Quigley offers has 16 comfortably furnished and recently refurbished en suite bedrooms, all with television and facilities for making tea and coffee. With a little notice, the staff can provide packed lunches for guests planning a day exploring the local places of interest. Felixstowe has a Blue Flag beach, a pier, good shopping, frequent bus and train services to Ipswich and the largest container port in Europe. To the north of town is Felixstowe Ferry, the original settlement and now a popular sailing centre on the Deben estuary .

- All day
- Bar snacks, English dishes and American Diner menu
- All the major cards
- 16 en suite rooms
- Car park, function room
- Regular quiz, live music and karaoke nights
- e-mail: ordnance@suffolkhotels.net website: www.ordnancehotel.com
- Felixstowe Ferry 1 mile, Landguard Fort and Point 2 miles, Ipswich 6miles

HIGH STREET, IXWORTH, BURY ST EDMUNDS, SUFFOLK IP31 2HN
TEL: 01359 230398

Directions: The inn stands on the main street of Ixworth, on the A143 about 7 miles northeast of Bury St Edmunds.

Dating back as far as 1530, **The Pykkerell** was a famous coaching inn on the London-Norwich route. The building has retained many interesting architectural features,

including the Stable, thought to have been built by John Garrard in about 1550. The rooms, which include public and lounge (library) bars, ooze old-world charm, with stripped panelling, heavily carved beams, a huge fireplace burning giant logs, and a mix of sturdy old tables and chairs. All this provides a wonderfully atmospheric setting for a drink or a meal and for enjoying the exceptional hospitality dispensed by mine host Tom Nicholson, who previously ran a pub in London's Fleet Street. An archway leads from the front of the inn to a stunning courtyard with outside seating, and the building that was once the courthouse for the village is now a function room.

Food is also a major factor in the Pykkerell's popularity, and the extensive à la carte menu is supplemented by daily blackboard specials that include several excellent fish dishes. There's always a good choice for vegetarians, and a selection of children's meals; Wednesday is Irish night, with a choice of traditional Irish dishes, and Thursday is steak night. Midweek lunches provide particularly good value for money, and the Sunday roast lunch is a guaranteed winner. The Pykkerell is located about 7 miles northeast of Bury St Edmunds in a typical old Suffolk village of considerable historic interest. Ixworth, its neighbour Pakenham and the surrounding area are well worth taking time to explore, and the inn is an excellent base from which to do it. The five comfortable guest bedrooms all have en suite facilities, television and hospitality tray.

- 🕐 12-3 & 5.30-11
- 🍴 A la carte menu
- 💷 Major cards accepted
- 🛏 5 en suite rooms
- Ⓟ Car park, courtyard garden, function room
- 🎵 Live jazz last Friday of the month
- @ Web: www.thepykkerell.com
- ❓ Pakenham 2 miles, Bury St Edmunds 7 miles

THE SORREL HORSE INN

OLD NORWICH ROAD, BARHAM, NR IPSWICH, SUFFOLK IP6 0PG
TEL: 01473 830327 FAX: 01473 833149

Directions: From the A14 down from Needham Market take the junction for the Norwich-bound A140 and return up the slip road; follow the signs for Barham. From the south, leave the A14 at the Great Blakenham junction and head for Claydon and Barham.

In a pleasant country setting **The Sorrel Horse Inn** has been owned and run for many years by Bridget (Breda) Smith and her sons Matthew and Philip. The 17th century building first became an inn in about 1840, and the interior boasts original features such as wall and ceiling beams and open fireplaces. Hewn log-style tables and rustic chairs assist the traditional look, and the dining areas feature interesting collections of miniatures and foreign banknotes.

Among the inn's many assets is a large lawned garden with plenty of picnic benches and parasols, and a children's play area complete with slide and bouncy castle. Expertly kept real ales – Adnams Bitter, Shepherd Neame Spitfire, Ridleys

Prospect – keep cask connoisseurs happy, and fresh-air appetites are satisfied with an excellent selection of home-cooked dishes. Lasagne, chicken curry, steaks and savoury pies are among the all-time favourites, and there's always a good choice of vegetarian dishes. Lighter options are available at lunchtime, and the inn is also open for breakfast.

With many popular attractions close by, the Sorrel Horse is an excellent base for touring the region, and eight bedrooms in a splendidly converted barn provide quiet, comfortable overnight accommodation. Most of the rooms have en suite facilities, and all are equipped with television, telephones and drinks trays. Ground-floor rooms are old-fashioned in style, with original beams, while those above are more modern looking, with pine furniture. One room has facilities for disabled guests.

- 🕐 11-3 & 5-11 (open all day Sat & Sun and every day for breakfast)
- 🍴 Lunch snacks, lunch and dinner à la carte, also open for breakfast
- £ All the major cards
- ⊟ 8 rooms, most en suite, 1 with disabled facilities
- Ⓟ Car park, garden, children's play area
- ❓ Shrublands Hall & Gardens next door, Ipswich 4 miles, Needham Market 4 miles

THE SWAN INN

THE STREET, LITTLE WALDINGFIELD, NR SUDBURY,
SUFFOLK CO10 0SQ
TEL: 01787 248584 FAX: 01787 247566

Suffolk

> **Directions:** From Sudbury, take the B1115 through Great Waldingham to Little Waldingham.

Pamela and Raymond Thompson are the new tenants at **The Swan Inn**, where the tradition of hospitality extends as far back as Tudor times. Standing near the parish church in Little Waldingham, this Grade II listed building is timber-framed beneath a peg-tiled roof, and recent refurbishment has enhanced its great appeal. The bar area is a happy marriage of traditional features such as the heavy beams, and the bright, cheerful modern paintwork. The inn is tastefully decorated throughout, and the walls in the dining area are adorned with photographs of Little Waldingfield in bygone times. Food is a major part of the success story here, and the excellent cooking draws diners not just from the village and the surrounding area but

increasingly from further afield.

The chef sets great store by fresh local ingredients, combining skill and imagination on wide-ranging menus that really do offer something for everyone, from traditional favourites like steaks, casseroles and fish pie to more elaborate and exotic offerings taking their inspiration from around the world. The wine list is equally impressive, and lovers of cask ales can choose between Greene King IPA and a regularly changing selection of guest ales. The region has a great deal to interest the visitor, and The Swan offers an ideal base for touring with two very comfortable and well equipped en suite bedrooms in the converted coach house. Lavenham, the most complete and original of the medieval 'wool towns', and Sudbury, the largest of them, are both an easy drive away.

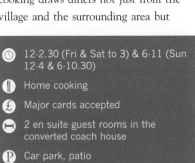

- 🕐 12-2.30 (Fri & Sat to 3) & 6-11 (Sun 12-4 & 6-10.30)
- 🍴 Home cooking
- 💷 Major cards accepted
- 🛏 2 en suite guest rooms in the converted coach house
- 🅿 Car park, patio
- ❓ Lavenham 3 miles, Sudbury 4 miles

THE TEN BELLS

THE STREET, STONHAM ASPAL, NR STOWMARKET, SUFFOLK IP14 6AF
TEL: 01449 711601

> **Directions:** The inn is on the main street of Stonham Aspal, on the A1120 1 mile east of the A140 at Earl Stonham.

Louise Lofts has been building up a loyal customer base since taking over the licence at **The Ten Bells**, which lies in the village of Stonham Aspal on the A1120, a short drive from the main A140. Behind the long yellow-painted frontage, a warm, genuine welcome awaits from Louise and Steve, and the cosy, well-stocked beamed bar offers a wide selection of cask ales, draught and bottled beers, lagers, wines and spirits. A tempting range of bar snacks is also available, and a full menu is served in the separate restaurant lunchtime and evening every day except Wednesday. The Ten Bells hosts a quiz on the last Friday of each month. Stonham Aspal was in the news in 1962, when the remains of a Roman bath house were unearthed. The parish

church has an unusual wooden top to its tower, an addition built to house the ten bells that gave their name to the pub.

Those interested in churches should find time to visit nearby Earl Stonham, where the Church of St Mary has a superb hammerbeam roof and a Jacobean pulpit with a row of hourglasses by which the preacher could time his sermon – or be timed! At Stonham Barns, the British Birds of Prey and Nature centre is home to every species of British owl, together with raptors from all over the world. This popular family attraction also has a Pets Paradise where children can make friends with meerkats, hamsters, parrots and piglets. All this sightseeing can generate a thirst, and Louise and Steve are ready and waiting at The Ten Bells. The pub has ample off-road parking and a pleasant beer garden.

- 12-3 & 5-11 (all day Sat & Sun)
- Bar and restaurant menus (no food Wed)
- Major cards accepted
- Car park, beer garden
- Quiz last Friday of the month
- British Birds of Prey and Nature Centre 1 mile, Earl Stonham 1 mile, Helmingham Hall 5 miles, Stowmarket 6 miles

HIGH ROAD, TRIMLEY ST MARY, NR FELIXSTOWE, SUFFOLK IP11 0TN
TEL/FAX: 01394 217999

Suffolk

> **Directions:** Trimley St Mary is on the A14 6 miles east of Ipswich towards Felixstowe.

By the A14 between Ipswich and Felixstowe, **The Three Mariners** is a popular local meeting place in the village of Trimley St Mary. Licensees Sharon White and Linda Green are working hard to enhance the inn's amenities, and owners the Unique Pub Company have recently completed a programme of

refurbishment. Behind the frontage painted in two shades of blue the bars have an inviting, traditional feel, with comfortably upholstered banquette seats and a feature brick fireplace. At the back is a patio with picnic benches, and beyond it a lawn with a children's play area. Shepherd Neame Spitfire is a popular choice among the cask ales and other beers and lagers on offer, and classic pub dishes include ploughman's platters, burgers, cod & chips and scampi; Sharon and Linda intend to expand the range of the menu as the dining area is extended.

The Three Mariners hosts a monthly quiz and fortnightly live music sessions, and there's a games room where pool, darts and dominoes are played. Trimley St Mary and Trimley St Martin are twin villages with two churches in a single churchyard. There is access on foot from Trimley St Mary to Trimley Marshes, home to an abundance of interesting plant life and to many species of wildfowl, waders and migrant birds. The coastal footpath that leads across the marshland goes on to Felixstowe, which has many attractions for holidaymakers as well as one of Europe's largest container ports.

- 🕐 12-11 (Sun to 10.30)
- 🍴 Bar snacks and meals
- 🅿 Car park, garden, children's play area
- 🎵 Quiz monthly, live music fortnightly, pool, darts, dominoes
- ❓ Walks down to the Orwell; Felixstowe 4 miles, Ipswich 6 miles

THE THREE TUNS COACHING INN

MAIN ROAD, PETTISTREE, NR WOODBRIDGE, SUFFOLK IP13 0HW
TEL: 01728 747979 FAX: 01728 746244

> **Directions:** The inn is on the main street of Pettistree, just off the A12 5 miles north of Woodbridge.

When Kirsty and Steve Lambert took over the management of the **Three Tuns Coaching Inn** early in 2004 they were continuing a long tradition of hospitality in this pleasant Suffolk village. The distinctive pub sign of three tuns (barrels) with an eagle perched on top is a relic of the days when the inn was owned by the now defunct Lacon Breweries. It was originally on the main route from Ipswich to Great Yarmouth, and the decor in the bar includes photographs of the coaches and charabancs that stopped here, and of the drivers and passengers who enjoyed the inn's facilities. The inn remains a great favourite with local residents and holidaymakers who pass this way. Four cask ales are always on tap in the bar, and there's a good selection of other beers, wines and malt whiskies.

Kirsty and Steve both cook, and the choice served throughout the day offers something for all tastes and appetites: sandwiches with mouthwatering fillings such as hot roast beef with red onion and horseradish; warm chicken liver & bacon salad as a starter or main course; fresh tuna salade niçoise; cod or haddock & chips; cauliflower & broccoli Stilton bake; lamb shanks cooked in a rosemary and red wine gravy; superb sausages from Revetts in nearby Wickham Market. The Three Tuns also serves morning coffee and afternoon tea. The inn is an ideal base for touring the Suffolk coast and countryside, and the 11 delightful and very comfortable en suite bedrooms will be increased to 28 for the 2005 season.

- 🕐 11.30-11 (Sun and Bank Holidays to 10.30)
- 🍴 Snack, à la carte and afternoon tea menus
- 💷 Major cards accepted
- 🛏 11 en suite rooms (more to be added)
- 🅿 Car park, beer garden
- @ e-mail: kirsty3tuns@aol.com website: www.threetuns-coachinginn.co.uk
- ❓ Woodbridge 5 miles, Wickham Market 1 mile

THE TRIPLE PLEA

BROADWAY, HALESWORTH, SUFFOLK IP19 8QW
TEL: 01986 874750

Suffolk

Directions: From the A12 take the A145, then the B1123 towards Halesworth, at the first roundabout turn right and the Triple Plea Inn is at the next roundabout on the right-hand side.

The Triple Plea is a handsome country inn just north of the town on the A145 Bungay road. The exterior is very appealing, with hanging baskets adding seasonal colour to the cream-painted brick frontage topped by a roof in patterned tiles. Completing the summery scene are picnic benches under parasols, and there are more of these at the back on a lawn that leads down to open countryside. The bars are neat and cheerful, with black beams contrasting with creamy white walls. Proprietors Venessa and Paul took over the inn in 2004 and with their son Gavin who manages the bar offer a fine choice of cask ales drawn straight from the barrels in the bar. They are supplied by Woodfords and Greene King and stock a good range of lagers, ciders and wines including a mini-cellar range.

Venessa, Paul and Gavin have been in the hospitality Industry for many years and have made many changes to the Triple Plea including a very smart non smoking lounge and re-vamped vaulted ceiling restaurant. Typical choices might be chicken & bacon melt, goujons of lemon sole, liver & bacon casserole, lasagne with a Mexican-style chilli kick and steaks from a first-class local butcher. Booking is strongly recommended for the Sunday roast lunch, with three meats, Yorkshire pudding and five fresh vegetables. The area is very popular with walkers and cyclists, and the inn has a camping site in the paddock beyond the garden. There's plenty to see in Halesworth, including two museums and an art gallery, and among many other local attractions are the magnificent 'Cathedral of the Marshes' at Blythburgh and the Earsham Otter Trust on the banks of the River Waveney.

- 🕐 11-11 (Sun 12-10.30)
- 🍴 Bar meals and à la carte menu 12-3.00 & 6-9.00
- 💷 All the major cards
- 🅿 Car park, garden, camping site
- @ website: www.thetripleplea.co.uk
- ❓ Cycling, walking, golf; Halesworth & District Museum 2 miles, Earsham Otter Trust 10 miles, Blythburgh 6 miles, Southwold 8 miles

THE WHITE HART INN

LONDON ROAD, BLYTHBURGH, NR SOUTHWOLD, SUFFOLK IP19 9LQ
TEL: 01502 478217

Directions: The inn lies right on the A12 at Blythburgh, 4 miles south of Southwold.

A former courthouse dating back to the 16th century, the **White Hart Inn** retains a number of fine original features, including ornate beams in the bar area and a large, handsome inglenook fireplace. The inn, whose frontage is adorned in spring and summer with cheerful hanging baskets, has been owned and run since 1999 by Mike Davis, who extends excellent hospitality and a fine range of food and drink to visitors. Traditional ales from Adnams head a long list of ales, lagers and ciders, and for the whole of October each year the inn hosts a beer festival, with more than two dozen cask ales to enjoy. Food is equally important, and the White Hart offers a great choice, from quick bar snacks to a children's menu and a full à la carte selection supplemented by dishes of the

day and not-to-be-missed fish specials.

This is a fine part of the world for exploring at leisure, and the White Hart provides an ideal base with four en suite chalets offering comfort, modern facilities and lovely views over Blyth estuary. Children and pets are welcome, and the inn has a patio and a beer garden. Blythburgh's Church of the Holy Trinity, known as the 'Cathedral of the Marshes', is one of the most memorable landmarks in the county, a stirring sight as it rises above the marshy estuary; visible for miles around, it is a particularly thrilling sight at night, when it is floodlit. This is also splendid walking country, and there are several nature reserves and bird sanctuaries in the region. The A12 provides easy access north and south, while a short distance to the east is Southwold, equally interesting to the historian and the holidaymaker, and to the west the fine old market town of Halesworth.

- 11·11 (Sun 12·10.30)
- Bar meals and à la carte served all day
- All the major cards
- 4 en suite chalets
- Car park
- Beer festival each year throughout October
- Blythburgh Church of Holy Trinity; Southwold 4 miles, Walberswick 4 miles, Halesworth 5 miles

THE WHITE HORSE

BURY ROAD, BEYTON, NR BURY ST EDMUNDS, SUFFOLK IP30 9AB
TEL: 01359 270324

Suffolk

Directions: From Bury St Edmunds take the A14 eastwards for about 5 miles. Turn off on to road signposted Tostock, Thurston and Beyton. Turn right at the junction in Beyton.

Motorists travelling between Bury St Edmunds and Stowmarket are well advised to make a small detour to seek out this delightful country pub. The pedigree of **The White Horse** is impeccable: the owners are the Suffolk brewery Greene King, Pub Company of the Year for the past three years, and the landlady is also one of the best in the business. Jane Waterman has held the reins since 1984, and the loyal clientele she has built up extends far beyond the surrounding villages. The outside of the pub is painted a delicate light green, with contrasting maroon and white door and window frames. The interior is equally attractive, both in the saloon with its wooden floor, polished wooden

tables and log-burning stove and in the comfortable carpeted restaurant area. Greene King IPA and Abbot head the list of cask ales, and the usual range of bitters, lagers, wines and spirits is always available.

Freshly prepared home-cooked dishes include many classic English favourites as well as some more unexpected choices such as lentil, hazelnut and mushroom pâté, crab thermidor and venison steaks. There's always an excellent choice of vegetarian dishes, and on Sunday, when booking is recommended, the weekday menu is joined by three traditional roasts. On the social side, pool is a popular pastime, and in summer the local cricket team and a troop of morris dancers make their base here. The White Horse is about to add another string to its bow in the shape of six letting bedrooms, including one with facilities for disabled guests, in a converted barn in the grounds.

🕐 11.30-3 & 6.30-11 (Sunday 12-3 & 7-10.30)

🍴 A la carte and bar menus

£ All majors except Amex

🛏 6 rooms planned for August 2005

🅿 Car park, patio, garden, disabled access (ramp), disabled toilets planned for 2005

🎵 Pool table

@ email: graclehelen@tiscali.co.uk

❓ Rougham Airfield 3 miles, Woolpit 2 miles, Bury St Edmunds 4 miles

Suffolk

THE WHITE HORSE INN

LONDON ROAD, CAPEL ST MARY, NR IPSWICH, SUFFOLK IP9 2JR
TEL/FAX: 01473 310261

Directions: The inn lies ¼ mile from the A12 5 miles south of Ipswich.

On a prominent corner site just yards from the A12, the **White Horse Inn** is a popular 'local' as well as a convenient and very agreeable stopping place for travellers and tourists. Roger Lee, who runs the pub with his wife Grace, was an actor

and director for many years before turning his hand to pulling pints, and he is rightly proud of what he has achieved at the White Horse since taking over this, his first pub, in 2003. A wide range of cask ales (Greene King IPA, Old Speckled Hen), beers, lagers, wines and spirits is served all day in the roomy bar, and the pub offers a straightforward

menu of popular dishes every lunchtime and evening except Mondays. There's a pool table in the lounge, while outside is a beer garden with an area for children to play. On the social side, the White Horse hosts a disco and karaoke on the last Friday of each month, and a cabaret on the last Saturday.

Capel St Mary has been much modernised since John Constable sketched here, but the Church of St Mary remains very much as he would have known it. All the main landmarks of Constable Country, including East Bergholt (his birthplace), Flatford Mill and Willy Lott's Cottage, are close by, and about three miles to the east of the pub lies Alton Water, a popular centre of waterborne leisure activity and a wildlife sanctuary.

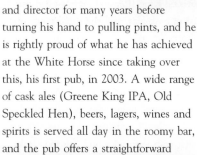
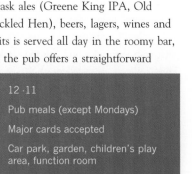

🕐 12·11

🍺 Pub meals (except Mondays)

💷 Major cards accepted

🅿 Car park, garden, children's play area, function room

🎵 Disco/karaoke last Friday of month, cabaret last Saturday

@ e-mail: leewh@tiscali.co.uk

❓ East Bergholt 3 miles, Alton Water 4 miles, Ipswich 5 miles, Colchester 8 miles

THE WHITE HORSE INN

TATTINGSTONE, NR IPSWICH, SUFFOLK IP9 2NU
TEL: 01473 328060

Suffolk

Directions: Tattingstone is situated 4 miles south of Ipswich off the A137.

The White Horse Inn is a very
attractive old slate-roofed building in a
village a short drive south of Ipswich.
The carved white horse that stands atop
a tall pole was rescued from a hotel in
Ipswich, and another interesting external
feature is an old hand pump that for
many years supplied the inn with water
from a well. Inside, black beams, brick
features, a log-burning stove and a bench
seat in an inglenook paint a delightfully
traditional picture and create a warm,
relaxing atmosphere in which to enjoy a
drink and a chat. Much credit for the
inn's appeal must go to Samantha
Rutherford, who took over the licence in
May 2004 and runs it with her mother
and stepfather. Samantha is in charge of
the cooking, and her menu tempts with
home-made pub classics such as cottage
pie, chicken curry or steak & ale pie.
Sunday lunch brings a choice of three

roasts. Burgers make tasty lighter snacks,
along with made-to-order hot and cold
sandwiches with a variety of generous
fillings. Drinks include a number of cask
ales and a range of wines available in
third-bottle size.

The inn is a popular meeting place not
just for the local community but also for
a number of clubs and societies,
including the local football team and an
owners' club for Wolseley 6/80s and
Morris Oxfords (MO and SO). Folk
singers gather every other Sunday, and
darts and cribbage are played
enthusiastically at any time. The inn has
no accommodation, but a field at the
back is available for caravans and tents –
Samantha plans to have showers
installed in time for the 2005 season.
Tattingstone lies at the western edge of
Alton Water, which offers a variety of
leisure facilities and holds the annual
Dragon Boat Regatta.

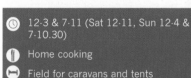

- 🕐 12-3 & 7-11 (Sat 12-11, Sun 12-4 & 7-10.30)
- 🍴 Home cooking
- 🚐 Field for caravans and tents
- 🅿 Car park
- 🎵 Darts, folk singing every other Sunday, quiz Sundays
- ❓ Alton Water (Dragon Boat Regatta, extensive leisure facilities) 2 miles, Ipswich 4 miles

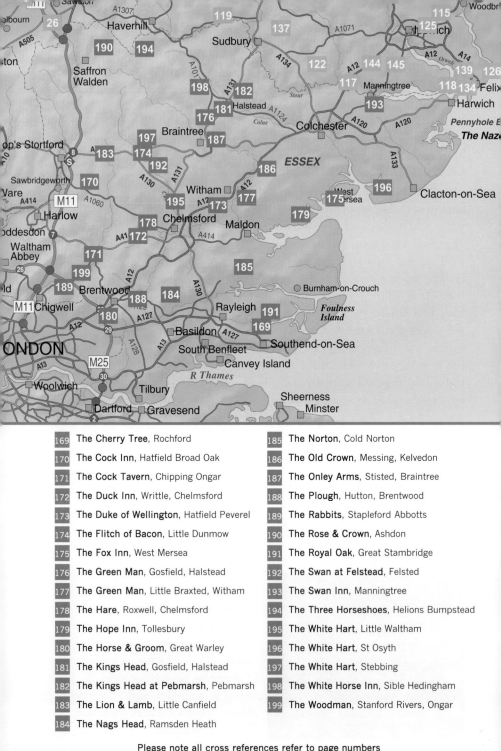

169	The Cherry Tree, Rochford		185	The Norton, Cold Norton
170	The Cock Inn, Hatfield Broad Oak		186	The Old Crown, Messing, Kelvedon
171	The Cock Tavern, Chipping Ongar		187	The Onley Arms, Stisted, Braintree
172	The Duck Inn, Writtle, Chelmsford		188	The Plough, Hutton, Brentwood
173	The Duke of Wellington, Hatfield Peverel		189	The Rabbits, Stapleford Abbotts
174	The Flitch of Bacon, Little Dunmow		190	The Rose & Crown, Ashdon
175	The Fox Inn, West Mersea		191	The Royal Oak, Great Stambridge
176	The Green Man, Gosfield, Halstead		192	The Swan at Felstead, Felsted
177	The Green Man, Little Braxted, Witham		193	The Swan Inn, Manningtree
178	The Hare, Roxwell, Chelmsford		194	The Three Horseshoes, Helions Bumpstead
179	The Hope Inn, Tollesbury		195	The White Hart, Little Waltham
180	The Horse & Groom, Great Warley		196	The White Hart, St Osyth
181	The Kings Head, Gosfield, Halstead		197	The White Hart, Stebbing
182	The Kings Head at Pebmarsh, Pebmarsh		198	The White Horse Inn, Sible Hedingham
183	The Lion & Lamb, Little Canfield		199	The Woodman, Stanford Rivers, Ongar
184	The Nags Head, Ramsden Heath			

Please note all cross references refer to page numbers

ESSEX

Northeast Essex has the true feel of East Anglia, particularly around the outstanding villages of the Stour Valley - which has come to be known as Constable Country. The inland villages and small towns here are notably historic and picturesque, offering very good touring and walking opportunities. A plethora of half-timbered medieval buildings, farms and churches mark this region out as of particular historical interest. Monuments to engineering feats past and present include Hedingham Castle, Chappel Viaduct and the postmill at Bocking Church Street. There are also many lovely gardens to visit, and the region's principal town, Colchester, is a mine of interesting sights and experiences.

The North Essex Coast has a distinguished history and a strong maritime heritage, as exemplified in towns like Harwich, Manningtree and Mistley. Further examples are the fine Martello Towers - circular brick edifices built to provide a coastal defence against Napoleon's armies - along the Tendring coast at Walton, Clacton, Jaywick and Point Clear. Dating from 1808 to 1812, each is mounted with a gun on the roof.

The Tendring Peninsula has a rich and varied heritage ranging from prehistoric remains to medieval churches and elegant Victorian villas. The Tendring Coast contains an interesting mix of extensive tidal inlets, sandy beaches and low cliffs.

PLACES OF INTEREST

Aythorpe Roding 149	Kelvedon Hatch 159
Braintree 149	Layer Marney 159
Brentwood 149	Maldon 159
Brightlingsea 150	Manningtree 160
Burnham-On-Crouch 150	Mersea Island 160
Canvey Island 150	Mistley 160
Castle Hedingham 150	Mountnessing 161
Chappel 151	North Weald 161
Chelmsford 151	Point Clear 161
Clacton-on-Sea 152	Saffron Walden 161
Coggleshall 152	Southend-on-Sea 163
Colchester 153	St Osyth 164
Cressing 155	Stansted Mountfitchet 164
Dedham 155	Thaxted 165
Frinton-on-Sea 155	Tilbury 165
Great Dunmow 156	Waltham Abbey 166
Hadleigh 156	Walton-on-the-Naze 167
Halstead 157	West Thurrock 168
Harlow 157	Wivenhoe 168
Harwich 158	
Hatfield Broad Oak 159	

Queen Elizabeth I Hunting Lodge, Epping

The Stour Estuary, Hamford Water and Colne Estuary are all renowned for seabirds and other wildlife. Many areas are protected nature reserves. The Manningtree-Ramsey road passes through some of the best coastal scenery in Essex, with some outstanding views of the Suffolk shore.

This is, of course, also the part of the county known as 'the sunshine holiday coast', where the resorts of Clacton, Frinton and Walton-on-the-Naze are to be found.

The small northwest Essex towns of Saffron Walden, Thaxted, Great Dunmow and Stansted Mountfichet are among the most beautiful and interesting in the nation. This area is also home to a wealth of picturesque villages boasting weatherboarded houses and pargeting. The quiet country lanes are perfect for walking, cycling or just exploring. This area also retains three beautiful and historic windmills, at Stansted Mountfichet, Aythorpe Roding and Thaxted. Visitors to southwest Essex and Epping Forest will find a treasure-trove of woodland, nature reserves, superb gardens and rural delights. Epping Forest dominates much of the far western corner, but all of this part of Essex is rich in countryside, forests and parks, including the magnificent Lee Valley Regional Park, Thorndon Country Park at Brentwood, and Weald Country Park at South Weald.

Bordering the north bank of the Thames, the borough of Thurrock has long been a gateway to London but also affords easy access to southwest Essex and to Kent. This thriving borough encompasses huge swathes of greenbelt country, and along its 18 miles of Thames frontage there are many important marshland wildlife habitats. History, too, abounds in this part of the county.

Henry VIII built riverside Block Houses at East and West Tilbury, which later became Coalhouse Fort and Tilbury Fort. It was at West Tilbury that Queen

Elizabeth I gave her most famous speech to her troops, gathered to meet the Spanish Armada threat. Both forts also played an important defensive role during the two World Wars. At the extreme southeast of the county, Southend is a popular and friendly seaside resort with a wealth of sights and amenities. The area surrounding the Rivers Blackwater and Crouch contains a wealth of ancient woodland and other natural beauties, particularly along the estuaries and the Chelmer and Blackwater Canal. This part of Essex affords some marvellous sailing, walking, cycling, birdwatching and other outdoor activities.

AYTHORPE RODING

Aythorpe Roding Windmill is the largest remaining post mill in Essex. Four storeys high, it was built around 1760 and remained in use up until 1935. It was fitted in the 1800s with a fantail which kept the sails pointing into the wind. It is open to the public on the last Sunday of each month from April to September, 2-5 p.m.

BRAINTREE

This town, along with its close neighbour Bocking, is sited at the crossing of two Roman roads and were brought together by the cloth industry in the 16th century. Flemish weavers settled here, followed by many Huguenots. One, Samuel Courtauld, set up a silk mill in 1816 and, by 1866, employed over 3,000 Essex inhabitants.

The magnificent former Town Hall is one of the many Courtauld legacies in the town. It was built in 1928 with panelled walls, murals by Grieffenhagen showing stirring scenes of local history, and a grand central tower with a five-belled striking clock. A smaller but no less fascinating reminder of Courtauld's generosity is the 1930s bronze fountain, with bay, shell and fish, near St Michael's Church.

The **Braintree District Museum** on Manor Street tells the story of Braintree's diverse industrial heritage and traditions. The **Town Hall Centre** is a Grade II listed building housing the Tourist Information Centre and the Art Gallery, which boasts a continuous changing programme of exhibitions and works.

BRENTWOOD

Brentwood Cathedral on Ingrave Road was built in 1991. This classically-styled church incorporates the original

Victorian church that stood on this spot. It was designed by the much-admired architect Quinlan Terry, with roundels by Raphael Maklouf (who also created the relief of the Queen's head used on current coins).

Brentwood Museum is a small and picturesque cottage museum concentrating on local and social interests during the late 19th and early 20th centuries.

BRIGHTLINGSEA

Brightlingsea has a long tradition of shipbuilding and seafaring and has the distinction of being the only limb of the Cinque Ports outside Kent and Sussex.

The 13th century **Jacobes Hall** in the town centre is one of the oldest occupied buildings in Essex. It is timber-framed with an undulating tile roof and an external staircase. Used as a meeting hall during the reign of Henry III, its name originates from its first owner, Edmund, Vicar of Brightlingsea, who was known locally as Jacob le Clerk.

All Saints Church, which occupies the highest point of the town on a hill about a mile from the centre, is mainly 13th century. Here are to be found some Roman brickwork and a frieze of ceramic tiles commemorating local residents whose lives were lost at sea. Its 97-foot tower can be seen from 17 miles out to sea. A light was once placed in the tower to guide the town's fishermen home.

Brightlingsea Museum offers an insight into the lives, customs and traditions of the area, housing a collection of exhibits relating to the town's maritime connections and the oyster industry.

BURNHAM-ON-CROUCH

Burnham-on-Crouch is attractively old-fashioned, and probably best known as a yachting venue. It is lively in summer, especially at the end of August when the town hosts one of England's premier regattas, Burnham Week.

CANVEY ISLAND

Canvey Island is a picturesque stretch of land overlooking the Thames estuary with views to neighbouring Kent. The island boasts two unusual museums: **Dutch Cottage Museum** is an early 17th century eight-sided cottage built by Dutch workmen for Dutch workmen and boasting many traditional Flemish features. **Castle Point Transport Museum**, in a 1930s bus garage, houses an interesting collection of historic and modern buses and coaches, mainly of East Anglian origin.

CASTLE HEDINGHAM

This town is named after its Norman **Castle**, which dominates the landscape. The impressive stone keep is one of the tallest in Europe, with four floors and rising over 100 feet, with 12-ft thick walls, and the banqueting hall and minstrels' gallery can still be seen.

The town itself is a maze of narrow streets radiating from Falcon Square,

Jousting at Castle Hedingham

comprehensive collection spanning 150 years of railway history, with period railway architecture, engineering and memorabilia in beautifully restored station buildings. Special steam days and other events are held throughout the year.

The dramatic 32-arched **Chappel Viaduct** standing 75 feet above the Colne Valley, a designated European Monument, was begun in 1846 and opened in 1849.

CHELMSFORD

Roman workmen cutting their great road linking London with Colchester built a fort at what is today called Chelmsford. Then called *Caesaromagus*, it stands at the confluence of the Rivers Chelmer and Can. The town has always been an important market centre and is now the bustling county town of Essex.

Christianity came to Essex with the Romans and again, later, with St Cedd (AD 654); in 1914 the diocese of Chelmsford was created. **Chelmsford Cathedral** in New Street dates from the 15th century and is built on the site of a church constructed 800 years ago. The cathedral is noted for the harmony and unity of its perpendicular architecture. John Johnson, a distinguished local architect, designed both the Shire Hall and the 18th century **Stone Bridge** over the River Can and also rebuilt the Parish Church of St Mary when most of its 15th century tower fell down. The church became a cathedral when the new

with many Georgian and 15th century houses comfortably vying for space, and the **Church of St Nicholas**, which is virtually completely Norman, with grand masonry and interestingly carved choir seats. At the **Colne Valley Railway and Museum**, a mile of the Colne Valley and Halstead line between Castle Hedingham and Great Yeldham has been restored and now runs steam trains operated by enthusiasts. These lovingly restored Victorian railway buildings feature a collection of vintage engines and carriages; short steam train trips are available.

CHAPPEL

Here, on a 4-acre site beside Chappel and Wakes Colne Station, is the **East Anglian Railway Museum**, a

Beach and Pier, Clacton-on-Sea

and businesses.

Three modern technologies - electrical engineering, radio, and ball and roller bearings - began in Chelmsford and at the **Engine House Project** at Sandford Mill Waterworks, museum collections from the town's unique industrial story provide a fascinating insight into the science of everyday things.

diocese of Chelmsford was created. Since then it has been enlarged and re-organised inside. The cathedral boasts memorial windows dedicated to the USAAF airmen who were based in Essex from 1942-5.

The Marconi Company, pioneers in the manufacture of wireless equipment, set up the first radio company in the world here in 1899. Exhibits of those pioneering days of wireless can be seen in the **Chelmsford Museum**, as can interesting displays of Roman remains and local history. Fine and decorative arts (ceramics, costume, glass), coins, natural history (live beehive, animals, geological exhibits) rub shoulders with displays exploring the history of the distinguished Essex Regiment. The museum is set in a lovely park complete with children's play area.

Also in the town, at Parkway, is **Moulsham Mill Business & Craft Centre**, set in an early 18th century water mill that has been renovated and now houses a variety of craft workshops

CLACTON-ON-SEA

Clacton is a traditional sun-and-sand family resort with a south-facing, long sandy beach, lovely gardens on the seafront and a wide variety of shops and places to explore. The Pier was constructed in 1871; at first paddle steamers provided the only mode of transport to the resort, the railway arriving in 1882. **The Pier** was widened from 30 feet to over 300 feet in the 1930s. As well as the traditional sideshows, big wheel, restaurants and fairground rides, the pier houses the fascinating **Seaquarium and Reptile Safari**. There are three Martello Towers along this bit of the Essex coast. Just south of the town, **Jaywick Sands** is the ideal spot for a picnic by the sea, boasting one of the finest natural sandy beaches in the county.

COGGESHALL

This medieval hamlet, a pleasant old

cloth and lace town, has some very fine timbered buildings. **Paycocke's House** on West Street, a delightful timber-framed medieval merchant's home dating from about 1500, boasts unusually rich panelling and wood carvings, and is owned by the National Trust. **Coggeshall Heritage Centre** displays items of local interest and features changing exhibitions on themes relating to the past of this historic wool town. There's an authentic, working wool loom on site.

The National Trust also owns the restored **Coggeshall Grange Barn**, which dates from around 1140 and is the oldest surviving timber-framed barn in Europe.

COLCHESTER

England's oldest recorded town, with more than 2,000 years of history. During the 1st century, Colchester's prime location made it an obvious target for invading Romans. The Roman Emperor Claudius accepted the surrender of 11 British Kings in Colchester. In AD60, Queen Boudicca helped to establish her place in history by taking revenge on the Romans and burning the town to the ground, before going on to destroy London and St Albans. Roman walls - the oldest in Britain - still surround the oldest part of town. Balkerne Gate, west

gate of the original Roman town, is the largest surviving Roman gateway in the country, and remains magnificent to this day.

Today the town is presided over by its lofty town hall and enormous Victorian water tower, nicknamed 'Jumbo' after London Zoo's first African elephant, an animal sold to P T Barnum (causing some controversy) in 1882. The tower has four massive pillars made up of one-and-a-quarter million bricks, 369 tons of stone and 142 tons of iron, all working to support the 230,000-gallon tank.

A good place to start any exploration of the town is **Colchester Castle** and its museum. When the Normans arrived, they built their castle on the foundations of the Roman temple of Claudius. Having used many of the Roman bricks in its construction, it boasts the largest Norman keep ever built in Europe - the only part still left standing. The keep houses the **Castle Museum**, one of the most exciting hands-on historical

Maiden Street, Dutch Quarter of Colchester

Essex

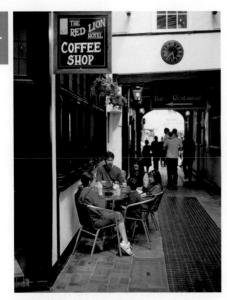

Colchester

attractions in the country. Its fascinating collection of Iron Age, Roman and medieval relics is one of the most important in the country.

Hollytrees Museum in the High Street is located in a fine Georgian house dating back to 1718. This award-winning museum houses a wonderful collection of toys, costumes, curios and antiquities from the last two centuries. Nearby, housed in the former All Saints' Church, is the **Natural History Museum**, with exhibits and many hands-on displays illustrating the natural history of Essex from the Ice Age right up to the present day. An arch in Trinity Street leads to **Tymperleys Clock Museum**, the 15th century timber-framed home of William Gilberd, who entertained Elizabeth I with experiments

in electricity. Today this fine example of architectural splendour houses a magnificent collection of 18th and 19th century Colchester-made clocks.

Close to the railway station are the ruins of **St Botolph's Priory**, the oldest Augustinian priory in the country. Its remains are a potent reminder of the bitterness of Civil War times, as it was here that Royalists held out for 11 weeks during the siege of Colchester, before finally being starved into submission.

On Bourne Road, south of the town centre just off the B1025, there's a striking stepped-and-curved gabled building known as **Bourne Mill**, now owned by the National Trust. Built in 1591 from stone taken from the nearby St John's Abbeygate, this delightful restored building near a lovely millpond was originally a fishing lodge, later converted (in the 19th century) into a mill - and still in working order.

Colchester Zoo, just off the A12 outside the town, has gained a well-deserved reputation as one of the best in Europe. Its award-winning enclosures allow visitors closer to the animals and provide naturalistic environments for the 170 species.

Colchester has been famous in its time for both oysters and roses. Colchester oysters are still cultivated on beds in the lower reaches of the River Colne, which skirts the northern edge of town. A visit to the **Oyster Fisheries** on nearby Mersea Island is a fascinating experience, and the tour includes complimentary fresh oysters and a glass of wine.

CRESSING

Cressing Temple Barns, set in the centre of an ancient farmstead, are two splendid medieval timber barns commissioned in the 12th century by the Knights Templar. They contain the timber of over 1,000 oak trees; an interpretive exhibition explains to visitors how the barns were made, as a special viewing platform brings visitors up into the roof of the magnificent Wheat Barn for a closer look. There's also a beautiful walled garden re-creating the Tudor style. Special events are held throughout the year.

DEDHAM

This is the heart of Constable country, and the village has several fine old buildings, especially the 15th century flint church, its pinnacled tower familiar from so many Constable paintings. There's also the school Constable went to, and good walks through the protected riverside meadows of Dedham Vale to **Flatford**, where **Bridge Cottage** is a restored thatched 16th century building housing a display about Constable, who featured this cottage in several of his paintings (his father's mill is across the river lock in Dedham).

Dedham Vale Family Farm on Mill Street is a nicely undeveloped 16-acre farm boasting a comprehensive collection of British farm animals. The **Art & Craft Centre** on Dedham's High Street is well worth a visit. **Marlborough Head**, a wool merchant's house dating back to 1475, and the **Toy Museum** has a fascinating collection of dolls, teddies, toys, games, doll houses and other artefacts of childhoods past.

At **Castle House**, approximately three-quarters of a mile from the village centre on the corner of East Lane and Castle Hill, The **Sir Alfred Munnings Art Museum** is housed in the former home, studios and grounds of the famous painter, who lived here between 1898 and 1920. The museum prides itself on the diversity of paintings and sculptures on view. The house itself is a mixture of Tudor and Georgian periods, carefully restored, and Munnings' original furniture is still in place.

FRINTON-ON-SEA

Once a quiet fishing village, this town

Frinton-on-Sea

was developed as a select resort by Sir Richard Cooper, and expanded in the 1880s to the genteel family resort it is today. Situated on a long stretch of sandy beach, Frinton remains peaceful and relatively unspoilt, and its grace and elegance are evidenced all round, as are hints of its distinguished past: Victorian beach huts still dot the extensive beach.

The **Church of Old St Mary** in the town contains some panels of stained glass in the East window designed by the Pre-Raphaelite artist Burne Jones.

A good example of 20th century English vernacular architecture is **The Homestead** at the corner of Second Avenue and Holland Road, built in 1905 by C F Voysey.

GREAT DUNMOW

The town is famous for the 'Flitch of Bacon', an ancient ceremony which dates back as far as the early 12th century. A prize of a flitch, or side, of bacon was awarded to the local man who, in the words of then-Lord Mayor Robert Fitzwalter;

'does not repent of his marriage nor quarrel, differ or dispute with his wife within a year and a day after the marriage'.

Amidst great ceremony, the winning couple would be seated and presented with their prize. The custom lapsed on the Dissolution of the Monasteries, was briefly revived in the 18th century, and became established again after 1885. 'Trials' to test the truth are all in good fun, and are carried out every leap year.

The successful couple are carried through the streets on chairs and then presented with the Flitch. The 'bacon chair' can be seen in Little Dunmow parish church. The **Great Dunmow Maltings**, opened to the public in 2000 after restoration, is the most complete example of a medieval timber-framed building of its type in the United Kingdom, and a focal point for local history in the shape of Great Dunmow Museum, with changing displays illustrating the history of the town from Roman times to the present day. H G Wells lived at **Brick House** in Great Dunmow, overlooking the **Doctor's Pond**, where in 1784 Lionel Lukin is reputed to have tested the first unsinkable lifeboat.

The **Flitch Way** is a 15-mile country walk along the former Bishop's Stortford-to-Braintree railway, taking in Victorian stations, impressive views, and a wealth of woodland wildlife.

HADLEIGH

Hadleigh Castle, built originally for Edward III, is owned by English Heritage and once belonged to Anne of Cleves, Catherine of Aragon and Katherine Parr. The ruins were also immortalised in a painting by Constable. The remains of this once impressive castle can still be seen. The curtain walls towers, which survive almost to their full height, overlook the Essex marshes and the Thames estuary.

Hadleigh Castle Country Park offers

a variety of woodland and coastal walks in grounds overlooking the Thames estuary.

HALSTEAD

The name 'Halstead' comes from the Anglo-Saxon for *healthy place*. Like Braintree and Coggeshall, Halstead was an important weaving centre. **Townsford Mill** is certainly the most picturesque reminder of Halstead's industrial heritage. Built in the 1700s, it remains one of the most handsome buildings in a town with a number of historic buildings. Today the Mill is an antiques centre, one of the largest in Essex, with thousands of items of furniture, porcelain, collectibles, stamps, coins, books, dolls, postcards, costume, paintings, glass and ceramics, old lace and clocks.

Somewhat improbably, Halstead's most famous product was once mechanical elephants. Life-sized and weighing half a ton, they were built by one W Hunwicks. Each one consisted of 9,000 parts and could carry a load of eight adults and four children at speeds of up to 12 miles per hour.

HARLOW

The 'New Town' of Harlow sometimes gets short shrift, but it is in fact a lively and vibrant place with a great deal more than excellent shopping facilities. There are some very good museums and several sites of historic interest. The **Gibberd Collection** in Harlow Town Hall offers a delightful collection of British watercolours featuring works by Blackadder, Sutherland, Frink, Nash and Sir Frederick Gibberd, Harlow's master planner and the founder of the collection.

Harlow Museum, in a Georgian manor house set in picturesque gardens, has extensive and important Roman, post-medieval and early 20th century collections, as well as a full programme of temporary exhibitions.

Mark Hall Cycle Museum and Gardens in Muskham Road offers a unique collection of cycles and cycling accessories illustrating the history of the bicycle from 1818 to the present day, including one made of plastic, one that folds, and one where the seat tips forward and throws its rider over the handlebars if the brakes are applied too hard. The museum is housed in a converted stable block within Mark Hall manor. Adjacent to the museum are three period walled gardens.

Gibberd Gardens, on the eastern outskirts of Harlow is well worth a visit, reflecting as it does the taste of its eponymous designer.

Harlow Study and Visitors Centre in Netteswellbury Farm is set in a medieval tithe barn and 13th century church. The site has displays outlining the story of Harlow New Town.

Parndon Wood Nature Reserve is an ancient woodland with a fine variety of birds, mammals and insects. Facilities include two nature trails with hides for observing wildlife, and a study centre.

HARWICH

During the French campaigns of the 14th and 15th centuries, Harwich was an important naval base. Later, the renowned Elizabethan seafarers Hawkins, Frobisher and Drake sailed from Harwich on various expeditions; in 1561 Queen Elizabeth I visited the town, describing it as 'a pretty place and want[ing] for nothing'. Christopher Newport, leader of the *Goodspeed* expedition which founded Jamestown, Virginia, in 1607, and Christopher Jones, master of the Pilgrim ship *The Mayflower*, lived in Harwich (the latter just off the quay in King's Head Street), as did Jones' kinsman John Alden, who sailed to America in 1620. The famous diarist Samuel Pepys was MP

for the town in the 1660s, when it was the headquarters of the King's Navy. Charles II took the first pleasure cruise from Harwich's shores, and other notable visitors included Lord Nelson and Lady Hamilton, who are reputed to have stayed at The Three Cups in Church Street.

Harwich remains popular as a vantage point for watching incoming and outgoing shipping in the harbour and across the waters to Felixstowe. Nowadays, lightships, buoys and miles of strong chain are stored along the front, and passengers arriving on North Sea ferries at Harwich International Port see the 90-foot high, six-sided **High Lighthouse** as the first landmark. Now housing the **National Vintage Wireless and Television Museum**, it was built in 1818 along with the **Low Lighthouse**. When the two lighthouses were in line they could indicate a safe shipping channel into the harbour. The Low lighthouse is now the town's **Maritime Museum**, with specialist displays on the Royal Navy and commercial shipping.

Two other museums in the town are the **Lifeboat Museum** off Wellington Road, which contains the last Clacton offshore 34-foot lifeboat and a history of the lifeboat service in Harwich, and the **Ha'penny Pier Visitor Centre** on the Quay, with information on everything in Harwich and a small heritage exhibition.

Another fascinating piece of the town's history is the **Electric Palace Cinema**, built in 1911 and now the

High Lighthouse, Harwich

oldest unaltered purpose-built cinema in Britain. It was restored by a trust and re-opened in 1981.

The importance of Harwich's port during the 19th century is confirmed by **The Redoubt**, a huge grey fort built between 1808 and 1810. Its design is an enlarged version of the Martello towers which dotted the English coast, awaiting a Napoleonic invasion that never came.

HATFIELD BROAD OAK

This very pretty village has many notable buildings for visitors to enjoy, including a church dating from Norman times, some delightful 18th century almshouses and several distinctive Georgian houses.

Nearby **Hatfield Forest** is a rare surviving example of a medieval Royal hunting forest. It has wonderful 400-year-old pollarded trees, two ornamental lakes and an 18th century shell house. The remaining 400 hectares are now protected by the National Trust and offer splendid woodland walks.

KELVEDON HATCH

A bungalow in the rural Essex village of Kelvedon Hatch is the deceptively simple exterior for the **Kelvedon Hatch Secret Nuclear Bunker**.

Built in 1952, it took 40,000 tons of concrete to create a base some 80 feet underground for up to 600 top Government and civilian personnel in the event of nuclear war. Visitors can explore room after room to see

communications equipment, a BBC studio, sick bay, massive kitchens and dormitories, power and filtration plant, government administration room and the scientists' room, where nuclear fall-out patterns would have been measured.

LAYER MARNEY

The mansion, which was planned to rival Hampton Court, was never completed, but its massive 8-storey Tudor gatehouse, known as **Layer Marney Tower**, is very impressive. Built between 1515 and 1525, it is one of the most striking examples of 16th century architecture in Britain. Its magnificent four red brick towers, covered in 16th century Italianate design, were built by Lord Marney, Henry VIII's Lord Privy Seal. They are surrounded by formal gardens designed at the turn of the century, with lovely roses, yew hedges and herbaceous borders. There is also on site a rare breeds farm, farm shop and tea room.

MALDON

Maldon's High Street has existed since medieval times, and the alleys and mews leading from it are full of intriguing shops, welcoming old inns and good places to eat. One of the most distinctive features of the High Street is the **Moot Hall**. Built in the 14th century for the D'Arcy family, this building passed into the hands of the town corporation and was the seat of power in Maldon for over 400 years. A few minutes' walk down one of the small roads leading from the High

Maldon Basin

Street brings you to the waterfront, where the old wharves and quays are still active. Moored at **Hythe Quay** are several Thames sailing barges, all over 100 years old and still boasting their traditional rigging and distinctive tan-coloured sails.

MANNINGTREE

The Walls, on the approach to Manningtree along the B1352, offer unrivalled views of the Stour estuary and the Suffolk coast, and the swans for which the area is famous. Lying on the River Stour amid beautiful rolling countryside, the scene has often been depicted by artists over the centuries.

Manningtree has been a market town since 1238, and is still a busy shopping centre. The smallest town in Britain, it has an intriguing past - as a river crossing, market, smugglers' haven and home of Matthew Hopkins, the reviled and self-styled Witchfinder General who struck terror into the local community

during the 17th century. Some of his victims were hanged on Manningtree's small village green.

Manningtree Museum in the High Street mounts two exhibitions a year, together with permanent photographs and pieces relating to the heritage of Manningtree, Lawford, Mistley and the district.

MERSEA ISLAND

Much of this island is a **National Nature Reserve**, home to its teeming shorelife. The island is linked to the mainland by a narrow causeway which is covered over at high tide. The towns of both East and West Mersea have excellent facilities for sailing enthusiasts. East Mersea is also a haven for birdwatchers, and West Mersea has long been a centre of the oyster industry.

MISTLEY

Here at the gateway to Constable Country, local 18th century landowner and MP Richard Rigby had grand designs to develop Mistley into a fashionable spa to rival Harrogate and Bath, adopting the swan as its symbol. Sadly, all that remains of Rigby's ambitious scheme is the Swan Fountain, a small number of attractive Georgian houses and **Mistley**

Towers, the remains of a church (otherwise demolished in 1870) designed by the flamboyant architect Robert Adams. From the waterfront, noted for its colony of swans, there are very pleasant views across the estuary to Suffolk.

Mistley Place Park Environmental & Animal Rescue Centre is 25 acres of parkland affording country walks, wildlife habitats, lake, farm animals and great views across the Stour Estuary. Over 2,000 rescued animals including rabbits, Vietnamese pigs and horses roam free.

MOUNTNESSING

This village has a beautifully restored early 19th century windmill as its main landmark, though the isolated church also has a massive beamed belfry. **Mountnessing Post Mill** was built in 1807 and restored to working order in 1983. Visitors can see the huge wooden and iron gears, and one pair of stones has been opened up for viewing.

NORTH WEALD

North Weald Airfield Museum and Memorial at Ad Astra House, Hurricane Way, North Weald Bassett is a small, meticulously detailed 'House of Memories' displaying the history of the famous airfield and all who served at RAF North Weald from 1916 to the present. Collections of photos and artefacts such as uniforms and the detailed records of all flying operations are on display.

POINT CLEAR

The **East Essex Aviation Society & Museum**, located in the Martello Tower at Point Clear, not only retains its original flooring and roof, but today contains interesting displays of wartime aviation, military and naval photographs, uniforms and other memorabilia with local and US Air Force connections. There are artefacts on show from the crash sites of wartime aircraft in the Tendring area, including the engine and fuselage section of a recovered P51D Mustang fighter. The museum also explores civil and military history from both World Wars.

SAFFRON WALDEN

Named after the Saffron crocus - grown in the area to make dyestuffs and fulfil a variety of other uses in the Middle Ages - Saffron Walden has retained much of its original street plan, as well as hundreds of fine old buildings, many of which are timbered and have overhanging upper floors and decorative plastering (known as pargeting). Gog and Magog (or, in some versions, folk-hero Tom Hickathrift and the Wisbech Giant) battle forever in plaster on the gable of the **Old Sun Inn**, where, legend has it, Oliver Cromwell and General Fairfax both lodged during the Civil War.

A typical market town, Saffron Walden's centrepiece is its magnificent church. **Saffron Walden Museum** was founded 'to gratify the inclination of all

Saffron Walden

was born in 1644. He is said to have held 'lighthouse trials' with a wooden lantern in the lavishly decorated 15th to 16th century church. The Lighthouse, and Winstanley with it, were swept away in a fierce storm in 1703.

To the north of the town are the **Bridge End Gardens**, a wonderfully restored example of early Victorian gardens, and the **Fry Public Art Gallery**, with a unique collection of work by 20th century artists and designers who lived in and around Saffron Walden. It also exhibits work by contemporary artists working in Essex today, demonstrating the area's continuing artistic tradition. Close to Bridge End is the **Anglo-American War Memorial** dedicated by Field Marshal the Viscount Montgomery of Alamein in 1953 to the memory of all the American flyers of the 65th Fighter

who value natural history'. It remains faithful to this credo, while widening the museum's scope in the ensuing years. Visitors can try their hand at corn grinding with a Romano-British quern, see how a medieval timber house would have been built, admire the displays of Native American and West African embroidery, and come face to face with Wallace the Lion, the museum's faithful guardian. On the local **Common**, once known as Castle Green, is the largest surviving Turf Maze in England. Only eight ancient turf mazes survive in England of the many that were constructed in the Middle Ages, and this one is believed to be some 800 years old.

Though many miles from the sea, it was here that Henry Winstanley - inventor, engineer and engraver, and designer of the first Eddystone Lighthouse at Plymouth -

Audley End House, Saffron Walden

Wing who lost their lives in the Second World War.

Audley End House was at one time the residence of the first Earl of Suffolk, and at one time home of Charles II. The original early 17th century house, with its two large courtyards, had a magnificence claimed to match that of Hampton Court. It was remodelled in the 18th century by Robert Adam, but unfortunately the subsequent earls lacked their forebears' financial acumen, and much of the house was demolished as it fell into disrepair. Nevertheless it remains today one of England's most impressive Jacobean mansions, its distinguished stone facade set off perfectly by Capability Brown's lake. The remaining state rooms retain their palatial magnificence and the exquisite state bed in the Neville Room is hung with the original embroidered drapes. The silver, the Dolls House, the Jacobean Screen and Robert Adam's painted Drawing Room are just among the many sights to marvel at, and the natural history collection features more than 1,000 stuffed animals and birds. There are paintings by Holbein, Lely and Canaletto, and this jewel also has a kitchen garden and grounds landscaped by Capability Brown, including the 'Temple of Concord' which Brown dedicated to George III. The Audley End Miniature Railway takes visitors through the beautiful private woods of the house.

Within the rolling parkland of the grounds there are several elegant outbuildings, some of which were designed by Robert Adam. Among these are an icehouse, a circular temple and a Springwood Column.

SOUTHEND-ON-SEA

The town is one of the best loved resorts in Britain, with miles of beaches and all the ingredients for a fun break by the sea. **Southend Pier and Museum** brings to life the fascinating past of the longest Pleasure Pier in the world. The Pier itself is 1.33 miles long; visitors can either take a leisurely walk along its length or take advantage of the regular train service.

Central Museum, Planetarium and Discovery Centre on Victoria Avenue is the only planetarium in the southeast outside London, and also features local history exhibits, archaeology and wildlife exhibits. **Beecroft Art Gallery** boasts

Beach, Southend-on-Sea

Seafront, Southend-on-Sea

the work of four centuries of artistic endeavour, with some 2,000 works including those by Lear, Molenaer, Seago and Constable.

Sealife Adventure employs the most advanced technology to close the wonders of British marine life, with concave bubble windows helping to make it seem that visitors are actually part of the sea-creatures' environment. Another exhibit features a walk-through tunnel along a reconstructed seabed, and the Shark Exhibition is not to be missed.

Prittlewell Priory Museum, slightly north of Southend town centre in Priory Park, is a well-preserved 12th century Cluniac Priory set in lovely grounds and housing collections of the Priory's history, natural history and the Caten collection of radios and communications equipment.

ST OSYTH

This pretty little village has a fascinating history and centres around its Norman church and the ancient ruins of **St Osyth Priory**, founded in the 12th century. The village and Priory were named by Augustinian Canons after St Osytha, martyred daughter of Frithenwald, first Christian King of the East Angles. Little of the original Priory remains, except for the magnificent late 15th century flint gatehouse, complete with battlements.

STANSTED MOUNTFITCHET

Though rather close to **Stansted Airport**, there are plenty of reasons to visit this village. Certainly pilots approaching the airport may be surprised at the sight of a **Norman Village**, complete with domestic animals and the reconstructed motte-and-bailey **Mountfitchet Castle**, standing just two miles from the end of the runway. The original castle was built after 1066 by the Duke of Boulogne, a cousin of the Conqueror. Siege weapons on show include two giant catapults. Next to the castle is **The House on the Hill Museum Adventure**, where there are three museums for the price of one. The Toy Museum is the largest of its kind in the world, and the Rock 'n' Roll, Film and Theatre Experience and the End-of-the-pier Amusement machine contribute to a grand day out in Stansted Mountfitchet.

Stansted Windmill is one of the best-preserved tower mills in the country. It dates from 1787, and most of the original machinery has survived.

THAXTED

Thaxted has a recorded history that dates back to before the *Domesday Book*, and its many beautiful old buildings contribute to its unique character and charm. It has numerous attractively pargeted and timber-framed houses, and a magnificent **Guildhall**, built as a meeting-place for cutlers around 1390. The demise of the cutlery industry in this part of Essex in the 1500s led it to becoming the administrative centre of the town. Restored in Georgian times, it became the town's Grammar School, as well as remaining a centre of administration.

The town's famous **Tower Windmill** was built in 1804 by John Webb. In working order until 1907, it had fallen into disuse and disrepair but has now been returned to full working order. It contains a rural life museum, and is well worth a visit.

Thaxted Church, which stands on a hill and soars cathedral-like over the town's streets, has been described as the finest Parish church in the country.

The composer Gustav Holst lived in Thaxted from 1914 to 1925, and often played the church organ. To celebrate his connection with the town there is a month-long music festival in late June/early July that attracts performers of international repute.

In Park Street, the **Thaxted Garden for Butterflies** has been developed with a view to pleasing birds, butterflies and other wildlife species - including humans. Displays depict the 22 native wild butterfly species that have visited the garden since its inception in 1988.

TILBURY

Tilbury Fort is a well-preserved and unusual 17th century structure with a double moat. The largest and best example of military engineering in England at that time, the fort also affords tremendous views of the Thames estuary. For a small fee visitors to the fort can fire a 1943 3.7mm anti-aircraft gun - a prospect most children and many adults find irresistible! Owned by English Heritage, the site was used for a military blockhouse during the reign of Henry VIII and was rebuilt in the 17th century. It remains one of Britain's finest examples of a star-shaped bastion

Morris Dancers, Thaxted

fortress. Extensions were made in the 18th and 19th centuries, and the Fort was still in active use in the Second World War.

WALTHAM ABBEY

The town of Waltham began as a small Roman settlement on the site of the present-day Market Square. The early Saxon kings maintained a hunting lodge here; a town formed round this, and the first church was built in the 6th century. By the 8th century, the town had a stone minster church with a great stone crucifix that had been brought from Somerset, were it had been found buried in land owned by Tovi, a trusted servant of the king. This cross became the focus of pilgrims seeking healing. One of those cured of a serious illness, Harold Godwinsson, built a new church, the third on the site, which was dedicated in 1060 - and it was this self-same Harold who became king and was killed in the Battle of Hastings six years later. Harold's body was brought back to Waltham to be buried in his church. The church that exists today was built in the first quarter of the 12th century, and incorporated an Augustinian Abbey. The town became known for the Abbey, which was one of the largest in the country and the last to be the victim of Henry VIII's Dissolution of the Monasteries, in 1540. Some remains of the Abbey are still visible, and the Crypt Centre houses an interesting exhibition explaining the history of both the Abbey

and the town, highlighting the religious significance of the site.

Along the Cornhill Stream, crossed by the impressive stone bridge, the town's **Dragonfly Sanctuary** is home to over half the native British species of dragonflies and damselflies.

A Tudor timber-framed house forms part of the **Epping Forest District Museum** in Sun Street. The wide range of displays includes exhibits covering the history of the Epping Forest District from the Stone Age to the present time. Tudor and Victorian times are particularly well represented, with some magnificent oak panelling dating from the reign of Henry VIII, and re-creations of Victorian rooms and shops. The Greenwich Meridian (0 degrees longitude) runs through Sun Street, marked out on the pavement and through the Abbey Gardens.

To the west of town, the **Lee Navigation Canal** offers opportunities for anglers, walkers, birdwatching and pleasure craft. Once used for transporting corn and other commercial goods to the growing City of London, and having associations with the town's important gunpowder industry for centuries, the canal remains a vital part of town life.

Gunpowder production became established in Waltham as early as the 1660s; by the 19th century the **Royal Gunpowder Mills** employed 500 workers, and production did not cease until 1943, after which time the factory became a research facility. In the spring of 2000, however, all this changed and the site was opened to the public for the

Epping Forest

first time. Of the 175 acres the site occupies, approximately 80 have been designated a Site of Special Scientific Interest, and two-thirds of the site is a Scheduled Ancient Monument, with many listed buildings, some of which date from the Napoleonic Wars.

Lee Valley Regional Park is a leisure area stretching for 26 miles along the River Lea (sometimes also spelled Lee) from East India Dock Basin, on the north bank of the River Thames in East London, to Hertfordshire. The Lee Valley is an important area of high biodiversity, sustaining a large range of wildlife and birds.

At the southern end of Lee Valley Park, **The House Mill**, one of two tidal mills still standing at this site, has been restored by the River Lea Tidal Mill Trust. It was built in 1776 in the Dutch style, and was used to grind grain for gin distilling.

Lee Valley Park Farms are two in number, **Hayes Hill** and **Holyfield Hall**. At Hayes Hill Farm, visitors can interact with the animals and enjoy a picnic or the children's adventure playground. This traditional farm also boasts old-fashioned tools and equipment, an exhibition in the medieval barn and occasional craft demonstrations. Holyfield Hall Farm is a working farm and dairy where visitors can see milking and learn about modern farming methods. Seasonal events such as sheep-shearing and harvesting are held, and there's an attractive farm tea room and a toy shop.

Myddleton House Gardens within Lee Valley Park is the place to see the work of the famous plantsman who created them - E A Bowles, the greatest amateur gardener of his time. Breathtaking colours and interesting plantings - such as the National Collection of award-winning bearded iris, the Tulip Terrace and the Lunatic Asylum (home to unusual plants) - are offset by a beautiful carp lake, two conservatories and a rock garden.

WALTON-ON-THE-NAZE

Walton-on-the-Naze is a traditional, cheerful resort with a good sandy beach, colourful gardens and a pier with all the usual seaside attractions. **The Backwaters** to the rear of Walton are made up of a series of small harbours and saltings, which lead into Harwich harbour. **The Pier**, first built in 1830, was originally constructed of wood and measured 330 feet long. It was extended to its present length of 2,610 feet in 1898, at the same time as the electric train service began.

The wind-blown expanse of **The Naze** just north of Walton is an extensive coastal recreation and picnic area, pleasant for walking, especially out of season when the visitor is likely to have the 150 acres all alone, with great views out over the water. The shape of the Naze is constantly changing, eroded by wind, water and tide. The octagonal brick-built **Naze Tower** was originally constructed as a beacon in 1720 to warn seamen of the West Rocks off shore. A nature trail has been created nearby, and the Essex Skipper butterfly and Emperor moth can be seen here.

The **Old Lifeboat House Museum** at East Terrace, in a building over 100 years old, houses an interpretive museum of local history and development, rural and maritime, covering Walton, Frinton and the Sokens.

Marina, Walton-on-the-Naze

WEST THURROCK

Immortalised by the film *Four Weddings and a Funeral*, little **St Clement's Church** occupies a striking location and is one of a number of picturesque ancient churches in the borough. Although this 12th century church is now deconsecrated, it was in its day a stopping point for pilgrims; visitors can see the remains of its original round tower. There is also a mass grave to the boys of the reformatory ship *Cornwall* who were drowned in an accident off Purfleet.

WIVENHOE

This riverside town on the banks of the River Colne was once renowned as a smugglers' haunt, and has a very pretty quayside that is steeped in maritime history.

The Wivenhoe Trail, by the river, is an interesting cycle track starting at the railway station and continuing along the river to Colchester Hythe. **Wivenhoe Woods** is dotted with grassy glades set with tables, the perfect place for a picnic.

East of the Quay, the public footpath takes visitors to the **Tidal Surge Barrier**, one of only two in the country. Volunteers run a ferry service operating across the River Colne between the Quay at Wivenhoe, Fingringhoe and Rowhedge. Nearby Wivenhoe Park has been the site of the campus for the University of Essex since 1962.

THE CHERRY TREE

STAMBRIDGE ROAD, ROCHFORD, ESSEX SS4 2AF
TEL/FAX: 01702 544426

> **Directions:** The inn is on the east side of Rochford, which is located about 3 miles north of Southend and the A127.

The Cherry Tree is a friendly, welcoming 18th century pub on the eastern side of Rochford, with a strong local following, both for its ambience and for its excellent food and drink. The

whitewashed facade is adorned in spring and summer with masses of flowers, and at one side of the main building is an attractive conservatory. At the back are a garden and an aviary, with countryside all around, and a barn is being converted to provide five en suite Bed & Breakfast rooms for 2005.

Freshly cooked meals are served every day, with local suppliers providing many of the ingredients, including a constantly changing selection of fish and shellfish.

There's a separate menu for children, and always a good choice for vegetarians. Two cask ales – Greene King IPA and Adnams Broadside – are joined by a guest ale or two, and the pub keeps a good choice of well-chosen wines.

When the bedrooms come on stream the Cherry Tree will be a good base for enjoying the various activities the area has to offer, including walks with sea views, golf, sailing and birdwatching. All the fun of the fair is available at nearby Southend-on-Sea, and the pub will provide a particularly convenient stopover for anyone flying to or from Southend Airport.

Mine hosts at the Cherry Tree are Tina and Colin Oliver, from a family long associated with owning pubs and restaurants.

- 12-3 & 7-11 (Sun to 10.30)
- Home cooking
- Major cards accepted
- 5 en suite rooms for 2005
- Car park, garden, children's play area
- Southend 3 miles

THE COCK INN

HATFIELD BROAD OAK, NR BISHOP'S STORTFORD,
HERTFORDSHIRE CM22 7HF
TEL/FAX: 01279 718306

Essex

> **Directions:** Hatfield Broad Oak lies 1 mile north of the A1060 at Hatfield Heath; 5 miles southwest of Great Dunmow on the B183.

The Cock Inn is a fine old redbrick building on the main street of Hatfield Broad Oak, a pretty village with a number of interesting old buildings. The oldest parts of the inn date back to the 17th century, and the interior has a very inviting, traditional appeal. David Sulway and Pam Holcroft have owned

and personally run the inn since 1994; they have been in the licensed trade in Essex, Kent and London for 30 years, and their experience and expertise have made The Cock Inn one of the best-known and best-loved hostelries in the area. Four real ales – Adnams Best, London Pride and two guests – are on tap in the bar, and top-quality food is served every session except Sunday evening.

David's regular trips to the London markets ensure that the very best ingredients go into the kitchen, and what comes out is some of the best pub cooking for miles around. Fish and seafood dishes are a speciality, with cod, salmon, battered calamari rings and Thai-style crab cakes among the favourites, but there's plenty more besides, with the likes of deep-fried jalapeno peppers stuffed with cream cheese, sausages with mash and onion gravy, moussaka and Tuscan bean bake satisfying for a wide variety of preferences. A private room seating up to 16 is available for parties and functions, and the enterprising owners also offer an outside catering service. Nearby Hatfield Forest, a rare surviving example of a royal hunting forest, is a perfect place to work up an appetite that can be satisfied in style at the Cock Inn.

- 🕐 12-3 & 5.30-11
- 🍴 Home cooking – many fish specialities
- 💷 Not Amex
- 🅿 Car park, patio, function room
- ❓ Hatfield Forest 1 mile, Aythorpe Roding 3 miles, Bishop's Stortford 5 miles, Great Dunmow 5 miles

THE COCK TAVERN

218 HIGH STREET, CHIPPING ONGAR, ESSEX CM5 9AB
TEL: 01277 362615

> **Directions:** The inn stands on the main street of Ongar, just off the A414.

For long a landmark on the main street of Ongar, the **Cock Tavern** is a very distinctive building. Inside, black beams and a feature brick fireplace take the eye, and there are plenty of comfortable bar stools and chairs for relaxing with a drink. Tenants Ian and Mary Goodman are very experienced licensees; Ian has been in the business all his working life and is a past chairman of the Licensed Victuallers Association. They know exactly what their customers want from their local and they provide it in abundance. Four real ales are always available, with Greene King IPA a permanent presence; the three guest ales change very frequently, so lucky regular customers can sample anything between 12 and 15 brews in a month!

Food is also taken very seriously at the

Cock Tavern, and hot and cold bar snacks and meals are served daily from the printed menu and the specials board, with roasts added to the choice on a Sunday. Those who appreciate hearty home cooking, generously served at kind prices, come from miles around to enjoy Ian's home-made pies – leek & chicken, steak & ale – and the likes of bacon & onion roll, beef and vegetable pasties, beef stews and chicken casseroles, or bubble & squeak with ham and eggs. A good appetite is needed to best appreciate these hearty, flavour-packed dishes, and a brisk walk round the sights of Ongar will help to generate it: only a mound and a moat remain of the Norman castle, but the ancient Church of St Mrtins still stands, and there are several other interesting buildings, some dating from Elizabethan times.

- 🕐 11-11, Sunday 12-10.30
- 🍴 Home cooking (pies a speciality)
- 💷 Major cards accepted
- 🅿 Car park, function room
- @ e-mail: thecocktavernph@hotmail.com website: www.thecocktavernongar.co.uk
- ❓ Blake Hall Gardens 2 miles, Fyfield Hall 2 miles, Willingale 3 miles, Kelvedon Hatch 4 miles

THE DUCK INN

NEWNEY GREEN, WRITTLE, NR CHELMSFORD, ESSEX CM1 3SF
TEL: 01245 421894 FAX: 01245 420855

Directions: Newney Green is reached from the A414 or the A1060 about 3 miles west of Chelmsford

Hardworking host and chef Simon Edwards sets great store by the quality of the freshness of the food he serves at **The Duck Inn**, and he has made his 18th century hostelry one of the most popular and successful destination pub restaurants in the region. Everything is prepared and cooked on the premises, even the ice cream, and the chalkboard menus always offer plenty of choice for diners in the roomy restaurant. Simon's signature duck dishes are famed far and wide, whether in a starter of rillettes or an elaborate, often exotic main course such as roasted breast with a filling of mango, chilli and tarragon, served with grated beetroot and a peach liqueur sauce. Other choices could include moules marinière, pork & thyme terrine, grilled fillet of plaice, mushroom and blue cheese ravioli, Cajun-spiced sausages and beef stroganoff. Food is served lunchtime and evening seven days a week, and booking is recommended at the weekend.

The fine cooking is complemented by a strong wine list that runs to more than 80 choices; for those who prefer ale there are three on tap from the Shepherd Neame Brewery – Masterbrew, Spitfire and Best Bitter. The inn itself is a classic of its kind, with a terrific ambience that comes not only from the host and the regulars but also from the superb period decor and furnishings. Outside is a garden with lawns, a pond and a children's play area. Simon also owns and runs The Keys, a contemporary-style hotel and restaurant located in Boyton Cross, 2 miles from the Duck Inn.

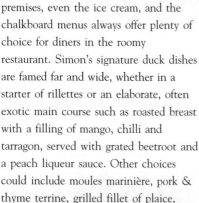

- 🕐 12-3 & 6-11
- 🍴 Home cooking
- £ Not Amex or Diners
- Ⓟ Car park
- @ e-mail: theduckwrittle@aol.com
  website: www.theduckwrittle.co.uk
- ❓ Writtle 1 mile, Chelmsford 3 miles

THE STREET, HATFIELD PEVEREL, NR CHELMSFORD, ESSEX CM3 2EA
TEL: 01245 380246

Directions: Hatfield Peverel is situated at the junction of the B1137 and B1019, right by the A12.

The Duke of Wellington is a traditional coaching inn, tasteful and welcoming, cosy and comfortable, with several original 18th century features. Charlie and Vivian Little, who took over in 2001 and have more than 20 years experience in the pub and hotel businesses, have created a really delightful ambience for enjoying a drink and a snack, or to sit down to a leisurely full meal. Head chef Jane, who was with the Littles at their previous pubs and hotels, has won several awards for her excellent cooking. She prepares a wide selection of dishes which can be taken in any of the beamed bar areas or in the 60-cover non-smoking restaurant. Locally

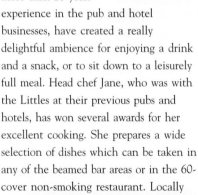

- 11-2.30 & 6-9.30 (Sun 12-8)
- Bar and à la carte menus
- Major cards accepted
- Car park
- Darts, golf society, quiz nights
- Witham 2 miles, Maldon 5 miles, Chelmsford 6 miles

brewed Ridleys ales are kept in tip-top condition, and there's a good selection of wines to complement a meal.

Families are welcome at the Duke of Wellington, and the large garden has an area where children can play in safety. The game of darts is taken very seriously here, and some of the top professional players are to be seen on the oche; the inn also hosts regular quiz nights and runs a golfing society. Hatfield Peverel lies at the junction of the B1137 (the old Roman road) and the B1019, almost alongside the A12, which now bypasses the village. Chelmsford is a short drive in the direction of London, Witham is just minutes away, and Maldon and the Blackwater estuary are easily reached along the B1019.

THE FLITCH OF BACON

THE STREET, LITTLE DUNMOW, NR GREAT DUNMOW, ESSEX CM6 3HT
TEL/FAX: 01371 820323

Directions: The inn lies in the village of Little Dunmow, 2 miles east of Great Dunmow immediately south of the A120.

On the main street of Little Dunmow, **The Flitch of Bacon** takes its name from the ancient ceremony that dates back as far as the early 12th century. The pub itself was built in the late 18th century, and in the summer of 2004 it welcomed new licensees Neil and Theresa Bacon. This is their first venture into the licensed trade, and they are enjoying the challenge of getting to know the locals and to expand their business. Behind the black-and-white frontage, with red-tiled roof and tall brick chimneys, the bar is warm and inviting, a very pleasant spot to relax with a drink and a chat. In the bar or in the restaurant at the back, diners can tuck into 'proper' pub food such as steaks, steak & kidney pie, bangers & mash and curries. Sandwiches, baguettes and jacket potatoes are available for lighter or

quicker snacks.

Upstairs are two en suite letting bedrooms, making the Flitch a comfortable, well-placed choice for an overnight or longer stay, whether on business or enjoying a leisurely tour of the area. The first port of call on any tour must be Little Dunmow's Church of St Mary, where in the chancel stands the Flitch Chair that was once used in the annual ceremony to find a local couple who married in church and managed to live for a year and a day without quarrelling or regretting their marriage. Their reward was a flitch – or side – of bacon. The ceremony, which has been consigned to history more than once, is currently celebrated every leap year in nearby Great Dunmow, which has several places of historical interest for the visitor.

- 🕐 12-3 & 5.30-11 (Sun 12-5 & 7-10.30); closed Monday lunchtime
- 🍴 Pub snacks and meals
- 💷 Major cards accepted
- 🛏 2 en suite bedrooms
- Ⓟ Beer garden
- ❓ Little Dunmow Church (Flitch Chair); Great Dunmow 2 miles

THE FOX INN

EAST ROAD, WEST MERSEA, ESSEX CO5 8SA
TEL: 01206 383391

> **Directions:** West Mersea lies on the southwestern end of Mersea Island, on the B1025 8 miles south of Colchester.

The Fox Inn is a fine cream-painted building dating back to the 17th century, with an extension that was added in the 1970s. It is situated in West Mersea on the eastern end of the island of Mersea and is reached by a narrow causeway (the B1025) that is covered over at high tide. Black beams aplenty and log fires add to the traditional feel in the carpeted dining areas and comfortable lounge, where Greene King IPA and two cask ales from the local Maldon Brewery are always on tap. There's a more modern look in the games room, where pool and darts are played by the regulars, and the Fox plays host to live music evenings every six weeks.

The Jowers family, well-known local farmers, took over the licence at The Fox in April 2004, and excellent steaks from their beef herd have quickly become one of the favourite dishes on the menu of home-cooked dishes served every lunchtime and Thursday to Saturday evenings. Daily specials supplement the printed menu, and the enjoyment level stays high to the end with some delicious home-made puddings. A site for touring caravans, with electrical hook-ups, is available nearby, a convenient base for exploring the island. Much of it is a National Nature Reserve, and the whole island offers great scope for birdwatching and bracing walks. Both East and West Mersea are popular sailing centres, and the latter is a famous centre of the oyster industry. From many points on the south coast of the island there are fine views across the Colne and Blackwater estuaries. Colchester is an easy drive up the B1025, and other places of interest on the mainland include Brightlingsea and Layer Marney.

- 🕐 11.30-11
- 🍴 Home cooking
- 💷 All the major cards
- 🅿 Car park
- 🎵 Live bands every 6 weeks, games room
- ❓ Cudmore Grove Country Park at East Mersea 3 miles, Colchester 8 miles

THE GREEN MAN

THE STREET, GOSFIELD, NR HALSTEAD, ESSEX CO9 1TP
TEL: 01787 472746

Directions: Gosfield lies on the A1017 about halfway between Braintree andSible Hedingham.

The Green Man (spot the jolly fellow on the sign) stands on a prominent corner site in the village of Gosfield, on the A1017 between Sible Hedingham and Braintree and a short distance west of the historic town of Halstead. The pub changed hands in October 2004, and the new tenants Debbie and Tony soon set

about refurbishing the interior. They also acquired the services of an excellent chef Mark Keenan, and the three of them expect to put the Green Man firmly among the top eating places in the district. The printed menu and daily changing blackboard specials put the emphasis on good fresh produce, the basis of a wide variety of dishes catering for all tastes. Those who like their pub food to be classic and traditional will enjoy the cod in beer batter, the home-made sausages, the fish pie and the steak

& kidney pudding, while the more adventurous might go for the chargrilled Mediterranean vegetables with toasted goat's cheese, the king prawns in filo pastry or a fragrantly subtle Thai curry.

There's a decent wine list to accompany the food, including several available by the glass. The pub has two cheerful little bars, where three cask ales are always available, and a beer garden at the back that's a pleasant spot for a drink in the summer. With plenty to see and do in the vicinity, the Green Man is a very pleasant place to pause on a tour of the towns and countryside. Halstead, Braintree and Sible Hedingham all have their own individual appeal, and Gosfield itself boasts the county's largest freshwater lake, now the Gosfield Lake Leisure Resort, in the grounds of a country mansion that belonged to the Courtauld family.

- 🕐 12·3 & 6·11
- 🍴 Home cooking
- 💷 Not Diners
- 🅿 Car park, beer garden
- @ website:
  www.thegreenmangosfield.co.uk
- ❓ Braintree 4 miles, Halstead 3 miles, Sible Hedingham 4 miles

THE GREEN MAN

KELVEDON ROAD, LITTLE BRAXTED, NR WITHAM, ESSEX CM8 3LB
TEL: 01621 891659

> **Directions:** Little Braxted is northeast of Chelmsford, signposted off the A12 after the Witham bypass on the B1389. Follow the small country lane for 2 miles, turn right at the 'T' junction and proceed for a further 500 yards.

Neil Pharaoh and Amanda Yelland were regular customers of the **Green Man** before taking over the licence in 2002. This exceptional 18th century country inn overlooking the green in the village of Little Braxted is a very civilised, relaxing spot. Behind the cream-painted, slate-roofed frontage, an interesting assortment of memorabilia adorns the walls, including carpenter's tools, horse brasses and artefacts associated with the Royal Marines. In the public bar, warmed by a wood-burning stove, are old photographs of the inn down the years and a collection of model cars in glass display cases. This is a Ridleys inn and is well known for the excellent condition of its ales, including IPA (3.5%ABV), Rumpus (4.5%) and Old Bob (5.1%).

The inn also keeps a good selection of wines to enjoy on their own or to accompany the home-cooked food that is served from 12 to 2 and 7 to 9 every day. Fresh produce, much of it local, is handled with skill to create generously served dishes such as the very popular steak & ale pie or braised lamb shanks – the meat, from a local butcher, is always top-quality, and the Sunday roasts are guaranteed to bring in the crowds. The menu always has a good choice for vegetarians, and home-made sweets such as treacle tart or bread & butter pudding followed by excellent coffee round things off in style. Meals are served throughout the pub or in the lovely tree-fringed garden, which has flower beds, a lawn and a pretty pond (families with children under 14 are allowed but only in the garden). The village itself has been a frequent winner or runner-up in the Best Kept Essex Village awards for the past 30 years.

- 🕐 11.30-3 & 6-11 (Sun 12-3.30 & 7-10.30)
- 🍴 Bar menu & daily specials board
- 💷 Visa, Mastercard
- 🅿 Car park, garden
- 🎵 Quiz nights held on first Sunday of the month throughout winter
- ❓ Birdwatching, golf; Little Braxted Church of St Nicholas; Maldon 4 miles, Witham 3 miles, Hatfield Peverel 3 miles, Kelvedon 4 miles, Cressing Temple Barns 4 miles

THE HARE

ROXWELL, NR CHELMSFORD, ESSEX CM1 4LU
TEL: 01245 248214

Directions: Roxwell lies about 3 miles west of Chelmsford on the A1060.

Once the Hare & Hounds, now just **The Hare**, this splendid 18th century inn stands back from the A1060 about 3 miles west of Chelmsford. Experienced leaseholders Peter and Ilona Sanderson took over in 2003, and with their head chef Diana have made this a very popular eating place, a destination restaurant for the local villagers, for the residents of Chelmsford and for a wider–flung clientele who have heard all the excellent reports. Behind the immaculate, long, white-painted frontage, the bars have a pleasantly contemporary rustic feel, and the garden has a safe area where children can play. Three real ales, including a regularly changing guest, are always available, and Diana's excellent dishes are served every lunchtime and evening in the spacious restaurant overlooking the River Can.

The restaurant has a large non-smoking section. The printed menu and the specials combine old favourites such as prawn cocktail, grilled trout or pepper steak with dishes not usually seen on pub menus: chicken liver and bacon salad; mozzarella, sun-dried tomato and basil in filo pastry; spicy red snapper; loin of pork with a honey and mustard glaze; and for vegetarians, cheesy pudding with a coarse tomato compote. Thursday is fish day, and it's best to book on Saturday and Sunday to be sure of a table.

Though close to big, bustling Chelmsford, this delightful inn has a real feel of the country, and its winning combination of rural charm, riverside setting and cooking that would grace a high-grade restaurant should ensure that the Hare will keep running for many years to come.

🕐 12-3 & 6-11 (all day Bank Holidays)

🍴 Home cooking

💷 Not Amex or Diners

🅿 Car park, riverside garden

@ e-mail: thehare@btclick.com
website: www.thehareroxwell.co.uk

❓ Chelmsford 3 miles

THE HOPE INN

HIGH STREET, TOLLESBURY, ESSEX CM9 8RG
TEL: 01621 869238

> **Directions:** The Hope Inn is situated on the main street of Tollesbury, 9 miles northeast of Maldon on the B1023.

New owners Dutchman Abraham Mooij and his wife have settled in well since taking over the **Hope Inn** in the spring of 2004. Behind the smart red-and-white brick-and-stone frontage they have made several major improvements, including a top-to-toe redecoration programme and taking the food up-market to appeal to a broader clientele. The public bar has been converted into a non-smoking restaurant, where the new French chef is showing his skills on a menu that caters for traditional and more contemporary tastes. Flying the flag for classic pub cuisine are ploughman's platters, ham & eggs, steaks and the Sunday roast, while warm chicken liver salad with raspberry vinaigrette and a cold meat platter with parma ham, pancetta and chorizo add a continental touch. Children's portions are available of all dishes.

Good food deserves good wine, and Abraham certainly knows his wines: the well-annotated list is predominantly French, and house wine can be ordered by the glass and two sizes of carafe. The Hope's accommodation has also been improved, with all the bedrooms recently modernised and two with en suite facilities. The marshland village of Tollesbury lies at the end of the B1023, at the mouth of the River Blackwater, and is a mecca for sailing enthusiasts. The marina has been designed very much with families in mind, as a well-equipped leisure centre for the crews and passengers of visiting yachts. In the marshlands beyond the village is located one of the area's largest RSPB reserves.

- 🕐 11-3 & 6-11
- 🍴 A la carte menu
- £ Major cards accepted
- 🛏 Modern en suite bedrooms
- 🅿 Car park adjacent
- ❓ Tollesbury Marina, RSPB marshes at end of village; Maldon 9 miles, Colchester 10 miles

180 THE HORSE & GROOM

WARLEY ROAD, GREAT WARLEY, NR BRENTWOOD, ESSEX CM13 3AE
TEL/FAX: 01277 220280

Directions: The inn lies in the village of Great Warley, on the B186 2 miles south of Brentwood.

With its elaborate gabled facade and small-paned windows, the **Horse & Groom** is an eyecatching landmark on a corner site in the village of Great Warley. Inside, it's equally striking, with bare floorboards and a long, wood-panelled bar counter topped with hopbines. This is very much a family business, with Sandra, her daughter Debbie and son-in-law Paul the leaseholders since September 2003. They've put a pub that was struggling back on its feet, appealing to a wide clientele with a combination of a warm, genuine welcome and excellent food and drink. The pub is open all day for drinks, which include Greene King IPA, Old Speckled Hen and a good selection of draught keg ales.

Sandra is a talented cook, and her dishes are served lunchtime and evening Wednesday to Saturday and until 6 o'clock Sunday to Tuesday. Classics such as prawn cocktail, chicken curry, roasts and spotted dick keep the customers happy, and booking is recommended on Saturday evening and Sunday to be sure of a table in the 25-cover non-smoking restaurant. The pub has plenty of off-road parking and a large rear garden with an aviary. Visitors to the White Horse should take time to look at Great Warley's Church of St Mary, with its marvellous early 20th century interior, and Warley Place, where a trail runs through a nature reserve with a fascinating variety of trees, shrubs and wildlife. Nearby Brentwood has extensive shopping and leisure facilities, a cottage museum and a cathedral built in classical style as recently as 1991.

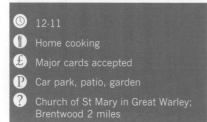

🕐 12-11

🍴 Home cooking

£ Major cards accepted

P Car park, patio, garden

❓ Church of St Mary in Great Warley; Brentwood 2 miles

THE KINGS HEAD

THE STREET, GOSFIELD, NR HALSTEAD, ESSEX CO9 1TP

TEL: 01787 474016

Directions: The inn is on the main street of Gosfield, which lies on the A1017 5 miles north of Braintree.

With its smartly renovated cream-and-black timbered facade, **The King's Head** is a stunning sight in the heart of picturesque Gosfield. Inside, the 16th century inn has been extensively restored and renovated throughout, creating a delightfully relaxed ambience with solid oak floors, leather sofas and armchairs, oak refectory tables, antique oak panelling and unobtrusive background music. Original artwork and a small selection of books add interest, and a fire in the huge original inglenook reinforce the warm welcome from Ali and Kate, who came here from the award-winning Settle Inn in Battersea, and their lovable Great Dane Scooby Blu. And on fine summer days the recently extended garden enjoys the sun all day, right up to a glorious sunset over Gosfield Lake.

- 🕐 12-3 & 6-11 (all day Sat & Sun in summer)
- 🍴 Bar and à la carte menus
- 💷 Major cards accepted
- 🅿 Car park
- @ website: www.thekingsheadgosfield.co.uk
- ❓ Gosfield Hall, Gosfield Lake Leisure Resort; Halstead 2 miles, Sible Hedingham 3 miles, Braintree 5 miles

Greene King IPA is the main cask ale on tap, and the inn keeps an impressive selection of wines from both Old and New Worlds. Under the new tenants, The Kings Head is building a reputation as a place for fine dining. Every dish is prepared to order, and diners can eat either in the bar or in the non-smoking dining area or conservatory. Baguettes, hot panini, aubergine parmigiana and an all-meat Moo Moo burger feature on the bar menu, while the à la carte menu is full of variety and tempting new ideas. Everything tastes as good as it sounds: chicken liver, chilli and lemon grass pâté; moules marinière with chips; seared duck breast with hasselback potatoes and a leek and courgette gratin; fillet steak with Lyonnaise potatoes, a brandy and peppercorn sauce and slow-roasted plum tomatoes; mango and ginger mascarpone crunch. Ali and Kate can recommend a chalet B&B a short walk away in the village.

THE KINGS HEAD AT PEBMARSH

THE STREET, PEBMARSH, NR HALSTEAD, ESSEX CO9 2NH
TEL: 01297 269306

Directions: The inn stands in the main street of Pebmarsh, about 1 mile east of the A131 Halstead-Sudbury road.

In pleasant countryside north of Earls Colne and Halstead, **The Kings Head** is a richly timbered free house dating from about 1450. Built as a drovers' inn, it stands in the beautiful North Essex village of Pebmarsh, a stone's throw from the 12th century church. A traditional country pub, with a welcome for the whole family from Jackie and Graham, it has a large bar with a log fire, a very inviting restaurant and a separate area with a pool table, darts and a gaming machine. Greene King IPA, Woodforde's Wherry, Blackthorn cider, Guinness, three premium lagers and constantly changing guest ales – the pub is CAMRA endorsed.

Food is a major part of the business here, served every lunchtime and evening and all day Sunday (the pub is closed on Monday). The menus provide the best choice of anywhere in the region, with fresh fish, Mexican and American dishes supplementing an impressive array of traditional English dishes including Sunday roasts, bargain two-course weekday lunches, children's dishes, home-made puddings and summer barbecues. The Kings Head's social calendar includes monthly quiz nights, occasional race nights and acoustic music sessions on the third Friday of every month. The front of the pub is a blaze of colour in spring and summer, and there are tables and chairs here and on the paved terrace at the back of the pub. The garden has a bouncy castle and other outdoor attractions to keep the little ones happy.

- 12-3 & 6-11 (Sun 12-10.30); closed Monday
- Home cooking on very varied menus
- Major cards accepted
- Garden, children's play area, pool table
- Monthly quiz, occasional race nights, live music 3rd Friday each month, annual charity weekend with all sorts of events
- Walking; Bures 3 miles, Halstead 4 miles, Earls Colne 4 miles, Sudbury 5 miles

THE LION & LAMB

STORTFORD ROAD, LITTLE CANFIELD, NR TAKELEY, DUNMOW,
ESSEX CM6 1SR
TEL: 01279 870257 FAX: 01279 870423

Directions: Leave the new A120 Stanstead Airport-Braintree road at Dunmow
West junction, and drive for about a mile on the B1256 towards Takeley. The inn
is on the right.

Hospitality is in generous supply at **The
Lion & Lamb**, which stands on the B1256
(previously the A120) at Little Canfield.
The new A120 has taken much of the
passing traffic away, giving this picture-
postcard inn a much more tranquil feel. It
is run by Mike Shields, whose belief in
traditional pub values has made the place
such a success. The immaculate interior –
a further tribute to Mike and his staff – has
a delightfully old-world appeal, with
masses of oak beams, open fires, red brick
features and rustic furniture.

In this cosy, inviting atmosphere,
Essex-brewed Ridleys ales are kept in
perfect condition, and an outstanding
selection of wines from around the world
can be enjoyed on their own or with a
meal. An excellent chef sets the
standard for cooking hereabouts, and his
menus, which are available all day long,
highlight prime produce, much of it
local. Salads and quiches provide
wholesome light meals, and other
choices run from pasta to daily fish
specials, meat dishes both plain and
sauced, and the popular Sunday roasts.
There are smoking and non-smoking
areas in the restaurant, and a self-
contained room with access to the
garden is an ideal venue for a private
party. The inn has a large car park, and
there are plenty of seats in the beer
garden for fair-weather sipping. Mike has
recently acquired a nearby house offering
Bed & Breakfast accommodation 1½
miles from Stansted Airport. The White
House, at Smiths Green, Dunmow Road,
Takeley, has three letting rooms, with
another 10 planned.

- 11-11 (Sun 12-10.30)
- Bar and restaurant menus
- Major cards accepted
- Car park, garden, function room, disabled access
- Live music monthly
- e-mail: info@lionandlambtakeley.co.uk website: www.lionandlambtakeley.co.uk
- Great Dunmow 3 miles, Bishops Stortford 4 miles, Stansted Airport 3 miles

THE NAGS HEAD

HEATH ROAD, RAMSDEN HEATH, NR BILLERICAY, ESSEX CM11 1HS
TEL: 01268 711875

Directions: Ramsden Heath is a village at the junction of two country roads 2 miles east of Billericay. Turn right off the B1007 or north from the A129.

In a village at the junction of two country roads east of Billericay, the **Nags Head** is a compact, attractive former private house in the shadow of some large, handsome trees. Inside, all is classically elegant, with striped wallpaper, heavy curtains at the windows, a wood-fronted bar counter and lots of gleaming brass and copper. The pub is open all day for drinks, which include Ridleys IPA and Old Bob, and good food is served every lunchtime. The choice runs from sandwiches and jacket potatoes to whitebait, beef or vegetable lasagne, chicken kiev, cod & chips, chilli con carne and steak & ale pie, with spotted dick or apple pie to round things off in style. Booking is recommended on Sundays, when the roast meats are always guaranteed to bring in the crowds.

Tenants Del and Denise, who took over the pub early in 2003, have made it one of the most popular venues in the region, particularly for lovers of jazz, rock and blues music. Jazz evenings take place on the second and fourth Thursday of each month, jam sessions on the first and third Thursdays, rock and blues on Fridays, and many well-known performers have entertained the customers here. There are plenty of interesting places to visit to combine with a trip to the Nags Head. In Billericay, the Chantry House was the home of the treasurer to the Pilgrim Fathers, while Norsey Wood, scene of a massacre during the Peasants Revolt of 1381, is a pleasant place for a stroll. The 100-acre wood around Hanningfield Reservoir is another good place to work up a thirst and appetite, while in the village of Stock the restored five-storey windmill is well worth a visit.

- 🕐 12-11
- 🍴 Home cooking (lunch only)
- 🅿 Car park
- 🎵 Regular music evenings – jazz, rock, blues
- @ website: www.pickapub.co.uk/nagshead
- ❓ Billericay 2 miles, Hanningfield Reservoir 2 miles, Stock 3 miles

THE NORTON

54 LATCHINGTON ROAD, COLD NORTON, ESSEX CM3 6JB
TEL: 01621 829569

> **Directions:** Cold Norton lies close to the B1010 5 miles south of Maldon.

The Norton is a fine-looking redbrick building with a conservatory extension, close to the B1010 a short drive south of Maldon or east of South Woodham Ferrers. Built in the late-19th century, the pub was originally called the Railway Tavern then the Norton Barge, and now it's just The Norton – the eyecatching pub sign is a vintage racing Norton motorcycle complete with goggled rider. Ben and Kerry, who bought the pub in October 2004, have immediately stamped their presence on the pub by creating a splendid new restaurant in striking black and white, with beams and high rafters and wagon wheels hanging from the ceiling.

The bar stocks a range of draught beers and fine wines, with three real ales, one from the local Crouch Vale Brewery, always on tap. Hot and cold bar food is available throughout the day, listed on a blackboard menu that is a real work of art. The choice runs from baguettes and jacket potatoes to salads, home-made chicken & mushroom and steak & ale pies, moussaka, Cajun chicken breast nachos, omelettes, steaks and a full traditional Sunday Roast. The non-smoking restaurant is open in the evenings and at weekends. It's early days for Ben and Kerry, but Ben has plenty of experience in the business, and The Norton is revving up to become one of the most popular pubs in the area, whether for a drink, a snack or a full meal. The village of Cold Norton is close to many attractions both inland and on the coast: Maldon is a ten-minute drive to the north, the new shops and amenities of the new town of South Woodham Ferrers are just to the west, and the towns of Southminster and Burnham-on-Crouch are to the east.

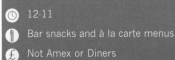

- 🕐 12-11
- 🍴 Bar snacks and à la carte menus
- 💷 Not Amex or Diners
- 🅿 Car park
- ❓ South Woodham Ferrers 3 miles, Maldon 5 miles, Southminster 9 miles, Burnham-on-Crouch 10 miles

THE OLD CROWN

MESSING, NR KELVEDON, ESSEX CO5 9TU
TEL: 01621 815575

Directions: From the B1024 at Kelvedon take the B1023 towards Tiptree; turn left after about a mile on to a minor road signposted Messing.

One mile east of Kelvedon (now bypassed by the A12), **The Old Crown** stands in the centre of the village where Boudicca is reputed to have fought her last battle against the invading Romans. Things have been much more peaceful since those times, and visitors to the 17th century inn will find a warm welcome and genuine hospitality from hosts Clive and Jill Bartram. Log fires keep things cosy in the comfortable, carpeted bar and lounge areas, where three cask ales from the Essex-based Ridleys Brewery are always on tap, along with a regularly changing guest ale and a good selection of wines and spirits.

The non-smoking restaurant specialises in tried-and-tested English classics on its menus. Traditional steak & ale pie, Old English fish pie, bangers & mustard mash with a rich onion gravy are among the favourites, along with steaks and a mighty mixed grill 'for the larger appetite'. The lunchtime menu offers sandwiches, jacket potatoes, salads, scampi and omelettes, with a choice of roasts on Sunday. The Old Crown has a large car park, and the garden has recently been expanded to provide views over the fields to the rear. The inn has a thriving social calendar that includes regular folk and jazz nights and monthly quizzes. Accommodation is available nearby, and the location is a good base for touring the area. The A12 provides easy access down to Witham and Chelmsford and up to Colchester, and other places of interest in the vicinity include Tiptree, Coggeshall and Layer Marney, which boasts the tallest Tudor gatehouse in Britain.

- 🕐 12-3 & 6-11
- 🍴 Snack and à la carte menus
- 💷 Major cards accepted
- 🅿 Car park
- 🎵 Live music; monthly quiz
- ❓ Kelvedon 2 miles, Tiptree 2 miles, Coggeshall 3 miles, Layer Marney Tower 3 miles

THE ONLEY ARMS

THE STREET, STISTED, NR BRAINTREE, ESSEX CM77 8AM
TEL: 01376 325204

Directions: Stisted is reached by minor roads off the A131 or A120 2 miles northeast of Braintree.

The Onley Arms is a delightful Ridleys pub in the main street of Stisted, reached by minor roads off the A131 or the A120. It's well worth seeking out, as tenants Paul Woodward and Sue Nightingale have greatly enhanced its appeal since arriving in 2003. The decor throughout has been refreshed and lightened, and the food, with USA-trained Paul heading the team at the stoves, is attracting a growing band of customers from all around. The atmosphere throughout is warm and inviting, and the bar is a good place to meet for a chat over a glass of Ridleys IPA or Old Tom.

The menu offers very good value, with light bites (baguettes and jacket potatoes) served at lunchtime, a Sunday roast in winter and an à la carte menu in the evening. Tried and tested favourites such as jumbo battered cod, lasagne, curries and steak & kidney pie are always in demand, and the pub holds regular theme nights featuring cuisines from around the world.

Pool, cribbage and darts are played in a room at the back, and there's a monthly quiz. The garden has a petanque pitch, and a children's play area with swings, a slide and goats to fondle and feed. Stisted is an interesting place for a stroll: All Saints Church, which dates from the 11th century, has some Flemish glass given by Onley family of Stisted Hall, and right opposite the pub is the Montefiore Institute, built as working men's club. Braintree, with its shops, museums and a magnificent Town Hall, is a short drive away, and nearby Coggeshall has two fine National Trust properties that are well worth a visit, including the oldest surviving timber-framed barn in Europe.

- 🕐 12-2.30 & 7-11 (Sun to 10.30); closed Monday lunchtime
- 🍴 Home cooking
- £ Major cards accepted
- 🅿 Car park, garden, children's play area, function room
- ❓ Braintree 2 miles, Bocking 2 miles, Coggeshall 3 miles, Halstead 6 miles

THE PLOUGH

570 RAYLEIGH ROAD, HUTTON, NR BRENTWOOD, ESSEX CM13 1SG
TEL: 01277 210255 FAX: 01277 204407

Directions: The inn is located in Hutton, by the A129 2 miles east of Brentwood towards Billericay.

Once you find yourself in the village of Hutton, there's no mistaking **The Plough**, a very distinctive building with a steeply raked tiled roof and tall chimneys. It's a pretty sight made even prettier by a wonderful year-round display of all kinds of flowers and shrubs and plants, a work of art that recently won the pub the runner-up spot in the Best Kept Pub (floral) awards in the area – there were 360 entrants, so this was no mean feat! The Plough has been run since 2001 by leaseholders Kevin and Lindsey and their experienced manager Lee. The traditionally styled beamed bar is adorned with a wealth of brass and cooper ornaments, a model sailing ship, tankards and pots and toby jugs, all

creating a very welcoming ambience in which to enjoy a drink – cask ales are Greene King IPA and two guests.

An extensive selection of well-priced, generously served dishes is available to enjoy anywhere in the pub, which has some non-smoking areas; the printed menu is supplemented by daily specials, and roasts are added on Sunday; the weekend is the busiest time, so booking is recommended, especially for Sunday lunch. A well-appointed marquee is permanently attached to the main building, providing an overflow at busy times or an attractive venue for a party or other special occasion. The Plough puts on an evening of entertainment every Thursday or Friday, with karaoke, a quiz, a race nights or live music.

- 🕐 12·11
- 🍴 Extensive à la carte menu
- £ Not Amex or Diners
- Ⓟ Car park
- 🎵 Weekly entertainment Thursday or Friday
- @ e-mail: kevin@amor1769.fslife.co.uk
- ❓ Brentwood 2 miles

THE RABBITS

STAPLEFORD ABBOTTS, NR ROMFORD, ESSEX RM4 1RP
TEL: 01708 688203

Directions: Stapleford Abbots lies on the B175 4 miles north of Romford.

If you spot a Triumph TR whizzing around the lanes north of Romford, there's a good chance that it's heading for **The Rabbits**, where a TR owners club holds regular meetings. A Beatrix Potter-style pub sign adorns the cream-and-black front of the pub, and recent refurbishment inside and out has preserved and enhanced its traditional appeal. Mugs, plates, horse brasses and pictures adorn the bars, where open coal fires keep winter at bay. Outside, a newly developed lawned garden offers a pleasant setting for summer drinking and contains an area where children can romp in safety. Greene King IPA, London Pride, Old Speckled Hen and rotating guest ales head the list of drinks, which also includes a good selection of wines (half a dozen house wines) and four champagnes.

Food is served all day in the bars or in the black-beamed dining area and offers a choice that runs from sandwiches and baguettes to a menu of traditional pub dishes using locally sourced produce as much as possible; the vegetables are fresh, the chips home-made and the prices keen. The Rabbits is managed by Geoff Hutter for the widely respected and multi-award-winning proprietor Peter Benefield, whose other pubs include The Woodman at nearby Stanford Rivers. With Epping Forest close by, walking, berrying and mushroom hunting are popular activities hereabouts, and golf and fishing are both available locally; among the other local attractions is the Nuclear Bunker at Kelvedon Hatch.

- 🕐 12·11
- 🍴 Traditional pub snacks and meals
- 💷 Major cards accepted
- 🅿️ Car park, garden, children's play area
- ❓ Walking, golf, fishing; Kelvedon Hatch Nuclear Bunker 4 miles, Romford 4 miles

THE ROSE & CROWN

ASHDON, NR SAFFRON WALDEN, ESSEX CB10 2HB
TEL: 01799 584337

Directions: Ashdon is reached by a minor road signposted northeast from Saffron Walden (about 3 miles).

Owner Paul Lewis spent some time in Australia before taking over at the **Rose & Crown**, which stands in the village of Ashdon a short drive north of Saffron Walden. The cream-painted roadside pub has a very traditional and convivial bar, a small lounge bar and a neat little restaurant; a huge log-burning stove ensures that things stay snug in the cooler months. Four cask ales are on tap to quench thirsts, and the pub also keeps a good selection of wines. On the food side, which is a very important part of the Rose & Crown's business, fresh seafood, excellent local lamb and big, juicy steaks are just a few of the menu options, and there's also an unusually generous choice of vegetarian dishes.

- 🕐 12·3 & 6·11
- 🍴 A la carte menu
- £ Major cards accepted
- Ⓟ Car park
- 🎵 Beer festival August Bank Holiday; occasional live music nights
- ❓ Ashdon Guildhall; Linton Zoo 3 miles, Bartlow Hills 3 miles, Saffron Walden 3 miles, Audley End 4 miles

The theme food nights are always well attended, as are the live music sessions that are held from time to time, but the main event in the Rose & Crown's calendar, and one that goes into many local diaries, is the popular beer festival held every August Bank Holiday. The inn is well placed for both town and country lovers. Saffron Walden is a wonderful old market town with delightful 15th and 16th century timber-framed buildings – some adorned with the East Anglian speciality of pargeting – and the largest church in Essex, the magnificent Church of St Mary, whose soaring 193ft spire dominates the town. Even closer to the Rose & Crown is the historic site of Bartlow Hills, whose 2nd century Roman burial mounds are said to be the largest of their kind in Europe.

THE ROYAL OAK

STAMBRIDGE ROAD, GREAT STAMBRIDGE, NR SOUTHEND-ON-SEA,
ESSEX SS4 2AX
TEL/FAX: 01702 258259

Directions: The Royal Oak lies in the village of Great Stambridge, about 5 miles
from Southend through Rochford.

Out in the countryside a short drive
northeast of Rochford, the **Royal Oak** is
a 17th century house, with later
additions, that has been a pub for almost
200 years. That long tradition of
hospitality is being carried on in fine
style by Lee Carter and Frances
Ransome, who have made it one of the
most popular pubs in the region.

Food is definitely the main part of the
business, and at the weekend as many as
200 flock from all over the area for
Sunday lunch. But any meal in the lofty
raftered restaurant is sure to be a treat,
with Lee at the head of a talented
kitchen team producing a wide selection
of dishes to suit most tastes and
appetites. Fish galore comes fresh from
Billingsgate, fruit and vegetables from
Covent Garden, meat from the best
butcher in the neighbourhood. The
choice is always supplemented by daily
specials: pie of the day might be chicken
and mushroom; curry of the day lamb
Madras; catch of the day skate or cod;
quiche of the day cheese & onion.
Mussels are prepared in a variety of ways,
there are plenty of pasta dishes, and most
of the dishes can be ordered in small or
large portions.

Courage Directors Bitter and Greene
King IPA are the permanent cask ales,
with Charles Wells Bombardier a popular
guest ale; there's also a good wine list.
The pub has plenty of off-road parking,
and at the back is a grassed area for
alfresco eating and drinking. The pub is
very child-friendly, and high chairs can
be provided in the restaurant. There are
plenty of ways of working up a thirst in
the vicinity, including walks by the
nearby River Roach.

- 🕐 12-3 & 6-11 (all day Sat & Sun)
- 🍽 Bar & restaurant menus
- 💷 Major cards accepted
- Ⓟ Car park
- 🎵 Live music once or twice a month
- @ website:
  www.theroyaloakstambridge.co.uk
- ❓ Rochford 2 miles, Southend 5 miles

THE SWAN AT FELSTED

STATION ROAD, FELSTED, NR GREAT DUNMOW, ESSEX CM6 3DG
TEL: 01371 820245 FAX: 01371 821393

Essex

Directions: Felsted is on the B1417 2 miles south of the A120 4 miles east of Great Dunmow.

Fifteen minutes from both Stansted Airport and Chelmsford, **The Swan** is a delightfully welcoming, well-run pub. Rebuilt in the Edwardian era after a devastating fire, it was tastefully modernised and totally refurbished in 2002 and enjoys a prominent place in the picturesque North Essex village of Felsted. Behind its redbrick and half-timbered facade, The Swan combines all the assets of a comfortable, traditional country pub and a high-quality restaurant, and mine host and proprietor Jono Clark is very proud of what he has achieved here.

The head chef and his team set great store by fresh produce in dishes that allow quality and true flavours to predominate. Their menus are well thought out and inventive without ever being outrageous,

and cater for the widest range of appetites and preferences. Sandwiches and salads have a menu to themselves, and the lunchtime menu offers a delicate balance of light, well-balanced dishes. The chefs demonstrate their talents to the full on the evening à la carte menu, which tempts with the likes of pan-fried scallops with roast courgettes and sun-dried tomatoes or lamb rump with flageolets and a rosemary jus, as well as old favourites including bangers & mash or haddock with chips and mushy peas. Desserts like chocolate risotto with a shortbread biscuit keep the enjoyment level high to the end, and the fine food is complemented by a superb wide-ranging wine list that includes lots by the glass and a good choice of bubbly for pushing the boat out. A private dining room for up to 16 guests is an ideal venue for a party or a family get together.

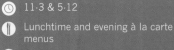

- 🕐 11·3 & 5·12
- 🍴 Lunchtime and evening à la carte menus
- £ Major cards accepted
- Ⓟ Car park
- @ e-mail: info@theswanatfelsted.co.uk website: www.theswanatfelsted.co.uk
- ❓ Great Dunmow 4 miles, Stansted Airport 8 miles, Chelmsford 8 miles

BROOK STREET, MANNINGTREE, ESSEX CO11 1DR
TEL: 01206 397042

> **Directions:** The Swan Inn is situated in the centre of Manningtree, which lies on the B1352 9 miles west of Harwich.

Manningtree is a delightful place to visit, and **The Swan Inn** is one of the most welcoming and sociable pubs not just in the town but in the whole region. The licensees are Peter Booth and Toni (Antonietta) Marchioni, and whether it's for a drink, a snack, a leisurely meal or an overnight stay, every visitor is treated like a friend. Three casks ales, including Canterbury Jack, are on tap in the well-stocked bar, and there's a good choice of well-priced wines to enjoy on their own or with a meal. Food is an important ingredient in The Swan's popularity, and Toni and the two chefs prepare a fine selection of dishes to enjoy every lunchtime and evening. The choice runs from bar snacks to full meals, with fish fresh landed at Harwich always

among the favourite orders. Specials like grilled sea bass on buttered lemon asparagus and plaice topped with prawns and cheese are guaranteed winners, and even lobster is sometimes available with a day's notice. Toni cooks some of her special Italian dishes, and on Sundays traditional roasts take centre stage. Desserts such as bread & butter pudding or pears poached in red wine make memorable endings to a memorable meal, and the menus are complemented by an excellent wine list.

The 60-cover restaurant is also available for private parties and functions. The Swan's busy social calendar embraces music nights, quiz nights, golf days and a fishing club. The guest accommodation includes en suite singles, doubles and family rooms, providing a practical, comfortable base for discovering the many attractions of what is officially England's smallest town.

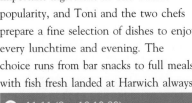

- 🕐 11-11 (Sun 12-10.30)
- 🍴 Bar and restaurant menus
- 💷 Major cards accepted
- 🛏 6 en suite rooms
- 🅿 Car park
- 🎵 Live music Saturday evening; quiz nights, golf days, fishing club
- @ e-mail: enquiries@theswanmanningtree.co.uk
- ❓ Walk to Flatford Mill starting at Manningtree Station, Manningtree Museum; Mistley 2 miles, Dedham 2 miles, East Bergholt 2 miles

THE THREE HORSESHOES

WATER LANE, HELIONS BUMPSTEAD, ESSEX CB9 7AL
TEL: 01440 730298

> **Directions:** From Haverhill take the B1057 to Sturmer, turn right on to the
> A1307, then first left on to minor road signposted Helions Bumpstead.

Since they took over **The Three
Horseshoes** in October 2003, Sue and
Les Anderson have made many new
friends at their fine old country inn near
Haverhill. Behind a smart black and
white facade, the ambience is
delightfully welcoming and traditional,
with beams and half-panelling, plates,
prints and photographs of bygone days,
horse brasses and a big brick hearth
bordered by various antique firearms,
badges, candlesticks and handsome
storage jars. There's always a choice of
three cask ales, including Greene King
IPA and Adnams Best, as well as other
draught and bottle beers and lagers,
ciders, wines and spirits. The non-
smoking dining area offers a good choice
of freshly prepared home-cooked food on
menus that mix pub classics with many
imaginative choices. Flying the old
favourites flag are steaks, rack of lamb

and simple grilled sole, along with the
much-loved double acts of cod & chips,
liver & bacon, sausage & mash and beef
& Guinness pie. More esoteric choices
might include sweet and savoury apple
tartlet, butterfly tiger prawns with
pernod and oriental sticky plum duck.
The inn has a long and interesting
history. Originally a row of three
cottages, it became an alehouse in 1846,
and since the landlord was a carpenter
he called it The Carpenters Arms. He
was succeeded by a blacksmith, who
naturally enough renamed it The
Horseshoes Inn. He nailed three
horseshoes to the pub sign, and ever
since it has been called The Three
Horseshoes. The next phase in the
owners' plans is for an extension to the
dining area, new toilets with disabled
facilities and four letting bedrooms due
for early 2005.

The inn has plenty of off-road parking
at the front, and at the rear is a spacious
garden with a children's play area.

- 🕐 12-3 & 7-11, closed Mon lunchtime
- 🍴 Lunch and evening menus
- 💷 All majors except Amex
- 🛏 4 rooms planned for early 2005
- 🅿 Car park, beer garden, children's play area
- 🎵 Dominoes, cribbage
- ❓ Haverhill 2½ miles, Linton Zoo 6 miles, Saffron Walden 6 miles

THE WHITE HART

THE STREET, LITTLE WALTHAM, NR CHELMSFORD, ESSEX CM3 3NY
TEL: 01245 360487

Essex

Directions: Little Waltham lies just off the A130 2 miles north of Chelmsford.

The White Hart is a homely, welcoming pub where Mo Gordon extends a friendly greeting to customers of all ages. The distinctive cream-and-red frontage on the main street of Little Waltham has three handsome bay windows, two of them fronting the public bar, where beamed ceilings, half-panelled walls and open fires create an invitingly traditional feel that's in keeping with the age of the pub – the records show that it was rebuilt after a fire in the 16th century. The pub is open all day except lunchtime on Tuesday for drinks, and excellent home-cooked dishes are served every session except Tuesday lunchtime and Monday evening.

The bar menu runs from filled cob rolls to jacket potatoes, salads and scampi, ham or cod and chips, while the restaurant menu features classic pub dishes such as garlic mushrooms. Cottage pie, gammon with pineapple and liver & bacon casserole; vegetarians are not forgotten with tasty offerings like lemon and asparagus risotto. The White Hart is very much at the heart of social life in Little Waltham, with darts and pool the popular pub games, live music every Saturday and a jam session on Thursday. It's also very family friendly, and there are swings and a slide to keep children happy in the large garden.

The banks of the nearby River Chelmer provide some lovely tranquil walks, and the bustling town of Chelmsford is just two miles away. As well as a full complement of shops, Chelmsford has plenty of historical interest, which can be discovered in the Cathedral, the Chelmsford &n Essex Museum and the Essex Regiment Museum.

- 🕐 12-11 (Tues from 5.30)
- 🍺 Home cooking
- 💷 Major cards accepted
- 🅿 Car park, garden, children's play area
- 🎵 Live music Saturday, jam session Thursday, pool, darts
- ❓ Chelmsford 2 miles

THE WHITE HART

Essex

MILL STREET, ST OSYTH, ESSEX CO16 8EN
TEL: 01255 820318

Directions: The inn lies west of Clacton off the B1027, on the road to Point Clear. From Colchester, take the A133 then the B1027.

The White Hart is a grand old inn located on the road from St Osyth to Point Clear, almost opposite the Brightlingsea estuary. The oldest parts of the inn date back to the 15th century, and the old-world look is reinforced by old beams and woodburning stoves in the bar. Tables and chairs are set out at the front, and the garden behind the pub has more seats, as well as swings and slides to keep young visitors happy. Karen Mallett and her son Simon who took over the licence in the summer of 2004, keep the grown-ups happy with a good selection of cask ales, beers, lagers, wines and spirits, and in the non-smoking dining area they serve a varied choice of favourite 'pub grub'. The meat from a local butcher is particularly good, and Tuesday night brings a selection of hearty, tasty meat pies and a vegetarian

version. Baguettes, jacket potatoes and salads provide lighter alternatives, and there's a separate children's menu.

One end of the bar is given over to darts, and once a month on a Saturday the pub hosts a live music evening. A road leads down past the pub to a little yacht basin and boatyard, and also within a short drive are a nature reserve – a popular spot with birdwatchers – and the East Essex Aviation Society's Museum housed in well-preserved Martello tower. St Osyth is best known for its Norman church and for the ruins of its 12th century Priory. The best surviving part of this once-grand establishment is the 15th century flint gatehouse, where visitors can see an interesting collection of jade and ceramics. Other attractions here include the Fitzwilliam art collection in the Georgian wing, with paintings by Reynolds, Stubbs and Van Dyck.

- 🕐 11-11
- 🍴 Traditional pub meals
- 💷 All the major cards
- 🅿 Car park, garden, children's play area
- 🎵 Music evenings once a month on Saturday
- @ web: www.thewhitehartstosyth.co.uk
- ❓ St Osyth Priory 1 mile, Clacton 3 miles

THE WHITE HART

HIGH STREET, STEBBING, NR GREAT DUNMOW, ESSEX CM6 3SQ
TEL: 01371 856383

> **Directions:** Stebbing is situated off the A120 2 miles east of Great Dunmow.

Two miles east of Great Dunmow off the Braintree road, the **White Hart** is tucked quietly away among some lovely little cottages. Built in the 16th century and still retaining great period charm, this is a really splendid example of a classic English country pub, and licensees Nick Eldred and Lynnette are committed to keeping it just the way they and their loyal customers want it. A large feature log fire keeps things cosy in the spotless oak-beamed bar, where the range of drinks includes Greene King IPA, Old Speckled Hen and guest ales, very good house wines and a selection of malts. Lynnette's home cooking is a major attraction, and her menus run from lunchtime snacks (jacket potatoes, omelettes, large baps with a choice of hot and cold fillings) to the Sunday roasts and tasty, satisfying daily specials like Ranch chicken or steak pie. With a

little notice, Lynnette can cater for special dietary needs.

The bar and non-smoking dining area are adorned with a number of interesting and unusual items, including a large collection of framed cigarette cards, a St Christopher charm left behind by Buddy Holly - and a piece of wood from Noah's Ark! The inn has a separate area with a pool table and bar billiards, there are quiz nights in winter and live music about 4 or 5 times a year on a Sunday afternoon. The White Hart has ample off-road parking and a large patio area, and for guests staying overnight there are two letting bedrooms upstairs. The historic town of Great Dunmow is a short drive away, and among many other local attractions are the Harold Peto-designed Gardens of Easton Lodge, and the rural museum and 14th century Church of St Mary the Virgin at Great Bardfield.

- 🕐 11-3 & 5-11 (Sat & Sun all day)
- 🍴 Home cooking
- 💷 Cash and cheques only
- 🛏 2 bedrooms
- 🅿 Car park, patio area
- 🎵 Quiz nights in winter
- ❓ Great Dunmow 2 miles, Easton Lodge 3 miles, Great Bardfield 4 miles, Thaxted 6 miles

CHURCH STREET, SIBLE HEDINGHAM, ESSEX CO9 3NT
TEL: 01787 460742

Directions: Sible Hedingham lies 3 miles northwest of Halstead. Take the A1124, then the A1017. Turn off at Rectory Road, White Horse is at the end.

Mentioned in the Domesday Book as part of the largest parish in England, Sible Hedingham is a charming village 3 miles north of Halstead. In the centre of the village stands **The White Horse**, where David Pearce took over the tenancy in April 2004. He and Kate have built up the trade at this cosy old country inn - the oldest parts date from the 15th century - with a combination of genuine hospitality and friendliness (even the ghost is well-behaved!), cask ales kept in tip-top condition and some tasty bar food. Redecorated in 2004, the interior has a traditional look enhanced by ancient beams, a large wood-burning stove in a vast brick hearth and a collection of lovely horse brasses.

The White Horse Inn has two bars, with pool and darts in the rear locals bar, and a non-smoking restaurant. The inn is family friendly throughout with the spacious lawned garden being a boon in summer, with plenty of picnic benches, a slide and swings and a bouncy castle. Greene King IPA and Abbot Ale are always on tap, and guest ales make an appearance in the summer months. Good-value lunchtime dishes, prepared to order, include basket bites (sausage, scampi, chicken), fish & chips, ploughman's platters, and huffers – large baps – with various fillings. The Sunday roasts are a popular weekly draw, and David and Kate specialise in steak meals on Thursday, Friday and Saturday evenings. Well worth a visit in Sible Hedingham is St Peter's Church, where one of the treasures is the tomb of the medieval knight Sir John Hawkwood, who was born in the village.

- 🕐 12-2.30 & 5-11 (Fri & Sat all day, Sun all day to 10.30)
- 🍴 Lunch menu – Thurs/Fri/Sat evenings
- 💷 Major cards accepted
- 🅿 Car park, garden, children's play area
- 🎵 Pool, darts, monthly music evenings
- ❓ Castle Hedingham 1 mile, Colne Valley Railway 1 mile, Halstead 3 miles, Earls Colne 4 miles, Braintree 8 miles

THE WOODMAN

LONDON ROAD, STANFORD RIVERS, NR ONGAR, ESSEX CM5 9QF
TEL: 01277 362019

> **Directions:** Stanford Rivers lies south of Ongar on the A113.

The oldest parts of **The Woodman** date back more than 900 years, and since it was the first building in the area, its address was No.1 London Road. Other parts were added in the 17th and 19th centuries, and the interior is rich in period charm, with patches of original wattle and daub, ancient beams, open fires and all sorts of ornaments, pictures and bric-a-brac. Outside is a large garden area with its own bar, a barbecue and a children's play area. The Woodman has been a popular place of refreshment down the centuries with wool merchants, highwaymen with goods to hide and landlords to bribe, farmers and farm workers, herdsmen, stage coach passengers, motorists and tourists. Dr Johnson and Daniel Defoe both expressed their enthusiastic approval, and today this outstanding inn ranks as

one of the best and most popular pub restaurants in the region, with a great range of excellent food, real ales and fine wines from around the world and a clientele that extends down into London and up into East Anglia.

The bar is stocked with a wide selection of drinks that includes Shepherd Neame's finest: Master Brew, Bishop's Finger and the superb Spitfire, first brewed in 1990 to commemorate the 50th anniversary of the Battle of Britain. Top-quality cooking brings the crowds from near and far to enjoy traditional English fare and pub classics such as pies, liver & bacon, lasagne, cod & chips, celebrated sausages (they call it 'the sausage pub' in the East End), steaks and scrumptious puds. The licensee is Peter Benefield, one of the best known and most respected proprietors in the business. He also runs the Rabbits Inn at nearby Stapleford Abbots.

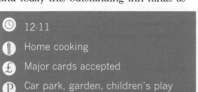

🕐 12-11

🍴 Home cooking

£ Major cards accepted

Ⓟ Car park, garden, children's play area

@ e-mail: sales@the-woodman-pub.co.uk
web: www.the-woodman-pub.co.uk

❓ Kelvedon Hatch Nuclear Bunker 3 miles, Greensted Church 3 miles, North Weald airfield 2 miles

ALPHABETICAL LIST
OF PUBS AND INNS

A

The Admiral's Head	Little Bealings, Woodbridge, Suffolk	115
The Angel Hotel	Halesworth, Suffolk	116
The Ark Royal	Wells-next-the-Sea, Norfolk	57

B

Baskerville's Hotel	Baston, Cambridgeshire	20
The Bell Inn	Salhouse, Norwich, Norfolk	58
The Black Horse	Stratford St Mary, Suffolk	117
The Black Swan	Farcet, Peterborough, Cambridgeshire	21
The Black Swan	Little Dunham, Swaffham, Norfolk	59
The Blue Lion	North Pickenham, Swaffham, Norfolk	60
The Boar Inn	Great Ryburgh, Norfolk	61
The Bridge Inn	Lenwade, Norwich, Norfolk	62
The Brisley Bell Inn	Brisley, Norfolk	63
The Bristol Arms	Shotley Gate, Ipswich, Suffolk	118
The Bull Inn	Cavendish, Suffolk	119

C

The Cherry Tree	Rochford, Essex	169
The Cherry Tree	Wicklewood, Wymondham, Norfolk	64
The Cherry Tree Inn	Woodbridge, Suffolk	120
The Cock Inn	Hatfield Broad Oak, Bishop's Stortford, Essex	170
The Cock Inn	Kentford, Newmarket, Suffolk	121
The Cock Inn	Polstead, Suffolk	122
The Cock Inn	Stanton, Bury St Edmunds, Suffolk	123
The Cock Tavern	Chipping Ongar, Essex	171
The Cross Keys	Dilham, North Walsham, Norfolk	65
The Crown	Gayton, Kings Lynn, Norfolk	66

D

The Dog & Duck	Campsea Ashe, Woodbridge, Suffolk	124
The Duck Inn	Writtle, Chelmsford, Essex	172
The Duke of Edinburgh	Bacton, Norfolk	67
The Duke of Wellington	Hatfield Peverel, Chelmsford, Essex	173

E

The Eels Foot Inn	Ormesby St Michael, Great Yarmouth, Norfolk	68

F

The Falcon	Rushmere St Andrew, Ipswich, Suffolk	125
The Ferry Boat Inn	Felixstowe, Suffolk	126
The Flitch of Bacon	Little Dunmow, Great Dunmow, Essex	174
The Fox	Pakenham, Suffolk	127
The Fox & Hounds	Filby, Great Yarmouth, Norfolk	69
The Fox Inn	West Mersea, Essex	175

G

The Gemini Pub & Restaurant	Dereham, Norfolk	70
The George Hotel	Chatteris, Cambridgeshire	22
The Golden Pheasant	Etton, Peterborough, Cambridgeshire	23
The Green Man	Gosfield, Halstead, Essex	176
The Green Man	Little Braxted, Witham, Essex	177
The Greyhound	Tibenham, Norwich, Norfolk	71
The Griffin Hotel	Attleborough, Norfolk	72

H

The Hare	Roxwell, Chelmsford, Essex	178
The Hill House	Happisburgh, Norfolk	73
The Hoops	Great Eversden, Cambridgeshire	24
The Hop Bind	Cottenham, Cambridgeshire	25
The Hope Inn	Tollesbury, Essex	179
The Horse & Groom	Great Warley, Brentwood, Essex	180
The Horse & Groom	Wrentham, Suffolk	128

J

The John Barleycorn	Duxford, Cambridgeshire	26
The John H Stracey	Briston, Melton Constable, Norfolk	74
The Jolly Farmers	North Creake, Norfolk	75
The Jolly Farmers	Swanton Abbott, Norwich, Norfolk	76

K

The Kings Head	Gosfield, Halstead, Essex	181
The Kings Head	New Buckenham, Norfolk	77
The Kings Head	Yoxford, Suffolk	129
The Kings Head at Pebmarsh	Pebmarsh, Halstead, Essex	182
The Kings Head Inn	Orford, Suffolk	130

L

The Lion & Lamb	Little Canfield, Takeley, Essex	183
The Little Wellington	Stowmarket, Suffolk	131
The Lobster	Sheringham, Norfolk	78

Alphabetical List of Pubs and Inns

M

The Marshlands Arms	Marshland St James, Wisbech, Norfolk	80
The Morning Star	Lowestoft, Suffolk	132

N

The Nags Head	Ramsden Heath, Billericay, Essex	184
The New Inn	Roughton, Norfolk	81
The Norton	Cold Norton, Essex	185

O

The Old Cannon Brewery	Bury St Edmunds, Suffolk	133
The Old Crown	Messing, Kelvedon, Essex	186
The Old Red Lion	Aldborough, Norfolk	82
The Oliver Twist Country Inn	Guyhirn, Wisbech, Cambridgeshire	27
The Onley Arms	Stisted, Braintree, Essex	187
The Ordnance Hotel	Felixstowe, Suffolk	134

P

The Plough	Hutton, Brentwood, Essex	188
The Prince of Wales	Hilton, Cambridgeshire	28
The Pykkerell	Ixworth, Bury St Edmunds, Suffolk	135

Q

The Queens Head	Harston, Cambridgeshire	29

R

The Rabbits	Stapleford Abbotts, Romford, Essex	189
The Railway Freehouse	North Elmham, Dereham, Norfolk	83
The Red Lion	Coltishall, Norfolk	84
The Red Lion	Needham, Harleston, Norfolk	85
The Rose & Crown	Ashdon, Saffron Walden, Essex	190
The Royal Oak	Great Stambridge, Southend on Sea, Essex	191

S

The Scole Inn	Scole, Diss, Norfolk	86
The Ship Inn	Mundesley, Cromer, Norfolk	87
The Sorrel Horse Inn	Barham, Ipswich, Suffolk	136
The Stables Restaurant	Sheringham, Norfolk	79
The Swan	Mattishall, Dereham, Norfolk	88
The Swan at Felstead	Felsted, Great Dunmow, Essex	192
The Swan Inn	Manningtree, Essex	193
The Swan Inn	Little Waldingfield, Sudbury, Suffolk	137

T

The Ten Bells	Stonham Aspal, Stowmarket, Suffolk	138
The Three Horseshoes	Turves, Whittlesey, Cambridgeshire	30
The Three Horseshoes	Helions Bumpstead, Essex	194
The Three Horseshoes	Roydon, Kings Lynn, Norfolk	89
The Three Mariners	Trimley St Mary, Felixstowe, Suffolk	139
The Three Tuns	Huntingdon, Cambridgeshire	31
The Three Tuns Coaching Inn	Pettistree, Woodbridge, Suffolk	140
The Triple Plea	Broadway, Halesworth, Suffolk	141

V

| The Vine | Coates, Cambridgeshire | 32 |

W

The Walpole Arms	Itteringham, Norwich, Norfolk	90
West End House	West End, Ely, Cambridgeshire	33
The White Hart	Little Waltham, Chelmsford, Essex	195
The White Hart	St Osyth, Essex	196
The White Hart	Stebbing, Great Dunmow, Essex	197
The White Hart Inn	Blythburgh, Southwold, Suffolk	142
The White Horse	Tilbrook, Cambridgeshire	34
The White Horse	Holme by the Sea, Hunstanton, Norfolk	91
The White Horse	Beyton, Bury St Edmunds, Suffolk	143
The White Horse at Longham	Dereham, Norfolk	92
The White Horse Inn	Capel St Mary, Ipswich, Suffolk	144
The White Horse Inn	Sible Hedingham, Essex	198
The White Horse Inn	Tattingstone, Ipswich, Suffolk	145
The White Swan	Conington, Fenstanton, Cambridgeshire	35
The White Swan	Woodnewton, Cambridgeshire	36
The Windmill	Somersham, Huntingdon, Cambridgeshire	37
The Woodman	Stanford Rivers, Ongar, Essex	199
The Woolpack	Terrington St John, Kings Lynn, Norfolk	93

SPECIAL INTEREST LISTS

Accommodation

CAMBRIDGESHIRE

Baskerville's Hotel	Baston, Cambridgeshire	20
The George Hotel	Chatteris, Cambridgeshire	22
The John Barleycorn	Duxford, Cambridgeshire	26
The Oliver Twist Country Inn	Guyhirn, Wisbech, Cambridgeshire	27
The Prince of Wales	Hilton, Cambridgeshire	28
The Three Tuns	Huntingdon, Cambridgeshire	31

ESSEX

The Flitch of Bacon	Little Dunmow, Great Dunmow, Essex	174
The Hope Inn	Tollesbury, Essex	179
The Swan Inn	Manningtree, Essex	193
The White Hart	Stebbing, Great Dunmow, Essex	197

NORFOLK

The Boar Inn	Great Ryburgh, Norfolk	61
The Bridge Inn	Lenwade, Norwich, Norfolk	62
The Duke of Edinburgh	Bacton, Norfolk	67
The Griffin Hotel	Attleborough, Norfolk	72
The Hill House	Happisburgh, Norfolk	73
The John H Stracey	Briston, Melton Constable, Norfolk	74
The Marshlands Arms	Marshland St James, Wisbech, Norfolk	80
The Old Red Lion	Aldborough, Norfolk	82
The Scole Inn	Scole, Diss, Norfolk	86
The White Horse at Longham	Dereham, Norfolk	92

SUFFOLK

The Angel Hotel	Halesworth, Suffolk	116
The Bull Inn	Cavendish, Suffolk	119
The Cherry Tree Inn	Woodbridge, Suffolk	120
The Dog & Duck	Campsea Ashe, Woodbridge, Suffolk	124
The Kings Head Inn	Orford, Suffolk	130
The Old Cannon Brewery	Bury St Edmunds, Suffolk	133
The Ordnance Hotel	Felixstowe, Suffolk	134
The Pykkerell	Ixworth, Bury St Edmunds, Suffolk	135
The Sorrel Horse Inn	Barham, Ipswich, Suffolk	136
The Swan Inn	Little Waldingfield, Sudbury, Suffolk	137
The Three Tuns Coaching Inn	Pettistree, Woodbridge, Suffolk	140
The White Hart Inn	Blythburgh, Southwold, Suffolk	142

All Day Opening

CAMBRIDGESHIRE

Baskerville's Hotel	Baston, Cambridgeshire	20
The George Hotel	Chatteris, Cambridgeshire	22
The Hoops	Great Eversden, Cambridgeshire	24
The Hop Bind	Cottenham, Cambridgeshire	25
The John Barleycorn	Duxford, Cambridgeshire	26
The Three Tuns	Huntingdon, Cambridgeshire	31

ESSEX

The Cock Tavern	Chipping Ongar, Essex	171
The Fox Inn	West Mersea, Essex	175
The Horse & Groom	Great Warley, Brentwood, Essex	180
The Lion & Lamb	Little Canfield, Takeley, Essex	183
The Nags Head	Ramsden Heath, Billericay, Essex	184
The Norton	Cold Norton, Essex	185
The Plough	Hutton, Brentwood, Essex	188
The Rabbits	Stapleford Abbotts, Romford, Essex	189
The Swan Inn	Manningtree, Essex	193
The White Hart	Little Waltham, Chelmsford, Essex	195
The White Hart	St Osyth, Essex	196
The Woodman	Stanford Rivers, Ongar, Essex	199

NORFOLK

The Ark Royal	Wells-next-the-Sea, Norfolk	57
The Blue Lion	North Pickenham, Swaffham, Norfolk	60
The Bridge Inn	Lenwade, Norwich, Norfolk	62
The Duke of Edinburgh	Bacton, Norfolk	67
The Eels Foot Inn	Ormesby St Michael, Great Yarmouth, Norfolk	68
The Fox & Hounds	Filby, Great Yarmouth, Norfolk	69
The Gemini Pub & Restaurant	Dereham, Norfolk	70
The Lobster	Sheringham, Norfolk	78
The Old Red Lion	Aldborough, Norfolk	82
The Railway Freehouse	North Elmham, Dereham, Norfolk	83
The Swan	Mattishall, Dereham, Norfolk	88
The White Horse	Holme by the Sea, Hunstanton, Norfolk	91

SUFFOLK

The Angel Hotel	Halesworth, Suffolk	116
The Black Horse	Stratford St Mary, Suffolk	117

Special Interest Lists

SUFFOLK (Cont.)

The Cock Inn	Kentford, Newmarket, Suffolk	121
The Morning Star	Lowestoft, Suffolk	132
The Ordnance Hotel	Felixstowe, Suffolk	134
The Three Mariners	Trimley St Mary, Felixstowe, Suffolk	139
The Three Tuns Coaching Inn	Pettistree, Woodbridge, Suffolk	140
The Triple Plea	Broadway, Halesworth, Suffolk	141
The White Hart Inn	Blythburgh, Southwold, Suffolk	142
The White Horse Inn	Capel St Mary, Ipswich, Suffolk	144

Childrens Facilities

CAMBRIDGESHIRE

The Golden Pheasant	Etton, Peterborough, Cambridgeshire	23
The John Barleycorn	Duxford, Cambridgeshire	26
The Vine	Coates, Cambridgeshire	32
The White Horse	Tilbrook, Cambridgeshire	34
The White Swan	Conington, Fenstanton, Cambridgeshire	35

ESSEX

The Cherry Tree	Rochford, Essex	169
The Kings Head at Pebmarsh	Pebmarsh, Halstead, Essex	182
The Onley Arms	Stisted, Braintree, Essex	187
The Rabbits	Stapleford Abbotts, Romford, Essex	189
The Three Horseshoes	Helions Bumpstead, Essex	194
The White Hart	Little Waltham, Chelmsford, Essex	195
The White Hart	St Osyth, Essex	196
The White Horse Inn	Sible Hedingham, Essex	198
The Woodman	Stanford Rivers, Ongar, Essex	199

NORFOLK

The Ark Royal	Wells-next-the-Sea, Norfolk	57
The Duke of Edinburgh	Bacton, Norfolk	67
The Eels Foot Inn	Ormesby St Michael, Great Yarmouth, Norfolk	68
The Swan	Mattishall, Dereham, Norfolk	88
The White Horse	Holme by the Sea, Hunstanton, Norfolk	91

SUFFOLK

The Cherry Tree Inn	Woodbridge, Suffolk	120
The Cock Inn	Polstead, Suffolk	122
The Fox	Pakenham, Suffolk	127
The Sorrel Horse Inn	Barham, Ipswich, Suffolk	136
The Three Mariners	Trimley St Mary, Felixstowe, Suffolk	139
The White Horse Inn	Capel St Mary, Ipswich, Suffolk	144

SPECIAL INTEREST LISTS

Credit Cards Accepted

CAMBRIDGESHIRE

Baskerville's Hotel	Baston, Cambridgeshire	20
The Black Swan	Farcet, Peterborough, Cambridgeshire	21
The George Hotel	Chatteris, Cambridgeshire	22
The Golden Pheasant	Etton, Peterborough, Cambridgeshire	23
The Hoops	Great Eversden, Cambridgeshire	24
The Hop Bind	Cottenham, Cambridgeshire	25
The John Barleycorn	Duxford, Cambridgeshire	26
The Oliver Twist Country Inn	Guyhirn, Wisbech, Cambridgeshire	27
The Prince of Wales	Hilton, Cambridgeshire	28
The Queens Head	Harston, Cambridgeshire	29
The Three Horseshoes	Turves, Whittlesey, Cambridgeshire	30
The Three Tuns	Huntingdon, Cambridgeshire	31
The White Horse	Tilbrook, Cambridgeshire	34
The White Swan	Conington, Fenstanton, Cambridgeshire	35
The White Swan	Woodnewton, Cambridgeshire	36
The Windmill	Somersham, Huntingdon, Cambridgeshire	37

ESSEX

The Cherry Tree	Rochford, Essex	169
The Cock Inn	Hatfield Broad Oak, Bishop's Stortford, Essex	170
The Cock Tavern	Chipping Ongar, Essex	171
The Duck Inn	Writtle, Chelmsford, Essex	172
The Duke of Wellington	Hatfield Peverel, Chelmsford, Essex	173
The Flitch of Bacon	Little Dunmow, Great Dunmow, Essex	174
The Fox Inn	West Mersea, Essex	175
The Green Man	Gosfield, Halstead, Essex	176
The Green Man	Little Braxted, Witham, Essex	177
The Hare	Roxwell, Chelmsford, Essex	178
The Hope Inn	Tollesbury, Essex	179
The Horse & Groom	Great Warley, Brentwood, Essex	180
The Kings Head	Gosfield, Halstead, Essex	181
The Kings Head at Pebmarsh	Pebmarsh, Halstead, Essex	182
The Lion & Lamb	Little Canfield, Takeley, Essex	183
The Norton	Cold Norton, Essex	185
The Old Crown	Messing, Kelvedon, Essex	186
The Onley Arms	Stisted, Braintree, Essex	187
The Plough	Hutton, Brentwood, Essex	188
The Rabbits	Stapleford Abbotts, Romford, Essex	189
The Rose & Crown	Ashdon, Saffron Walden, Essex	190

The Royal Oak	Great Stambridge, Southend on Sea, Essex	191
The Swan at Felstead	Felsted, Great Dunmow, Essex	192
The Swan Inn	Manningtree, Essex	193
The Three Horseshoes	Helions Bumpstead, Essex	194
The White Hart	Little Waltham, Chelmsford, Essex	195
The White Hart	St Osyth, Essex	196
The White Horse Inn	Sible Hedingham, Essex	198
The Woodman	Stanford Rivers, Ongar, Essex	199

NORFOLK

The Ark Royal	Wells-next-the-Sea, Norfolk	57
The Bell Inn	Salhouse, Norwich, Norfolk	58
The Black Swan	Little Dunham, Swaffham, Norfolk	59
The Boar Inn	Great Ryburgh, Norfolk	61
The Bridge Inn	Lenwade, Norwich, Norfolk	62
The Brisley Bell Inn	Brisley, Norfolk	63
The Cherry Tree	Wicklewood, Wymondham, Norfolk	64
The Crown	Gayton, Kings Lynn, Norfolk	66
The Duke of Edinburgh	Bacton, Norfolk	67
The Eels Foot Inn	Ormesby St Michael, Great Yarmouth, Norfolk	68
The Gemini Pub & Restaurant	Dereham, Norfolk	70
The Griffin Hotel	Attleborough, Norfolk	72
The Hill House	Happisburgh, Norfolk	73
The John H Stracey	Briston, Melton Constable, Norfolk	74
The Jolly Farmers	North Creake, Norfolk	75
The Jolly Farmers	Swanton Abbott, Norwich, Norfolk	76
The Lobster	Sheringham, Norfolk	78
The Marshlands Arms	Marshland St James, Wisbech, Norfolk	80
The New Inn	Roughton, Norfolk	81
The Railway Freehouse	North Elmham, Dereham, Norfolk	83
The Red Lion	Coltishall, Norfolk	84
The Red Lion	Needham, Harleston, Norfolk	85
The Scole Inn	Scole, Diss, Norfolk	86
The Ship Inn	Mundesley, Cromer, Norfolk	87
The Stables Restaurant	Sheringham, Norfolk	79
The Swan	Mattishall, Dereham, Norfolk	88
The Three Horseshoes	Roydon, Kings Lynn, Norfolk	89
The Walpole Arms	Itteringham, Norwich, Norfolk	90
The White Horse	Holme by the Sea, Hunstanton, Norfolk	91
The White Horse at Longham	Dereham, Norfolk	92
The Woolpack	Terrington St John, Kings Lynn, Norfolk	93

Credit Cards Accepted

SUFFOLK

The Admiral's Head	Little Bealings, Woodbridge, Suffolk	115
The Angel Hotel	Halesworth, Suffolk	116
The Black Horse	Stratford St Mary, Suffolk	117
The Bristol Arms	Shotley Gate, Ipswich, Suffolk	118
The Bull Inn	Cavendish, Suffolk	119
The Cherry Tree Inn	Woodbridge, Suffolk	120
The Cock Inn	Kentford, Newmarket, Suffolk	121
The Cock Inn	Polstead, Suffolk	122
The Cock Inn	Stanton, Bury St Edmunds, Suffolk	123
The Dog & Duck	Campsea Ashe, Woodbridge, Suffolk	124
The Falcon	Rushmere St Andrew, Ipswich, Suffolk	125
The Ferry Boat Inn	Felixstowe, Suffolk	126
The Fox	Pakenham, Suffolk	127
The Kings Head	Yoxford, Suffolk	129
The Kings Head Inn	Orford, Suffolk	130
The Old Cannon Brewery	Bury St Edmunds, Suffolk	133
The Ordnance Hotel	Felixstowe, Suffolk	134
The Pykkerell	Ixworth, Bury St Edmunds, Suffolk	135
The Sorrel Horse Inn	Barham, Ipswich, Suffolk	136
The Swan Inn	Little Waldingfield, Sudbury, Suffolk	137
The Ten Bells	Stonham Aspal, Stowmarket, Suffolk	138
The Three Tuns Coaching Inn	Pettistree, Woodbridge, Suffolk	140
The Triple Plea	Broadway, Halesworth, Suffolk	141
The White Hart Inn	Blythburgh, Southwold, Suffolk	142
The White Horse	Beyton, Bury St Edmunds, Suffolk	143
The White Horse Inn	Capel St Mary, Ipswich, Suffolk	144

Garden, Patio or Terrace

CAMBRIDGESHIRE

Baskerville's Hotel	Baston, Cambridgeshire	20
The Black Swan	Farcet, Peterborough, Cambridgeshire	21
The George Hotel	Chatteris, Cambridgeshire	22
The Golden Pheasant	Etton, Peterborough, Cambridgeshire	23
The Hoops	Great Eversden, Cambridgeshire	24
The Hop Bind	Cottenham, Cambridgeshire	25
The John Barleycorn	Duxford, Cambridgeshire	26
The Prince of Wales	Hilton, Cambridgeshire	28
The Queens Head	Harston, Cambridgeshire	29
The Three Horseshoes	Turves, Whittlesey, Cambridgeshire	30
The Three Tuns	Huntingdon, Cambridgeshire	31
The Vine	Coates, Cambridgeshire	32
West End House	West End, Ely, Cambridgeshire	33
The White Horse	Tilbrook, Cambridgeshire	34
The White Swan	Conington, Fenstanton, Cambridgeshire	35
The White Swan	Woodnewton, Cambridgeshire	36
The Windmill	Somersham, Huntingdon, Cambridgeshire	37

ESSEX

The Cherry Tree	Rochford, Essex	169
The Cock Inn	Hatfield Broad Oak, Bishop's Stortford, Essex	170
The Duck Inn	Writtle, Chelmsford, Essex	172
The Duke of Wellington	Hatfield Peverel, Chelmsford, Essex	173
The Flitch of Bacon	Little Dunmow, Great Dunmow, Essex	174
The Green Man	Gosfield, Halstead, Essex	176
The Green Man	Little Braxted, Witham, Essex	177
The Hare	Roxwell, Chelmsford, Essex	178
The Horse & Groom	Great Warley, Brentwood, Essex	180
The Kings Head	Gosfield, Halstead, Essex	181
The Kings Head at Pebmarsh	Pebmarsh, Halstead, Essex	182
The Lion & Lamb	Little Canfield, Takeley, Essex	183
The Nags Head	Ramsden Heath, Billericay, Essex	184
The Old Crown	Messing, Kelvedon, Essex	186
The Onley Arms	Stisted, Braintree, Essex	187
The Plough	Hutton, Brentwood, Essex	188
The Rabbits	Stapleford Abbotts, Romford, Essex	189
The Royal Oak	Great Stambridge, Southend on Sea, Essex	191
The Three Horseshoes	Helions Bumpstead, Essex	194
The White Hart	Little Waltham, Chelmsford, Essex	195

Garden, Patio or Terrace

The White Hart	St Osyth, Essex	196
The White Hart	Stebbing, Great Dunmow, Essex	197
The White Horse Inn	Sible Hedingham, Essex	198
The Woodman	Stanford Rivers, Ongar, Essex	199

NORFOLK

The Ark Royal	Wells-next-the-Sea, Norfolk	57
The Bell Inn	Salhouse, Norwich, Norfolk	58
The Black Swan	Little Dunham, Swaffham, Norfolk	59
The Blue Lion	North Pickenham, Swaffham, Norfolk	60
The Boar Inn	Great Ryburgh, Norfolk	61
The Bridge Inn	Lenwade, Norwich, Norfolk	62
The Brisley Bell Inn	Brisley, Norfolk	63
The Cherry Tree	Wicklewood, Wymondham, Norfolk	64
The Cross Keys	Dilham, North Walsham, Norfolk	65
The Crown	Gayton, Kings Lynn, Norfolk	66
The Eels Foot Inn	Ormesby St Michael, Great Yarmouth, Norfolk	68
The Fox & Hounds	Filby, Great Yarmouth, Norfolk	69
The Gemini Pub & Restaurant	Dereham, Norfolk	70
The Greyhound	Tibenham, Norwich, Norfolk	71
The Griffin Hotel	Attleborough, Norfolk	72
The Hill House	Happisburgh, Norfolk	73
The John H Stracey	Briston, Melton Constable, Norfolk	74
The Jolly Farmers	North Creake, Norfolk	75
The Jolly Farmers	Swanton Abbott, Norwich, Norfolk	76
The Kings Head	New Buckenham, Norfolk	77
The Lobster	Sheringham, Norfolk	78
The Marshlands Arms	Marshland St James, Wisbech, Norfolk	80
The New Inn	Roughton, Norfolk	81
The Old Red Lion	Aldborough, Norfolk	82
The Red Lion	Coltishall, Norfolk	84
The Red Lion	Needham, Harleston, Norfolk	85
The Ship Inn	Mundesley, Cromer, Norfolk	87
The Swan	Mattishall, Dereham, Norfolk	88
The Three Horseshoes	Roydon, Kings Lynn, Norfolk	89
The Walpole Arms	Itteringham, Norwich, Norfolk	90
The White Horse	Holme by the Sea, Hunstanton, Norfolk	91
The White Horse at Longham	Dereham, Norfolk	92
The Woolpack	Terrington St John, Kings Lynn, Norfolk	93

SUFFOLK

The Admiral's Head	Little Bealings, Woodbridge, Suffolk	115
The Angel Hotel	Halesworth, Suffolk	116
The Black Horse	Stratford St Mary, Suffolk	117
The Bristol Arms	Shotley Gate, Ipswich, Suffolk	118
The Bull Inn	Cavendish, Suffolk	119
The Cherry Tree Inn	Woodbridge, Suffolk	120
The Cock Inn	Polstead, Suffolk	122
The Cock Inn	Stanton, Bury St Edmunds, Suffolk	123
The Dog & Duck	Campsea Ashe, Woodbridge, Suffolk	124
The Falcon	Rushmere St Andrew, Ipswich, Suffolk	125
The Ferry Boat Inn	Felixstowe, Suffolk	126
The Fox	Pakenham, Suffolk	127
The Horse & Groom	Wrentham, Suffolk	128
The Kings Head	Yoxford, Suffolk	129
The Little Wellington	Stowmarket, Suffolk	131
The Morning Star	Lowestoft, Suffolk	132
The Old Cannon Brewery	Bury St Edmunds, Suffolk	133
The Ordnance Hotel	Felixstowe, Suffolk	134
The Pykkerell	Ixworth, Bury St Edmunds, Suffolk	135
The Sorrel Horse Inn	Barham, Ipswich, Suffolk	136
The Swan Inn	Little Waldingfield, Sudbury, Suffolk	137
The Ten Bells	Stonham Aspal, Stowmarket, Suffolk	138
The Three Mariners	Trimley St Mary, Felixstowe, Suffolk	139
The Three Tuns Coaching Inn	Pettistree, Woodbridge, Suffolk	140
The Triple Plea	Broadway, Halesworth, Suffolk	141
The White Hart Inn	Blythburgh, Southwold, Suffolk	142
The White Horse	Beyton, Bury St Edmunds, Suffolk	143
The White Horse Inn	Capel St Mary, Ipswich, Suffolk	144
The White Horse Inn	Tattingstone, Ipswich, Suffolk	145

SPECIAL INTEREST LISTS

Live Entertainment

CAMBRIDGESHIRE

Baskerville's Hotel	Baston, Cambridgeshire	20
The Hop Bind	Cottenham, Cambridgeshire	25
The Three Horseshoes	Turves, Whittlesey, Cambridgeshire	30
The Three Tuns	Huntingdon, Cambridgeshire	31
The Vine	Coates, Cambridgeshire	32
The Windmill	Somersham, Huntingdon, Cambridgeshire	37

ESSEX

The Fox Inn	West Mersea, Essex	175
The Kings Head at Pebmarsh	Pebmarsh, Halstead, Essex	182
The Lion & Lamb	Little Canfield, Takeley, Essex	183
The Nags Head	Ramsden Heath, Billericay, Essex	184
The Old Crown	Messing, Kelvedon, Essex	186
The Plough	Hutton, Brentwood, Essex	188
The Rose & Crown	Ashdon, Saffron Walden, Essex	190
The Royal Oak	Great Stambridge, Southend on Sea, Essex	191
The Swan Inn	Manningtree, Essex	193
The White Hart	Little Waltham, Chelmsford, Essex	195

NORFOLK

The Duke of Edinburgh	Bacton, Norfolk	67
The Eels Foot Inn	Ormesby St Michael, Great Yarmouth, Norfolk	68
The Fox & Hounds	Filby, Great Yarmouth, Norfolk	69
The Gemini Pub & Restaurant	Dereham, Norfolk	70
The Greyhound	Tibenham, Norwich, Norfolk	71
The Jolly Farmers	Swanton Abbott, Norwich, Norfolk	76
The Old Red Lion	Aldborough, Norfolk	82
The Red Lion	Coltishall, Norfolk	84
The Ship Inn	Mundesley, Cromer, Norfolk	87
The Swan	Mattishall, Dereham, Norfolk	88

SUFFOLK

The Black Horse	Stratford St Mary, Suffolk	117
The Bristol Arms	Shotley Gate, Ipswich, Suffolk	118
The Cherry Tree Inn	Woodbridge, Suffolk	120
The Cock Inn	Stanton, Bury St Edmunds, Suffolk	123
The Little Wellington	Stowmarket, Suffolk	131

SUFFOLK (Cont.)

The Morning Star	Lowestoft, Suffolk	132
The Ordnance Hotel	Felixstowe, Suffolk	134
The Pykkerell	Ixworth, Bury St Edmunds, Suffolk	135
The Three Mariners	Trimley St Mary, Felixstowe, Suffolk	139
The White Horse Inn	Capel St Mary, Ipswich, Suffolk	144
The White Horse Inn	Tattingstone, Ipswich, Suffolk	145

SPECIAL INTEREST LISTS

Restaurant or Dining Area

CAMBRIDGESHIRE

Baskerville's Hotel	Baston, Cambridgeshire	20
The Hoops	Great Eversden, Cambridgeshire	24
The Queens Head	Harston, Cambridgeshire	29
The Three Horseshoes	Turves, Whittlesey, Cambridgeshire	30
The Vine	Coates, Cambridgeshire	32
The White Horse	Tilbrook, Cambridgeshire	34
The White Swan	Conington, Fenstanton, Cambridgeshire	35
The White Swan	Woodnewton, Cambridgeshire	36

ESSEX

The Duck Inn	Writtle, Chelmsford, Essex	172
The Duke of Wellington	Hatfield Peverel, Chelmsford, Essex	173
The Flitch of Bacon	Little Dunmow, Great Dunmow, Essex	174
The Hare	Roxwell, Chelmsford, Essex	178
The Hope Inn	Tollesbury, Essex	179
The Horse & Groom	Great Warley, Brentwood, Essex	180
The Kings Head	Gosfield, Halstead, Essex	181
The Kings Head at Pebmarsh	Pebmarsh, Halstead, Essex	182
The Lion & Lamb	Little Canfield, Takeley, Essex	183
The Norton	Cold Norton, Essex	185
The Old Crown	Messing, Kelvedon, Essex	186
The Rabbits	Stapleford Abbotts, Romford, Essex	189
The Rose & Crown	Ashdon, Saffron Walden, Essex	190
The Royal Oak	Great Stambridge, Southend on Sea, Essex	191
The Swan at Felstead	Felsted, Great Dunmow, Essex	192
The Swan Inn	Manningtree, Essex	193
The White Hart	Little Waltham, Chelmsford, Essex	195
The White Hart	St Osyth, Essex	196
The White Hart	Stebbing, Great Dunmow, Essex	197
The White Horse Inn	Sible Hedingham, Essex	198
The Woodman	Stanford Rivers, Ongar, Essex	199

NORFOLK

The Bell Inn	Salhouse, Norwich, Norfolk	58
The Black Swan	Little Dunham, Swaffham, Norfolk	59
The Boar Inn	Great Ryburgh, Norfolk	61
The Bridge Inn	Lenwade, Norwich, Norfolk	62
The Cherry Tree	Wicklewood, Wymondham, Norfolk	64

Restaurant or Dining Area

The Crown	Gayton, Kings Lynn, Norfolk	66
The Duke of Edinburgh	Bacton, Norfolk	67
The Eels Foot Inn	Ormesby St Michael, Great Yarmouth, Norfolk	68
The Gemini Pub & Restaurant	Dereham, Norfolk	70
The Greyhound	Tibenham, Norwich, Norfolk	71
The Hill House	Happisburgh, Norfolk	73
The Jolly Farmers	North Creake, Norfolk	75
The Jolly Farmers	Swanton Abbott, Norwich, Norfolk	76
The Lobster	Sheringham, Norfolk	78
The Marshlands Arms	Marshland St James, Wisbech, Norfolk	80
The New Inn	Roughton, Norfolk	81
The Railway Freehouse	North Elmham, Dereham, Norfolk	83
The Red Lion	Needham, Harleston, Norfolk	85
The Scole Inn	Scole, Diss, Norfolk	86
The Ship Inn	Mundesley, Cromer, Norfolk	87
The Stables Restaurant	Sheringham, Norfolk	79
The Walpole Arms	Itteringham, Norwich, Norfolk	90
The White Horse	Holme by the Sea, Hunstanton, Norfolk	91
The White Horse at Longham	Dereham, Norfolk	92
The Woolpack	Terrington St John, Kings Lynn, Norfolk	93

SUFFOLK

The Angel Hotel	Halesworth, Suffolk	116
The Black Horse	Stratford St Mary, Suffolk	117
The Bristol Arms	Shotley Gate, Ipswich, Suffolk	118
The Bull Inn	Cavendish, Suffolk	119
The Cock Inn	Kentford, Newmarket, Suffolk	121
The Cock Inn	Polstead, Suffolk	122
The Cock Inn	Stanton, Bury St Edmunds, Suffolk	123
The Dog & Duck	Campsea Ashe, Woodbridge, Suffolk	124
The Fox	Pakenham, Suffolk	127
The Kings Head	Yoxford, Suffolk	129
The Kings Head Inn	Orford, Suffolk	130
The Old Cannon Brewery	Bury St Edmunds, Suffolk	133
The Ordnance Hotel	Felixstowe, Suffolk	134
The Sorrel Horse Inn	Barham, Ipswich, Suffolk	136
The Ten Bells	Stonham Aspal, Stowmarket, Suffolk	138
The Three Mariners	Trimley St Mary, Felixstowe, Suffolk	139
The Triple Plea	Broadway, Halesworth, Suffolk	141
The White Horse	Beyton, Bury St Edmunds, Suffolk	143

PLACES OF INTEREST

Places of Interest

A
Aldeburgh   97
Arrington   5
Attleborough   41
Aylsham   41
Aythorpe Roding 149

B
Beccles   98
Blakeney   41
Blythburgh   98
Braintree   149
Brandon   99
Brentwood   149
Bressingham   42
Brightlingsea   150
Burghley   5
Burnham Market   42
Burnham Thorpe   42
Burnham-On-Crouch   150
Bury St Edmunds   100

C
Caister-on-Sea   43
Cambridge   5
Canvey Island   150
Carlton Colville   101
Castle Hedingham   150
Cavendish   102
Chappel   151
Chelmsford   151
Clacton-on-Sea   152
Clare   102
Coggleshall   152
Colchester   153
Coltishall   43
Cressing   155
Cromer   44
Crowland   8

D
Dedham   155
Diss   44
Dunwich   102
Duxford   8

E
Earsham   103
East Bergholt   103
Ely   8

F
Fakenham   45
Felixstowe   103
Fenstanton   10
Flixton   104
Framlingham   104
Frinton-on-Sea   155

G
Godmanchester   10
Grafham   10
Grantchester   11
Great Dunmow   156
Great Yarmouth   45

H
Hadleigh   104
Hadleigh   156
Halstead   157
Harlow   157
Harwich   158
Hatfield Broad Oak   159
Haverhll   105
Holkham   46
Horringer   105
Hunstanton   46
Huntingdon   11

I
Ipswich   105

K
Kelvedon Hatch   159
Kersey   106
Kessingland   106
Kimbolton   12
King's Lynn   47

L
Lavenham   107
Layer Marney   159
Leiston   108

Linton   12
Lode   12
Long Melford   108
Lowestoft   109

M

Madingley   13
Maldon   159
Manningtree   160
March   13
Mersea Island   160
Mildenhall   109
Mistley   160
Mountnessing   161

N

Newmarket   110
North Weald   161
Norwich   47

O

Orford   110

P

Pakenham   111
Peterborough   13
Point Clear   161
Potter Heigham   51
Prickwillow   15

R

Ramsey   15

S

Saffron Walden   161
Sandringham   51
Sheringham   52
Shotley   111
Snettisham   52
Somerleyton   111
South Walsham   52
Southend-on-Sea   163
Southwold   112
St Ives   16
St Neots   16
St Osyth   164
Stansted Mountfitchet   164
Stonham Aspal   112
Stowmarket   112
Stratford St Mary   113
Sudbury   113
Swaffham   53

T

Terrington St Clement   53
Thaxted   165
Thetford   53
Thorney   17
Thorpeness   113
Tilbury   165

W

Waltham Abbey   166
Walton-on-the-Naze   167
Waterbeach   18
Wells Next-the-Sea   55
Welney   18
West Runton   55
West Thurrock   168
Whittlesey   18
Wicken   18
Wisbech   19
Wivenhoe   168
Woodbridge   113
Wymondham   55

Travel Publishing

The Hidden Places

Regional and National guides to the less well-known places of interest and places to eat, stay and drink

Hidden Inns

Regional guides to traditional pubs and inns throughout the United Kingdom

Off the Motorway

This very popular guide follows the junctions of each of the country's leading motorways and provides detailed information on places to stop close to each junction.

COUNTRY LIVING
MAGAZINE
RURAL GUIDES

Regional and National guides to the traditional countryside of Britain and Ireland with easy to read facts on places to visit, stay, eat, drink and shop

For more information:

Phone: 0118 981 7777
e-mail: adam@travelpublishing.co.uk

Fax: 0118 982 0077
website: www.travelpublishing.co.u

Easy-to-use, Informative
Travel Guides on the British Isles

Order Form

ORDER FORM

To order any of our publications just fill in the payment details below and complete the order form. For orders of less than 4 copies please add £1 per book for postage and packing. Orders over 4 copies are P & P free.

Please Complete Either:

I enclose a cheque for £ _____ made payable to Travel Publishing Ltd

Or:

Card No: _____ Expiry Date: _____

Signature: _____

Name: _____

Address: _____

Tel no: _____

Please either send, telephone, fax or e-mail your order to:

Travel Publishing Ltd, 7a Apollo House, Calleva Park, Aldermaston, Berkshire RG7 8TN Tel: 0118 981 7777   Fax: 0118 982 0077
e-mail: karen@travelpublishing.co.uk

Hidden Places Regional Titles	Price	Quantity
Cambs & Lincolnshire	£8.99	....
Chilterns	£8.99	....
Cornwall	£8.99	....
Derbyshire	£8.99	....
Devon	£8.99	....
Dorset, Hants & Isle of Wight	£8.99	....
East Anglia	£8.99	....
Gloucs, Wiltshire & Somerset	£8.99	....
Heart of England	£8.99	....
Hereford, Worcs & Shropshire	£8.99	....
Kent	£8.99	....
Lake District & Cumbria	£8.99	....
Lancashire & Cheshire	£8.99	....
Lincolnshire & Notts	£8.99	....
Northumberland & Durham	£8.99	....
Sussex	£8.99	....
Yorkshire	£8.99	....

Hidden Places National Titles	Price	Quantity
England	£11.99	....
Ireland	£11.99	....
Scotland	£11.99	....
Wales	£11.99	....

Hidden Inns Titles	Price	Quantity
East Anglia	£7.99	....
Heart of England	£7.99	....
Lancashire & Cheshire	£7.99	....
North of England	£7.99	....
South	£7.99	....
South East	£7.99	....
South and Central Scotland	£7.99	....
Wales	£7.99	....
Welsh Borders	£7.99	....
West Country	£7.99	....
Yorkshire	£7.99	....

Country Living Rural Guides	Price	Quantity
East Anglia	£10.99	....
Heart of England	£10.99	....
Ireland	£11.99	....
Scotland	£11.99	....
South of England	£10.99	....
South East of England	£10.99	....
Wales	£11.99	....
West Country	£10.99	....

Total Quantity _____

Post & Packing _____

Total Value _____

READER REACTION FORM

The *Travel Publishing* research team would like to receive reader's comments on any visitor attractions or places reviewed in the book and also recommendations for suitable entries to be included in the next edition. This will help ensure that the *Hidden Inns Series* continues to provide its readers with useful information on the more interesting, unusual or unique features of each inn or place ensuring that their visit to the local area is an enjoyable and stimulating experience. To provide your comments or recommendations would you please complete the forms below and overleaf as indicated and send to:

The Research Department, Travel Publishing Ltd,
7a Apollo House, Calleva Park, Aldermaston, Reading, RG7 8TN.

Your Name:

Your Address:

Your Telephone Number:

Please tick as appropriate:

Comments ☐   Recommendation ☐

Name of Establishment:

Address:

Telephone Number:

Name of Contact:

READER REACTION FORM

Comment or Reason for Recommendation:

READER REACTION FORM

The *Travel Publishing* research team would like to receive reader's comments on any visitor attractions or places reviewed in the book and also recommendations for suitable entries to be included in the next edition. This will help ensure that the *Hidden Inns Series* continues to provide its readers with useful information on the more interesting, unusual or unique features of each inn or place ensuring that their visit to the local area is an enjoyable and stimulating experience. To provide your comments or recommendations would you please complete the forms below and overleaf as indicated and send to:

**The Research Department, Travel Publishing Ltd,
7a Apollo House, Calleva Park, Aldermaston, Reading, RG7 8TN.**

Your Name:

Your Address:

Your Telephone Number:

Please tick as appropriate:

           Comments ☐   Recommendation ☐

Name of Establishment:

Address:

Telephone Number:

Name of Contact:

READER REACTION FORM

Comment or Reason for Recommendation:

READER REACTION FORM

The *Travel Publishing* research team would like to receive reader's comments on any visitor attractions or places reviewed in the book and also recommendations for suitable entries to be included in the next edition. This will help ensure that the *Hidden Inns Series* continues to provide its readers with useful information on the more interesting, unusual or unique features of each inn or place ensuring that their visit to the local area is an enjoyable and stimulating experience. To provide your comments or recommendations would you please complete the forms below and overleaf as indicated and send to:

The Research Department, Travel Publishing Ltd,
7a Apollo House, Calleva Park, Aldermaston, Reading, RG7 8TN.

Your Name:

Your Address:

Your Telephone Number:

Please tick as appropriate:

Comments ☐   Recommendation ☐

Name of Establishment:

Address:

Telephone Number:

Name of Contact:

READER REACTION FORM

Comment or Reason for Recommendation: